The Geography of International Terrorism

An Introduction to Spaces and Places of Violent Non-State Groups

The Geography of International Terrorism

An Introduction to Spaces and Places of Violent Non-State Groups

Richard M. Medina and George F. Hepner

CRC Press is an imprint of the
Taylor & Francis Group, an **informa** business

CRC Press
Taylor & Francis Group
6000 Broken Sound Parkway NW, Suite 300
Boca Raton, FL 33487-2742

Printed on acid-free paper
Version Date: 20130208

International Standard Book Number-13: 978-1-4398-8686-1 (Hardback)

Library of Congress Cataloging-in-Publication Data

Medina, Richard M.
The geography of international terrorism : an introduction to spaces and places of violent non-state groups / Richard M. Medina and George F. Hepner.
p. cm.
Includes bibliographical references and index.
ISBN 978-1-4398-8686-1 (alk. paper)
1. Terrorism. 2. Violence. I. Hepner, George F. II. Title.

HV6431.M4336 2013
363.325--dc23 2012044329

Visit the Taylor & Francis Web site at
http://www.taylorandfrancis.com

and the CRC Press Web site at
http://www.crcpress.com

Contents

Preface

The approach of this book is different from those of other books on terrorism published by geographers and other scholars. First of all, both of us are educated in the science and technology of the geospatial information revolution of the last 20 years. Our research records are founded in the technical geography areas of geographic information science (GISc), especially geospatial statistics and modeling, geographic information systems (GIS), and remote sensing. The result is a book on the traditional geographic aspects of terrorism informed by recent technological and analytical tools and procedures.

We have only scratched the surface on the use of geographic theory, concepts, and tools of analysis in this book. This is a vast, largely underdeveloped area of scholarly investigation. On the practical side, terrorism is a covert undertaking; thus, much relevant information is not readily available. Additionally, much of the geospatial intelligence information, maps, and imagery that could make this a more informative book is classified or "for official use only." We have had to rely on unrestricted, published sources and our own experience, knowledge, and research.

This book has evolved out of the Geography of Terrorism courses that both of us teach at our respective universities. Over the last 6 years of offering this course, the lack of a book that focuses on the explicit geographic contributions to the study of terrorism has become apparent. The course offerings allowed us to hone the topical logic of the book, which we hope is both a contribution to the research domain and a possible text for a similar course. Numerous class discussions informed us of the need to address the multiple geographic scales of terrorism. The vertical linkage between topics at the high-resolution level, such as sense of place and cultural identity of a clan or tribe with regional and global geographic-scale issues, is critical to understanding twenty-first century international terrorist groups.

We wish to thank the university and research organizations that have supported our research and scholarship over the years. These include Oak Ridge National Laboratory, CalTech/JPL, and Lawrence Livermore National Laboratory, along with George Mason University and the University of Utah. On a personal note, many individuals in the field have been supportive of our efforts, most importantly Nevin Bryant, CalTech/JPL; Wayne McCormack, University of Utah; Bruce Hoffman, Georgetown University; and Rohan Gunaratna, Nanyang Technological University. And, of course, we would like to thank our families for support, inspiration, and understanding throughout the book-writing process.

The Authors

Richard M. Medina is an assistant professor in the Department of Geography and GeoInformation Science and faculty in the Center for Geospatial Intelligence at George Mason University. His research focuses on terrorism and homeland security, hazards and vulnerability, geographic information systems and science (GIS/GISc), and complex social systems. He previously worked as a research scientist at Oak Ridge National Laboratory and has recent publications on terrorist group operations in hybrid space, spatial analysis of terrorist attacks in Iraq, and vulnerable dynamic populations.

George F. Hepner is a professor and chair of the Department of Geography at the University of Utah in Salt Lake City, Utah. His major areas of research involve geographical analysis using remote sensing and geographic information systems (GIS), hazard response and mitigation, and international environmental assessment. His research has received specific attention in the areas of the use of spatial field representation in GIS applied to cross-country movement of vehicles and the vulnerability of humans to hazardous gas plumes, the early use of artificial neural networks for image processing, and the fusion of hyperspectral imagery with other GIS data. Most recently, his research has been in the areas of geospatial analysis to the geographical dimension of international terrorism. Hepner served as president of the American Society for Photogrammetry and Remote Sensing (ASPRS) in 2001–2002.

He has been a research fellow and consultant to the Image Processing Laboratory at the NASA Jet Propulsion Laboratory, California Institute of Technology, and the Risk and Response Management Program at Lawrence Livermore National Laboratory.

1

The Links between Terrorism and Geography

INTRODUCTION

Much of the research and scholarship on terrorism has focused on the vitally important historical record—political organizational and social psychological perspectives of terrorists and their groups (Crenshaw 1995). These political, social, and psychological perspectives contain implicit recognition and use of geographic theories, concepts, and analytical tools. The terrorist literature uses geographic concepts of region, relative location, distance decay, core periphery, insurgent state, geographic diffusion of ideas, technology and people, and sense of place as an underpinning for political or social explanations of terrorists and terrorist group beliefs and actions. However, these are not explicitly described or recognized as the primary constituents and vehicles for explanation and understanding.

The study of terrorism is often based on the notion of security, defined as military security of the state from a Western point of view—not encompassing economic, social, and environmental security of indigenous cultural people and traditions (Smith 2005). Military security of the state or political theories are not the major concern of tribal groups in the Niger River Delta being destroyed by environmental insecurity, or the Uighur group in Xinjiang, China, being culturally decimated by Han Chinese migrants and governmental policy. This limited view of security and, therefore, terrorism has resulted in much of the scholarship and resulting policy not being done at higher spatial resolutions within a state, where geographic differences in ethnicity, religion, physical landscape features, and resource capacities are critical influences on group dynamics and behavior, including terrorism.

Terrorists operate in various spaces, interact in spaces and at places, and maybe most important, terrorists are typically fighting for control of territory and the people within that territory (Rock 2006). Motivations for terrorism are geopolitical in nature, focusing on specific regions under the control of a larger, more powerful opponent. Target locations are selected for various reasons, including symbolic value, psychological effects, or potential damages (human and physical), that can be geospatially modeled and mapped. Many instances of terrorism have sociocultural underpinnings that have specific human geographic characteristics. Geographically referenced data (geospatial data) are interpreted to create geospatial information for investigation of spatial patterns from which underlying processes can be inferred, analyzed, and explained within a geographic information system (GIS). In some cases, this information creates knowledge, conveyed as integrated maps, images, spatiotemporal models of change, and predictive assessments. This is the core of geospatial intelligence and the broader geographic perspective.

This book uses the geographic perspective in a more explicit manner than previous treatments of the terrorism topic have done. While it is not believed that geography determines human behavior, the influence of physical and human geography on terrorist motivations, behaviors, options, and activities is a primary consideration in understanding terrorism. Terrorism is a complex phenomenon and is best studied through multidisciplinary approaches. Geography acts as a science of convergence, where many other disciplines intersect in the study of phenomena and processes in a geographic context. Understanding terrorism in a more complete, multidisciplinary fashion using the most current analytical tools is essential to preempting and countering terrorism in the future.

BRIEF ACCOUNT OF GEOGRAPHY OF PRESENT-DAY TERRORISM IN NIGERIA

Nigeria is a nation of great natural resources and many cultural and ethnic differences that have driven conflict and terrorism. In Nigeria, the character of terrorist activity is greatly influenced by relative location of petroleum, tribal groups, and political and economic control. Under British colonial rule in the nineteenth and twentieth centuries, the British sustained control using three governance regions. This regional governance allowed the British to use the existing ethnic and tribal differences to lessen opposition and to ensure control by the tribes of the northern region. This allowed the

British preferential access to the oil-rich Niger River delta and continued control of the oil after independence. Terrorism has manifested very differently in the north and the south and reflects political, economic, and cultural challenges faced in the different areas. Investigation of the human and physical geography of the nation makes evident the important insights into terrorism in Nigeria and the role of geography in terrorism.

The South

Over half the residents of Nigeria live in poverty (World Bank 2012), while a small percentage enjoy great wealth due to petroleum resources. In southern Nigeria's Niger River Delta, oil is abundant. Nigeria is on the small list of great oil producers in the world and, since 1971, a member of the Organization of the Petroleum Exporting Countries (OPEC). In and around the Niger Delta, there are many on- and offshore oil facilities, including those from multinational corporate giants Chevron, Shell, Agip, and ExxonMobil. The oil infrastructure in the Niger Delta is shown in Figure 1.1.

The extraction of oil in the region by multinational companies has been viewed by Niger Delta residents as exploitation. They see rich foreign companies coming in as oil resources and money leave. Political control of the nation and the southern oil is maintained in the north. In addition, the state is plagued by corruption (Smith 2008). Extraction efforts by Nigerian firms, lacking technical resources and investment capital, would most likely be unfruitful. This has created the reliance on foreign firms. Compensation for oil extraction rarely trickles down to the residents of the south, who have been marginalized from the process.

Many people of the Niger Delta region are dependent on farming and fishing for sustenance. Environmental effects from oil-based activities can render an area hazardous. In December 2011, the largest oil spill in Nigeria since 1998 occurred at the Bonga oil tanker facility run by Royal Dutch Shell (not shown in Figure 1.1) (Reuters 2011).

The result is that the people of the region suffer from air and water contamination and resultant health problems and destruction of their traditional way of life without receiving the benefits of the petroleum production. This discontent has led to the formation of several terrorist groups. The largest and most popular is the Movement for the Emancipation of the Niger Delta (MEND). MEND has been fighting against the foreign development of petroleum extraction for years. Their main goal is to expel all oil companies from the region. In doing this, they hope to bring the

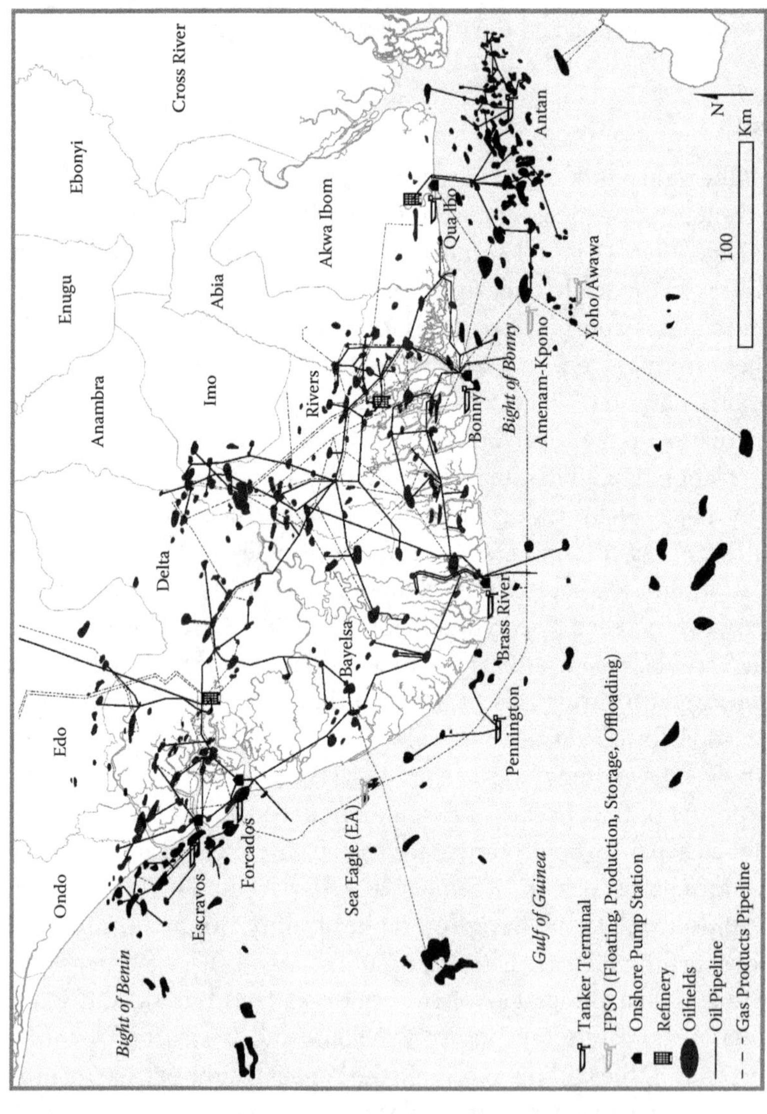

FIGURE 1.1
Nigeria Delta oil infrastructure. (Adapted from the Energy Information Administration, 2011.)

money made from oil in the region back to the people, build infrastructure in support of basic services, and save the environment from further degradation. MEND's main target focus is on the oil companies; however, demands in 2006 included participation in local politics and oil-based business decisions, development, and a reduction of military presence in the region (Asuni 2009).

MEND operations typically focus on oil and international oil-company-based targets, including tankers, pipelines, and employees. The MEND organization is well known for taking hostages from local businesses and construction sites, as well as from oil tankers and other related sites. Those that are often targeted work for oil or construction companies. In most cases, ransoms are paid and the hostages are returned unharmed. The organization is also active in bombings and other types of traditional terrorist activities.

One of their popular attack strategies is to attack offshore oil rigs with speedboats, which are small and quick and can outrun and outmaneuver the larger naval boats that chase them along the complex coastline of the Niger Delta. Mobility is always a concern for terrorist organizations and is partially dependent on the environment. Like the exploitation of the Toyota minitruck by the Taliban to react quickly and cover large areas, nationalist terrorists in Nigeria utilize speedboats to attack offshore oil facilities and escape from authorities. The Nigerian terrorists are well armed with AK-47s and RPGs and are better equipped than local authorities. In a 2008 attack, the Bonga oil platform built by Shell was fired upon and, as a response, closed for weeks. The platform was constructed over 100 km offshore and thought to be unreachable by terrorists. The perpetrators attacked this oil platform specifically to send the message that no facility is "untouchable" (Lloyd-Roberts 2009).

The ethnic foundation of the MEND organization is the Ijaw people of the Niger Delta region (National Consortium for the Study of Terrorism and Responses to Terrorism 2012). The Ijaw people comprise one of the largest ethnic groups in the Niger Delta, which is home to approximately 140 ethnic groups. Other ethnic groups that have greatly been affected by oil extraction include the Ogonis, Okrikans, and Elemes. The people of the Niger Delta have fought against the oil companies for decades. Some have estimated the number of violent actors in the region to be as many as 60,000 (Asuni 2009).

Oil extraction by foreign companies has brought further conflict between ethnic groups. Resulting from early colonialism, ethnic conflict exists throughout Nigeria. Various tribes are now experiencing power struggles over ownership of land and resources used for agriculture and oil extraction. These animosities are responsible for the continuation of future violence in the region (Joab-Peterside 2007). On the other hand, many in the Niger Delta region are united against those they consider to be exploiting their homeland. In a region stricken by poverty and cultural strife, relative geographies of resources, cultural identity, and inequities of political power have created an environment ripe for the growth of terrorism. This brief description of terrorist activities in southern Nigeria is simplified greatly, but provides an overview of one situation of terrorism in Nigeria.

The North

The terrorism and conflict in northern Nigeria are much different from those of the southern part, although the emergence of terrorism stems from the same issues of poverty and marginalization. Oil has not been found in commercial quantities, so the residents are not fighting against foreign companies. The main source of terrorism in the north is based on ethnic and religious conflict. Figure 1.2 shows the relative location of Nigeria with respect to the Muslim world, as defined by percentages of Muslims per country.

While Nigeria's population as a whole is at 41% to 60% Muslim, there is a well-defined split within the country. The northern half of Nigeria is majority Muslim and the southern half is majority Christian and other religions. Figure 1.3 shows that about half the area of the country uses or abides by Sharia law in one form or another (Center for Religious Freedom 2002).* There are several Islamist terrorist organizations in the northern part of the country that are fighting for political and religious change. Presently, the most powerful is Boko Haram, also known as the Nigerian Taliban.

It is widely believed that the name Boko Haram translates into English as "Western education is a sin"; however, the leader of the group in a 2009 interview stated that the name's meaning is "Western civilization

* Sharia law is a collection of rules and punishments based on interpretations of Islamic text. It is applied in many aspects of life, including finances, education, and daily routines (Johnson and Vriens 2011). It is based on the Quran, which is interpreted as the word of God, and the Sunna and Hadith, which are the lessons and words of Muhammad and his companions. The rules set forth by Sharia law can be confusing due to differing interpretations of the foundational texts by religious scholars (ulama) (Hunt 2007).

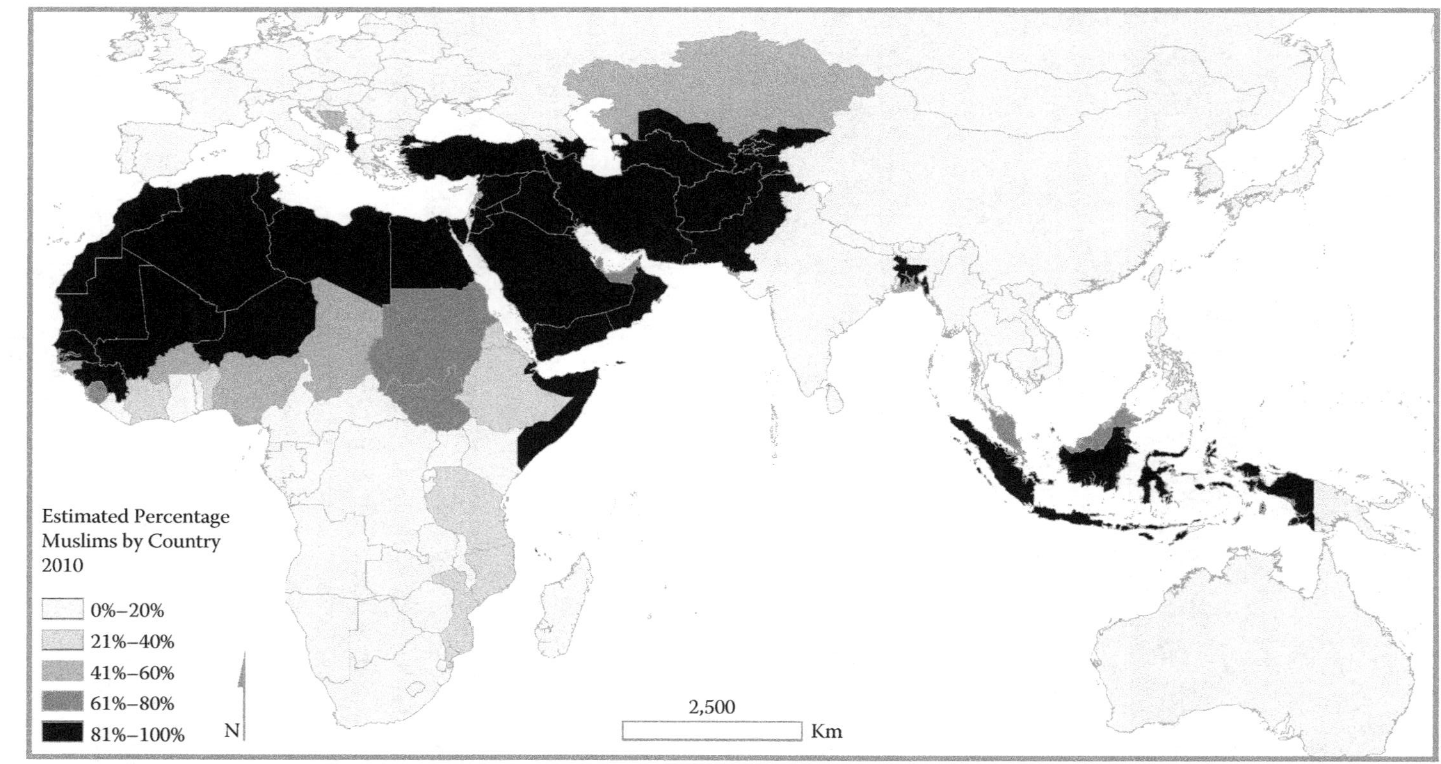

FIGURE 1.2
The Muslim world as defined by percentages of Muslims. (Data sources: Pew Research Center, 2011, political boundaries—ESRI, 2011.)

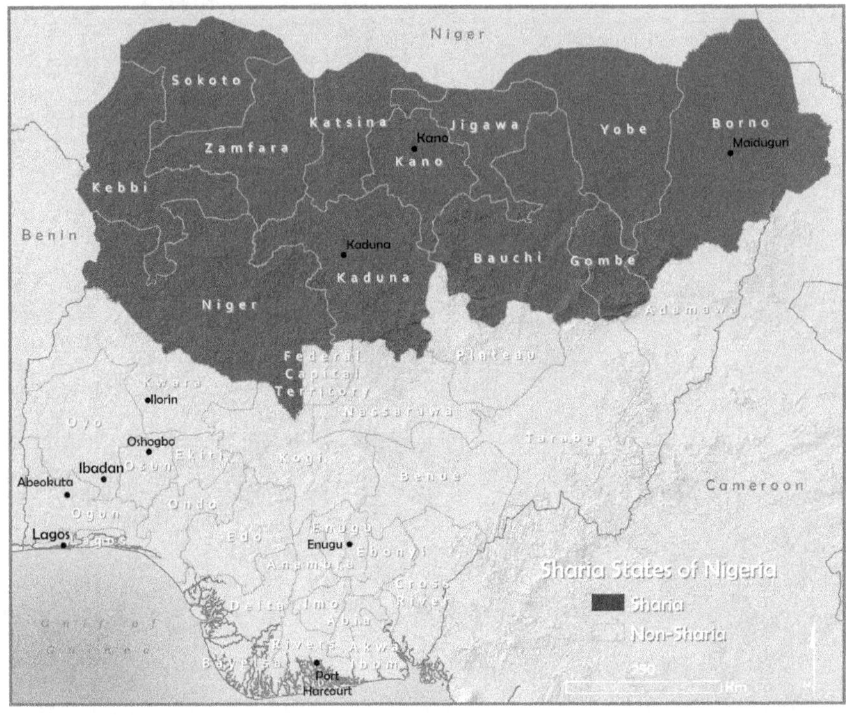

FIGURE 1.3
The Sharia states of Nigeria. (Data sources: Adapted from the Center for Religious Freedom, 2002, political boundaries—ESRI, 2011.)

is forbidden." This is a broader view intended to impose a wider control of fundamental Islamic rule. Members of Boko Haram believe that the Nigerian people have been polluted by Western ideals and ideologies and intend to bring rule by Sharia law to the entire country. The organization has been active since 1995 and violently active since 2000. The connection to the Taliban is self-imposed. In a 2003 attack on police and government in Yobe state, the organization raised the flag of the Taliban and established a base in Yobe named Afghanistan. Boko Haram is responsible for many violent attacks in northern Nigeria on police, government, and religious (Muslim and Christian) targets (Onuoha 2012).

The Muslim/Christian split in Nigeria is not precisely demarcated and there remain Christian minorities in the north and Muslim groups in the south. In 2011, an extremist Christian group named Akhwat Akwop began the fight against Boko Haram and Muslim rule as a whole by threatening to attack nationals of countries that support the Islamist terror organizations' activities in Nigeria. Akhwat Akwop's main grievance is with the

Hausa/Fulani people that are, according to the terrorist group, oppressing the minorities in northern Nigeria. The Hausa/Fulani are a major Islamic ethnic group. They make up approximately 25% to 30% of the country's population, and about 65% of northern Nigeria. They have held political control since Nigeria's independence from British rule in 1960 and have facilitated today's rule by Sharia law in the north.

In the south, few Muslims support the terrorism of Boko Haram. As long as the Muslim ethnic groups of southern Nigeria, especially the Yorubas, continue to deny Boko Haram logistical support in the southern zones, Boko Haram's attempts to strike targets in the south will likely remain isolated, infrequent, and ineffectual. In Nigeria, terrorism has manifested in two completely different ways based on the relative geographies of the physical and human environments.

DEFINING TERRORISM

The intent is not to dwell on the multifaceted and sometimes subjective concepts of terrorism, insurgencies, and criminal acts. These concepts have been analyzed and debated by experts in history and political science. There are many important questions one could ask about terrorism; the first and foremost is "What is terrorism?" With a consistent standard definition of terrorism, acts of violence can then be classified as either terrorist or non-terrorist. Another important question is, "Who are the terrorists?" Both questions here have proven to be difficult to answer and vary based on the political or rhetorical agenda. The intent here is to use these terms in a generally accepted and consistent manner.

There are many definitions of terrorism, which vary from country to country and even within country agencies, such as the Federal Bureau of Investigation, the Department of Homeland Security, and the Department of Defense in the United States. Each of these agencies has its own definition for terrorism (Hoffman 2006a). But among all the definitions some commonalities exist. Generally speaking, definitions of terrorism are composed of similar concepts including violence, fear, and motivation toward change. In its most general form, terrorism can be defined as "the deliberate creation and exploitation of fear through violence or the threat of violence in the pursuit of political change" (Hoffman 2006a, p. 40). Inherent in this definition is the concept that terrorism is a strategy or tactic for violence against non-combatants. It is typically used by individuals or smaller groups of people to fight against a larger, more heavily armed opponent and is aimed against non-combatants. Terrorists do not typically organize into strict militaristic structures, they tend to avoid enemy forces, and they have limited resources, which forces them to resort to more terroristic (i.e., non-combatant based) attacks.

The concept of terrorism is typically perceived as a negative act. Because of the negative nature of the term, a terrorist never labels himself or herself as a terrorist. Terrorists are always fighting on the self-proclaimed side of freedom, liberation, and truth, and thus label themselves freedom fighters. For example, in a video released by the As-Sahab Media Foundation, the media branch of al-Qaeda, American-born terrorist Adam Gadahn celebrates attacks within the United States and gives lessons on how to wage war against the West:

> Everything our enemies are, we are not, and everything we are, they are not. We are people of courage, honor, decency, chivalry and ethics who selflessly sacrifice themselves for the noblest cause on earth, and that is why every Muslim and every Mujahid must continue to take the high road and protect the moral high ground which we have fought so long and hard to secure (NEFA Foundation 2010, p. 4).

Al-Qaeda-affiliated terrorists, as well as those from many other organizations, believe they are fighting a moral and righteous war against evil, and that they are the victims. Because of this and the negative connotations that the term *terrorist* brings, they install this label on others. In 2007, Osama bin Laden, the leader of al-Qaeda, placed blame on major corporations as the "real tyrannical terrorists" (NEFA Foundation 2007, p. 4), in part because of their responsibility for global warming and its effects on humans. It is common for terrorist organizations to redirect the terrorist label onto their enemies.

The perception of righteousness of terrorist ideas and activities is reflected in organizational titles such as the Moro Islamic Liberation Front (MILF) in the Philippines, the Palestine Liberation Organization (PLO) in Palestine, and the Basque Fatherland and Freedom (ETA) in Spain. These names project a sense of freedom and good intention, and they reassure those involved that they are working toward a better life for themselves and others. Acts of terrorism can be waged for what some may consider good causes, but neither the intentions of the actors, nor the perceived goodness of the cause can change the category of the action.

Terrorism is a strategy and nothing more—an approach to violence, albeit an irregular one.

In their present form, terrorist organizations have taken advantage of global financial and communications networks and ubiquitous media, in some cases to construct international structures that facilitate violent and non-violent activities. Information age technologies have "shrunken the world" in the sense that the non-physical reachability between people has been greatly enhanced. With the combination of greater potential for information exchange and the earlier realization by terrorist organizations that worldwide attention to their cause is possible through attacks that are publicized, terrorists have moved into the twenty-first century.

Today's approach to international terrorism is the product of the PLO hijacking of an Israeli flight from Rome to Tel Aviv on July 22, 1968. This attack signaled the future of terrorism with key innovations, such as a hijacking; the choice of flight was politically driven, rather than merely a destination; communications with Israel being driven by the event, where previously communications with terrorists were avoided; and the ability to reach a widespread audience through the global media by targeting civilians (Hoffman 2006a). Communications technologies have come a long way since 1968. As the information age progresses, communications technology advancements in the speed of transmission, reduction of transmission costs, and increased capabilities for transmission of complex data will continue (Zanini and Edwards 2001). These ideas have major implications for the future of terrorism and counterterrorism.

TERRORISTS, INSURGENTS, OR CRIMINALS?

Having reviewed the definition of terrorism, the next step is to discuss the differences between terrorists, insurgents, and criminals. Some violent actors are at times misrepresented as terrorists. All three terms are at times used interchangeably (and sometimes, incorrectly), as the three groups often employ the same tactics in search of political change or profit. Though in many cases there is justification to use multiple categories for substate violent actors, these actors can span all three groups, especially as they evolve over time.

Insurgents typically operate in larger groups. They operate in a more coordinated, militaristic structure, whereas terrorists often operate in smaller groups of cells or individually. The insurgents' militaristic power allows them primarily to target opposing military forces in direct action, while terrorists primarily target non-combatants, using hit-and-run tactics. For insurgents, the long-term control of territory and the people within that territory is much more of a concern than with terrorists. They often incorporate propaganda and psychological warfare into their efforts and their main strategy tends to be the acquisition of popular support. An example of an insurgency is the Iraqi insurgency against the Iraqi government and the opposing coalition forces who occupied the state from 2004 to 2011 (North Atlantic Treaty Organization 2012). The insurgency remained in operation against government forces even after the coalition troops returned home.

There are many cases where violent actors are both insurgents and terrorists. There is a fine line between the two that is based on targeting. At times terrorists target government entities and insurgents target civilians. There are regions where both insurgent and terrorist organizations are active. Determining the classification of violent organizations can prove to be difficult, as some groups may operate as both.

Criminals can use many of the same tactics as insurgents or terrorists, including guerrilla warfare, but the main defining factor is that criminals operate for profit—and only profit. Neither insurgents nor terrorists have the end goal of profit, although terrorists do seek profit at times, as terrorism requires money. In many parts of the world there exist crime–terror nexuses where criminal and terrorist organizations operate symbiotically for mutual benefit. With criminals, the end goal remains profit.

An example of a type of criminal organization that is relatively difficult to categorize is the narcoterrorist group. Narcoterrorists, like terrorists and insurgents defined here, attack either non-combatants or government entities in search of political change. While narcoterrorists may adopt some political power in a region, their end goal remains profit, and efforts to subdue authority are also in the name of profit. Because of this, narcoterrorists may be more accurately defined as criminals.

GEOGRAPHY OF THE DEFINITION

There are many issues to consider when defining terrorism, some of which are described in the previous sections. A key point in the geography of understanding the meaning of terrorism is the spatial distribution of the definitions. There is a geography and spatial variance among formally stated definitions. Countries and organizations within them rarely agree on definitions of terrorism. This leads to a lack of agreement on how to deal with and punish terrorists. Each country's definition of a terrorist is designed specifically with their previous experiences in mind. For example, Israel is concerned to a great extent with the spread of propaganda and ideas. Activity in a terrorist organization is defined by Israel as

> A person performing a function in the management or instruction of a terrorist organization or participating in the deliberations or the framing of the decisions of a terrorist organization or acting as a member of tribunal of a terrorist organization or delivering a propaganda speech a public meeting or over the wireless on behalf of a terrorist organization shall be guilty of an offense and shall be liable on conviction to imprisonment for a term not exceeding twenty years (Israel Ministry of Foreign Affairs 1948).

In Pakistan, many more specific criminal activities are mentioned, some of which are sexual in nature. In some regions of the world, rape and other sexual offenses are termed conflict crimes. The definition of terrorism here is found in the Pakistan Anti-Terrorism (Amendment) Ordinance (Pakistani government 1999):

> Terrorist act—A person is said to commit a terrorist act if he
>
> (a) in order to, or if the effect of his actions will be to, strike terror or create a sense of fear and insecurity in the people, or any section of the people, does any act or thing by using bombs, dynamite or other explosive or inflammable substances, or such fire-arms or other lethal weapons as may be notified, or poisons or noxious gases or chemicals, in such a manner as to cause, or be likely to cause, the death of, or injury to, any person or persons, or damage to, or destruction of, property on a large scale, or a widespread disruption of supplies of services essential to the life of the community, or threatens with the use of force public servants in order to prevent them from discharging their lawful duties; or
> (b) commits a scheduled offense, the effect of which will be, or be likely to be, to strike terror, or create a sense of fear and insecurity in the people, or any section of the people, or to adversely affect harmony among different sections of the people; or
> (c) commits an act of gang rape, child molestation, or robbery coupled with rape as specified in the Schedule to this Act; or
> (d) commits an act of civil commotion as specified in section A. (Pakistani government 1999).

For Italy, terrorism is specifically defined in *Article 270 bis* as affecting democratic order:

> *Article 270 bis*: Associations whose aim is terrorism and subversion of the democratic order
>
> Whoever promotes, establishes, organizes, or heads associations that propose to carry out violent acts with the purpose of subverting the democratic order shall be punished with imprisonment for a period of four to eight years (United Nations 2002).

Updates to the aforementioned definition of terrorism by Italy are offered in *Decree Law 374/2001*, whereby it states, "Anyone promoting, instituting, organizing, managing, or financing organizations whose purpose is to propose acts of violence for the purposes of terrorism or for subverting the democratic order shall be liable for a term of imprisonment of between seven and fifteen years" (United Nations 2005).

These definitions differ greatly from the all-encompassing definition used in the USA Patriot Act (2001):

> The primary domestic legislation is the Uniting and Strengthening America by Providing Appropriate Tools Required to Intercept and Obstruct Terrorism Act, known as the USA PATRIOT Act 2001. This Act defines "terrorism" as activities that:
>
> involve violent acts or acts dangerous to human life that are a violation of the criminal laws of the United States or of any State, or that would be a criminal violation if committed within the jurisdiction of the United States or of any State;
>
> appear to be intended to intimidate or coerce a civilian population; to influence the policy of a government by intimidation or coercion; or to affect the conduct of a government by mass destruction, assassination, or kidnapping.

Variations in definitions of terrorism are typically found in the amount of detail/specifics within the definition, motivations for violence, and types of activities considered terroristic. These definitions directly reflect experiences in each region or a symbol of what is important to those in power. It is also worth noting that definitions of terrorism are deeply political and subjective. While countries throughout the world cannot agree on one unifying definition of terrorism, within-state organizations, such as the CIA, FBI, and Department of State in the United States have varying definitions based on their operations and goals.

MOTIVATIONS FOR TERRORISM

Terrorists are classified by their motivations. The motivations focus on a desire for political change, as the definition of terrorism suggests. While all motivations for terrorism are based on philosophy or doctrine, they can be divided into three different categories of nationalist/separatist, cultural/religious, and ideological. These three categories are not mutually exclusive, but rather are defined by their dominant motivation. Terrorists in all three categories can show differing organizational structures, preference for attack types and targets, and use of violence. To varying degrees all terrorists, regardless of their motivations, are primarily concerned with territories, the people living within those territories, and the ways those territories and people are governed.

Nationalist/Separatist

Nationalist/separatist terrorists are driven to force a change in state policies or a separation from the state to create a sovereign entity. In this motivation, nationalists/separatists work to force the state to turn over control of a territory defined by the terrorists. Attacks for nationalist terrorists are typically directed at state or foreign occupational targets. Because this is the case, agreements by the state and terrorist organizations can be made, where territories are conceded to end the violence (Sanchez-Cuenca 2007).

The primary motivation of Hamas, or the Islamic Resistance Movement, is nationalism/separatism. Their goal is the establishment and global acceptance of Palestine.* They can also be seen as a cultural/religious organization, but are used here in the discussion of nationalist/separatist motivations. Hamas has been in operation since the late 1980s and began as splinter group of the Muslim Brotherhood. Hamas won political leadership of Palestine by election, beating out the former ruling party, Fatah. It remains the "largest and most influential Palestinian militant movement" (Masters 2011). The stated goals of this organization are the destruction of Israel, the conversion of the West Bank and Gaza to an Islamist state, and the spread of Islam throughout Palestine. In the past, Hamas

* Hamas is a designated terrorist organization by the US Department of State and appears in the current list of designated foreign terrorist organizations (US Department of State 2012), though many other organizations, such as the Council on Foreign Relations, do not consider Hamas to be a terrorist organization and may see the group rather as an organization of service and charity (Masters 2011).

has been known to utilize suicide bombing as a form of terrorism, but the organization also spends an estimated $70 million in charity annually and is involved with social services including educational and recreational facilities. Hamas's military branch is believed to have over one thousand active members, and the organization is supported by many thousands (Masters 2011; Mishal and Sela 2000). The political boundaries of Israel, areas considered to be Palestinian (West Bank and Gaza Strip), and surrounding countries are shown in Figure 1.4.

Cultural/Religious

Cultural/religious terrorism is an attempt to build and implement a new social structure for a given region, territory, or state based on previously defined cultural or religious beliefs. With the advent of Islamist terrorism, and especially al-Qaeda in the late twentieth century, cultural/religious terrorism is arguably the most dangerous form of terrorism. This may be attributed to (Piazza 2009):

- Dehumanization of targets
- Focus on spiritual reward rather than earthly ones
- A much larger scale of attack (i.e., attacks are directed at multiple nations, rather than just one)
- Violence being the end, not the means (e.g., suicide terrorism is much more prevalent)

Also, since the goal is often based on perceived righteousness, these terrorists can rarely be negotiated with. They operate on an all-or-nothing agenda. This category includes antiabortion bombers in the United States and Aum Shinrikyo, religious terrorists in Japan.

An example of a religious terrorist organization is the Armed Islamic Group (GIA) in Algeria. The GIA was active in the 1990s into the 2000s and fought for a fundamental Islamic rule for the state. It was responsible for many attacks against journalists, intellectuals, liberated women, and foreign nationals, as well as a hijacking in 1994 and Metro station bombings in Paris in 1995. The last attack by the GIA was most likely in 2001. This group seems no longer to be active, though many of its members may have joined al-Qaeda in the region and continue religiously motivated terrorist activities (Vriens 2006).

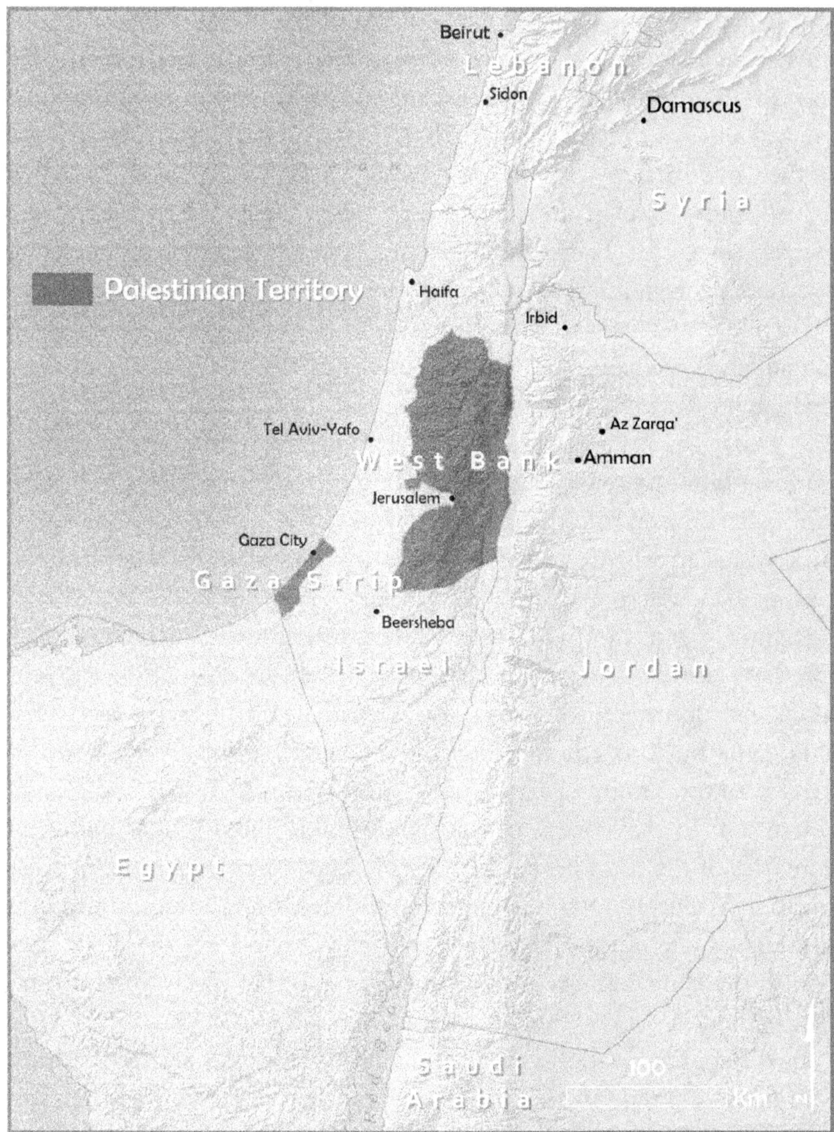

FIGURE 1.4
Israel, Palestine, and surrounding countries. (Data source: ESRI, 2011.)

Ideological

Ideological terrorists want to construct a new social order based on their political doctrine. These terrorists are motivated by the embrace of an idealized form of government, such as communist or socialist, or an idealized form of antigovernment anarchy. Unlike nationalist terrorists, whose goals are a complete restructuring of the state's social order, for most cases, agreements cannot be reached through the concession of territory (Sanchez-Cuenca 2007). Examples of ideologies in this context are Naxalites in India, Shining Path in Peru, and the Aryan Brotherhood in the United States.

Ideological terrorist organizations are often organized into *leftist* and *rightist* categories. Leftist organizations typically follow communist or socialist ideologies and have idealist/utopian political visions. An example of a leftist terrorist organization is the Revolutionary Armed Forces of Columbia (FARC). The FARC was founded in 1964 on Marxist ideology and supported the Columbian Communist Party as the military wing. The group has been involved in many violent activities aimed at government and economic targets and has connections to drug production and trafficking. While the FARC remains active, it has been weakened by counterterrorist/insurgent activities by the Columbian government (National Counterterrorism Center 2012).

Rightist organizations typically follow fascist or racist agendas. Targets for these terrorists are often chosen according to race, ethnicity, religion, and immigrant status. An example of a rightist terrorist organization is the Ku Klux Klan in the United States. Presently, the Klan, also known as the Knights Party, claims to be "committed to a non-violent resolution" to the "race war against whites" (Robb 2012), though past activities of the Klan have proven to be much more violent. This organization is deeply religious—specifically, Christian based. The Klan's ideology is one of fascism/racism, whereby they believe the white race within the United States to be in jeopardy and that their efforts are led by God.

Terrorist organizations can have any combination of motivations. For example, many of the present day Islamist organizations can also be seen as nationalist and vice versa, as previously seen with Hamas. Religious terrorists in the present are increasingly concerned with territorial control. Organizations can exist as motivational hybrids and can also transition from one motivation to another over time. Many terrorist organizations want to establish a sovereign state based on their beliefs or to unite with neighboring countries (Kydd and Walter 2006). This goal is of a geopolitical nature, as are others that focus on changing the beliefs of people within some geographic boundary.

CONTEXT OF PRESENT-DAY INTERNATIONAL TERRORISM

The world in the late twentieth and early twenty-first centuries has seen great changes that are affecting global order. The information revolution has changed the game. The nature of human activity has been forever altered. Within human activity, trends in war have also changed. A natural move toward networked forms of social organization, where power is redistributed away from traditional state-based entities to substate groups, is occurring. Those that wish to keep up must adapt. Also, communication and information in conflict settings have become much more important. The use of propaganda and, largely, perception management is a key trait of present-day conflict. The way in which information is distributed and accessed has changed. It is much easier now to reach more people (Arquilla and Ronfeldt 2001). This makes it difficult to stop Westernization. Thus, antiglobalization-focused terrorists may be fighting a losing battle, but the conflicts will persist.

For many throughout the world, connections to globalization are unreachable, so they remain disconnected. Ultimately, this creates a global environment of haves and have-nots. Figure 1.5 shows state weakness in the developing world, which includes 141 countries. The numerical values in the figure represent a normalized index of weakness from 0.00 to 10.00. State weakness here is designated by government responses and activities in political, economic, social welfare, and security spheres. All countries shown in various shades of gray and black are relatively weak. The countries without data in Figure 1.5 (shown in white) have already developed economically and are relatively stronger in comparison to the developing nations. In general, weaker states have less opportunity, fewer resources, and less ability to connect to the globalizing world.

To be disconnected from the globalizing world can mean different things. It can mean that a country has few resources for complementary trade, is unwilling to adopt new globalized ways of life, or lacks technologies necessary to remain connected effectively. Most of all, being disconnected is economic, in that countries that do not progressively integrate their economies with the world economy can remain behind as the rest of the world moves forward (Barnett 2004).

Poverty and the lack of opportunity provide a situation conducive for instability and terrorism to take root. State weakness diminishes the possibility of constructive governmental responses to the formation of

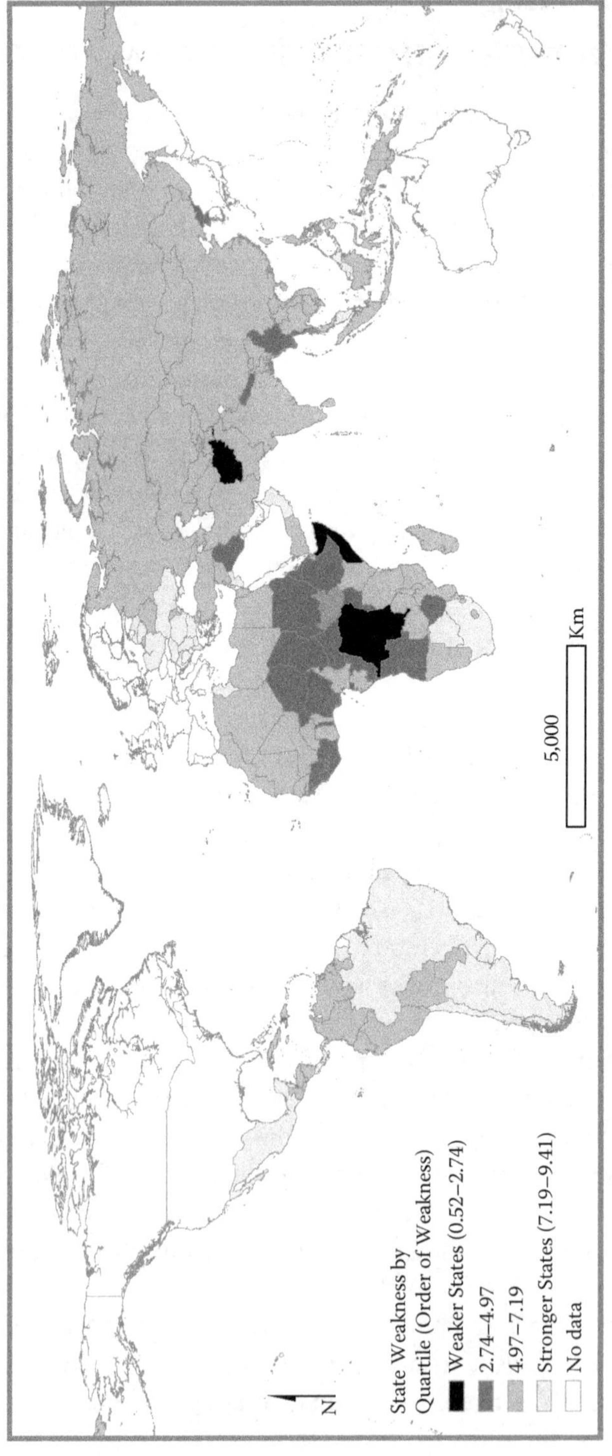

FIGURE 1.5
State weakness in the developing world by quartile. (Data source: Rice, S. E. and Patrick, S., 2008, political boundaries—ESRI, 2011.)

terrorist groups in the nation. This appears to be the case even more so for ideological and nationalistic terrorist groups, where the existing national political system is seen as the major impediment to success of the ideological or nationalistic movement.

Regions can benefit in some ways from being connected, but they can also suffer. Connection to the world means giving up total autonomy in exchange for participation. Joining the globalized world leads to the adoption of new rule sets, loss of tradition and culture, adaptation of new ideas and ideals that may not harmonize well with the present state of the country, and a wider field of competition (Barnett 2004). These are effects that some may not consider worth trading to be part of the globalized world. When they are imposed, resentment and conflict can develop. These grievances with progress in an unwanted direction can result in terrorism.

Today's terrorist organizations focus largely on "antiglobalization" platforms—a struggle to keep things the same or to return things to the way they used to be. For many, the world is changing too fast, and those that are having trouble keeping up are on the fringe of development. Much of the activity has been against US- or Western-based policies, ideologies, cultures, and other sweeping changes brought on by globalization (Cronin 2002/2003). Much of today's terrorist violence is a response to the breakdown of global order beginning in the late twentieth century and the unstoppable march of globalization.

WHERE IS TERRORISM LOCATED TODAY?

When considering terrorist incidents from 2007 through 2011, the majority occurred in states of Africa, Europe, the Middle East, and Asia (see Figure 1.6). The majority of countries that have experienced relatively high numbers of terrorist incidents are within the non-integrated gap. This gap includes nations that are economically and politically unstable, largely due to disconnection from the global economy (Barnett 2004). Not all terrorism can be explained by integration or lack thereof. Terrorist attacks can result in rich countries by foreign attackers, from homegrown terrorists that are marginalized in a social sense, or just from people who differ in political opinion.

Figure 1.7 shows the top 20 countries/regions (Note: the Palestinian territory is split into the West Bank and the Gaza Strip) for terrorist incidents. The terrorist incidents in Iraq, Afghanistan, Somalia, Indonesia, the Philippines, and Pakistan reflect Islamist or anti-Western activity of

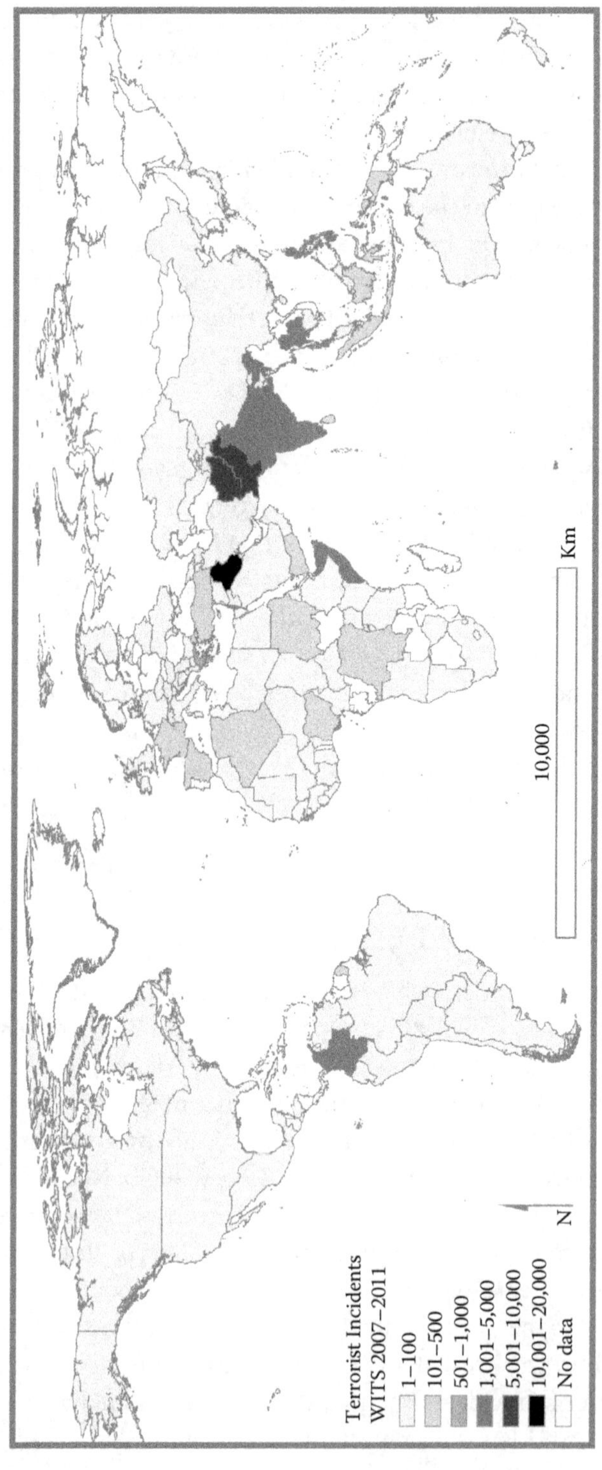

FIGURE 1.6
Terrorist incidents from 2007 to 2011. (Data sources: terrorist incidents—National Counterterrorism Center, 2012, political boundaries—ESRI, 2011.)

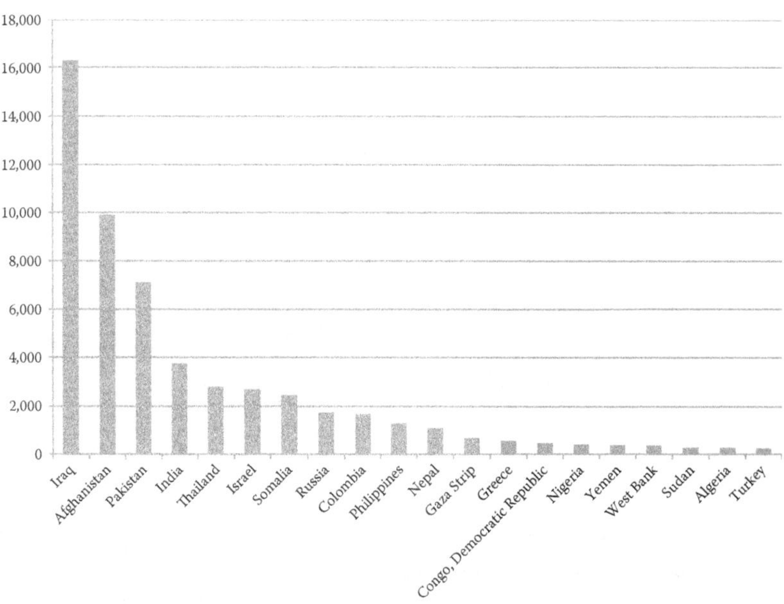

FIGURE 1.7
Top 20 countries of terrorist attacks from 2007 to 2011. (Data source: National Counterterrorism Center, 2012.)

al-Qaeda and affiliated organizations. Terrorism in Africa stems from ethnic conflict, poverty, and resource exploitation. In Thailand, there are many separatist groups in the south; in Columbia, much of the terrorism is ideology interconnected with drug production and sale.

Terrorism manifests itself in various forms throughout the world. Post 9/11 focus on terrorism is given largely to al-Qaeda style terror. Religious terrorism is considered to be the fourth wave of terrorism following the anarchist wave in the 1880s, the anticolonial wave in the mid-1900s, and the new left wave in the late 1900s (Rapoport 2002). Even in this fourth wave there are many other types of terrorism, which can be seen in many countries throughout the world.

GEOGRAPHY, THEORIES OF SPACE AND PLACE, AND APPLICATIONS TO TERRORISM RESEARCH

Geography is the study of spaces, places, and the phenomena that occur within or at them. It has many different manifestations for researching. The

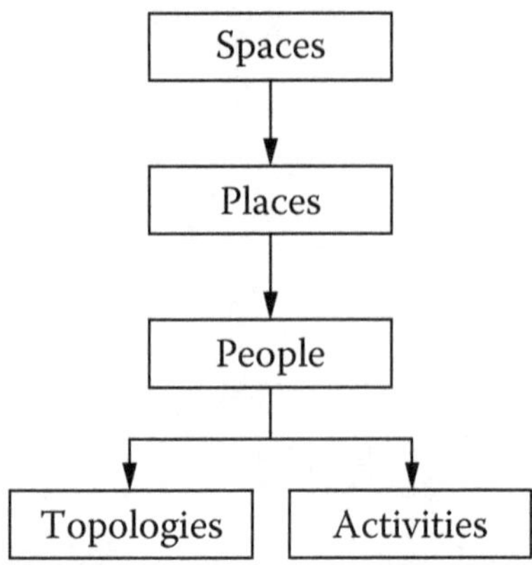

FIGURE 1.8
Geography thematic hierarchy in the context of terrorism.

geographic perspective is necessary to understand terrorism and terrorist activities that take place in the physical world. What geographers provide is expertise with the geographic perspective, or spatial thinking. There are two main components: physical geography and human geography (Knight 1992). These components are composed of subcategories of more specialized study, such as earth environments and geomorphology in physical geography, and political geography, and economic geography in human geography.

Geography as a discipline focuses on aspects of space and place, as well as the people, objects, and phenomena that exist in spaces and at places. Figure 1.8 illustrates the geography thematic hierarchy in the context of terrorism. It begins with spaces that bound all other parts of the hierarchy. Terrorists operate in various spaces, depending on goals. Places exist in spaces and exist as locations that people visit or have a connection to. People include terrorists, counterterrorists, local populations, potential radicals, etc. Topologies are the social, financial, or infrastructural connections that bind people. Networks are constructed from nodes and connections. In the case of terrorist networks, the nodes and connections can be people and social links, targets and roads that connect them, or banks with virtual money transfers. Activities include all those necessary to operate a terrorist organization or to carry out a terrorist attack. These can also be counterterrorist activities or any other activity that influences/affects the terrorist organization.

Space and place are social constructs (Harvey 1995). Space is not a thing, but instead a necessity of reason where people and things exist and interact—though, theoretically, the existence of things or people is not a necessity for a space. Spaces can take many different forms, some of which include physical (geographic) space, socioeconomic space, and behavioral space (Couclelis 1992). All these spaces are constructed to define and describe human experiences, activities, interactions, and accessibilities.

Places exist within spaces and are typically referred to as geographic locations, but they can also be used to describe a social or temporal location. Places are constructs in locations where activities happen (Couclelis 1992; Tuan 1996). They require the stimulation of all human senses and are typically connected to ideas or emotions and occur at many scales. When one contemplates one's concept of "home," it is typically accompanied by thoughts of family, childhood, activities, and, in general, a notion of what it "felt" like to be at that geographic (and temporal) place: a sense of place.

The constructs of space and place are always evolving as new spaces and places have meaning to us as humans. The information age has extended space and place to a virtual arena where communications can be managed and maintained. With the onset of the Internet in the late twentieth century, constructs of virtual spaces have become as relevant to everyday life as the other spatial constructs. Some principles of geographic places are relevant to actions and activities in virtual places. Activities in virtual space have replaced activities in geographic space in many cases. For example, purchases can be made online without a trip to the mall, books and articles can be read online without a trip to the library, and social connections can be built without coincidence in space and time. Because this is the case, geographic connotations have been applied to the Internet since its conception. Understanding many human social systems now requires research in geographic and virtual spaces. Virtual spaces and activities have great implications for activities in geographic space.

While virtual "places" may simulate real places at different levels, they lack the perception of physical interaction and are not yet considered places by some, though this may change in the future. Still, virtual places deserve attention from the geographic community, as they are increasingly approaching the realism experienced in geographic spaces and may one day stimulate physical senses (Adams 1998). Often, in science fiction movies, virtual places are imagined to be much more real to human perception, and total immersion into virtual places will most likely be a goal of the future. Take, for example, futuristic movies such as *The Matrix* and *Tron,* where people are able to enter the virtual world, or *Star Wars,* where, for meetings, people can be virtually coincident in space and time with the use of holograms. While virtual places may not be very "real" in their present state, they do present a platform for many information-based activities and flows, and studying activities within them provides information on properties of the systems that occupy them.

SPACES OF TERRORISM

In conflict and terrorism analysis, one must consider activities in specific spaces. There exist conceptualizations of high-level spaces: geographic space (bounds everything physical or geographic), social space (bounds all social interaction), virtual space (the space created by the Internet and the World Wide Web in the information age), and perceptual space (bounds human perception of reality). Everything happens in physical space, even social interactions, though it is often beneficial for our understanding to draw a specific space bounding human interaction; hence, social space is valuable. Terrorists physically live, interact, and attack in geographic space, while the communicative interactions that facilitate terrorist networks take place in layered social and virtual spaces. A hybrid space comprising geographic, social, and virtual space activities will also be discussed here, as many operations require the use of multiple spaces to be effective.

Geographic Space

Geographic space is the real, physical land and landscape of the Earth. The most important spatial concerns in terrorist network research are geographic spaces, where terrorists reside, plan, train, and attack. It is in geographic space that victims get killed and wounded by terrorist attacks, albeit sometimes with help from social and virtual space sources. Terrorist activities occur at and can be traced to places in geographic space. Even virtual space activities of computer-based communications are initiated from some geographic location where computer keys are pressed.

Social Space

Social space refers to the conceptual space of all social interaction including communication flows in virtual space. It is of vital importance to the understanding of terrorism and terrorist networks. These organizations cannot survive without communications, recruitment efforts, financial transactions, ideological diffusion, and local support—all of which require topological structures and activities in social space.

In most cases, it is simple to render physical activities onto maps. Rendering social connections and interactions has proven to be a bit more difficult, as it is more difficult to conceptualize the complexities of social interaction as geographic phenomena. Social interactions can be transferred from a network "graph" to a representation of geographic space, as shown in Figure 1.9, which illustrates a rendering of the global Islamist terrorist network in both spaces (Medina and Hepner 2011).* Redrawing a social network graph onto a representation of a geographic space provides more information. Clusters of people and directions of connections are evident. With more information, narratives can begin to be constructed to tell an operational story that is not possible through social space analysis only.

Virtual Space

Virtual space is defined in this book as the space bounded by Internet infrastructure and the World Wide Web (WWW). As the information age moves forward, more people are trading in their physical interactions for those in the virtual world. Virtual spaces, like physical spaces, are experienced by individuals in a relative manner. Virtual locations and interactions will have varying impacts on different individuals (Massey 1995). Accessibility within virtual space is unequal and leads some to benefit from the decentralization and interconnectedness of the information age and others to experience *virtual disparities* (i.e., disadvantages from lack of or poor connections to the virtual environment).

Al-Qaeda, sitting at the core of the Islamist terrorist system, has learned to wield the power of flows and connectivity of the information age. By controlling this power, the terrorist organization has effectively joined forces of many like-minded terrorist organizations and individuals throughout the globe. Al-Qaeda and other organizations in the Islamist terrorist system have embraced the Internet and other media outlets. Many terrorist organizations have sophisticated media arms, such as al-Qaeda's As-Sahab and the Taliban's Islamic Emirate of Afghanistan Media, as well as their own websites (US Committee on Homeland Security and Government

* A graph is a representation of a network composed of nodes (entities, not necessarily people) and links (connections or relationships between the entities) typically used for analysis and visualization (Wasserman and Faust 1994).

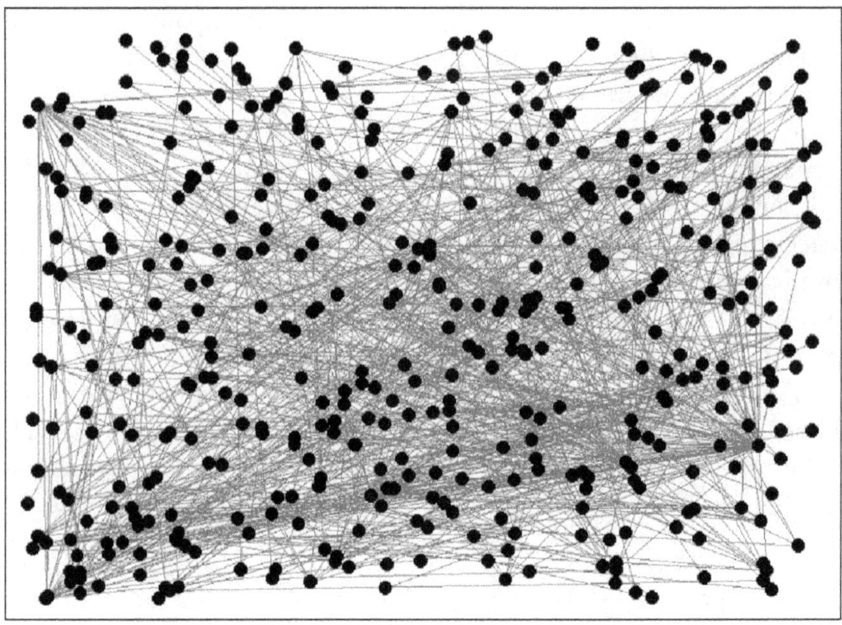

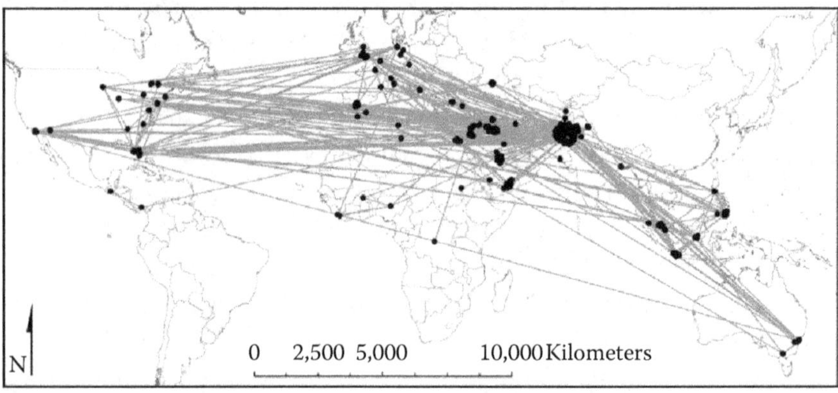

FIGURE 1.9
Representations of social space data in social (upper) and geographic (lower) spaces. (Social network graph created with UCINet; political boundary data—Garcia, N., Rala, A., Maunahan, A., Wieczorek, J., and Kapoor, J. 2011. GADM Database of Global Adminstration Areas. From Medina, R. M. and Hepner, G. F., 2011, *Transactions in GIS* 15 (5): 577–597. With permission.)

Affairs 2008; Kohlmann 2009; Zanini and Edwards 2001; Weimann 2004). The Internet serves as a center for distribution, collection, and connection. Terrorist organizations use these outlets to spread propaganda and ideology, conduct psychological warfare, disseminate logistic information and instruments of instruction and training, conduct fundraising, facilitate planning efforts, and maintain general social connectivity and social networking (Weimann 2004; Hoffman 2006b; Rogan 2006).

Virtual space has been coupled with terrorist activities so much in recent years that some even question the significance of physical havens, though this book argues for the importance of geographic activities and face-to-face interactions (Pillar 2009). Leaders of the Islamist network are aware of the importance of virtual space, which includes the present media battle, as well as terrorist activities (US Senate Committee on Homeland Security and Government Affairs 2008).

The importance of information and its spread through media and other outlets is recognized by Islamists and has been conceptualized as a "media battle for the hearts and minds" (West Point, Combating Terrorism Center 2005, p. 10). The time of release and content of official information by terrorist organizations is well planned. Recorded information by al-Qaeda's As-Sahab must be approved by a clearinghouse before release to the public. The benefits are to (1) provide authenticity of information, and (2) facilitate efficient distribution to previously used information flows (for example, to specific websites and forums) (US Senate Committee on Homeland Security and Government Affairs 2008).

The usefulness of posts, discussions, and interaction using online resources is theorized to help the cause in two ways:

- To convert secularist members to the mujahidin cause by changing opinions and to promote sympathy for oppressed Muslims in a type of *digital missionary* process, so that the Internet acts as a "virtual extremist *madrassa*" (US Senate Committee on Homeland Security and Government Affairs 2008, p. 8)
- By creating jihadist cells for action, although constructing terrorist cells strictly through actions online may be quite difficult

Concerns of attachment to the global jihad through the Internet are amplified by cases such as the "Jihad Jane" case in 2010. Colleen LaRose (aka Jihad Jane and Fatima LaRose) and Jamie Paulin-Ramirez, two American women, allegedly planned to travel to Sweden to assassinate a cartoonist for depicting the prophet Mohammed as a dog. LaRose had been contacting potential supporters through the Internet, as she contacted Paulin Ramirez (Foley 2010). LaRose contacted her target and became a member of his online community, and through the virtual introduction, she was able to move to his artist colony in Sweden (Khan et al. 2010). This shows a good example of hybrid space activity integrating geographic, virtual, and social spaces. Members of the cell are from the United States, Algeria, Libya, Croatia, and Palestine (Foley 2010).

Perceptual Space

Perceptual space involves the subjectivity of places, activities, and interactions considered (i.e., what exists in perceptual space is totally dependent on the minds of people). For example, some groups involved in activities to destroy the state of Israel, such as Hezbollah in Lebanon, do so because it is perceived by the group to be Muslim land. These perceptions are based on many factors, including social interactions, past experiences, and environmental effects. Much of Hezbollah's disdain for Israel stems from the Israeli invasion of Lebanon in 1982 (*BBC News* 2010).

Because perceptions are built on experiences, it can be difficult for others to share the same perceptions. Some perceptions can be shared by people, though that typically involves shared experiences within geographic or physical spaces at some time, or points in time. Often, perceived spaces can be more important than geographic spaces, as people act on their perceptions and not necessarily the actual reality of situations.

Another example of perceptual space activities with respect to terrorism today is the goal of the global caliphate, often alluded to by Islamist ideologists and strategists. The global caliphate is the idea of world rule through Islam and by Islamic leaders, and it has been practiced many times throughout history on a much more regional basis—for example, during the Umayyad Caliphate that was in power from 661 to 750. During the Ottoman Empire, caliphate rule stretched from Spain down through North Africa and east to Pakistan in Asia (Arnold 1967; Kennedy 2005). Today, many secularist Westerners understand the concept of the global caliphate as overbearing religious intrusion into society; in contrast, some in the Middle East see the caliphate as a viable and historically proven alternative to a government that has failed them.

Finally, this last example of perceived spaces lies in the symbolic meaning of a place. In a letter from Ayman al-Zawahiri, at the time second in command of al-Qaeda, to Abu Mussab al-Zarqawi, one-time leader of al-Qaeda in Iraq, al-Zawahiri describes what he believes to be "the heart of the Islamic world" as being "like a bird whose wings are Egypt and Syria, and whose heart is Palestine" (West Point, Combating Terrorism Center 2005)

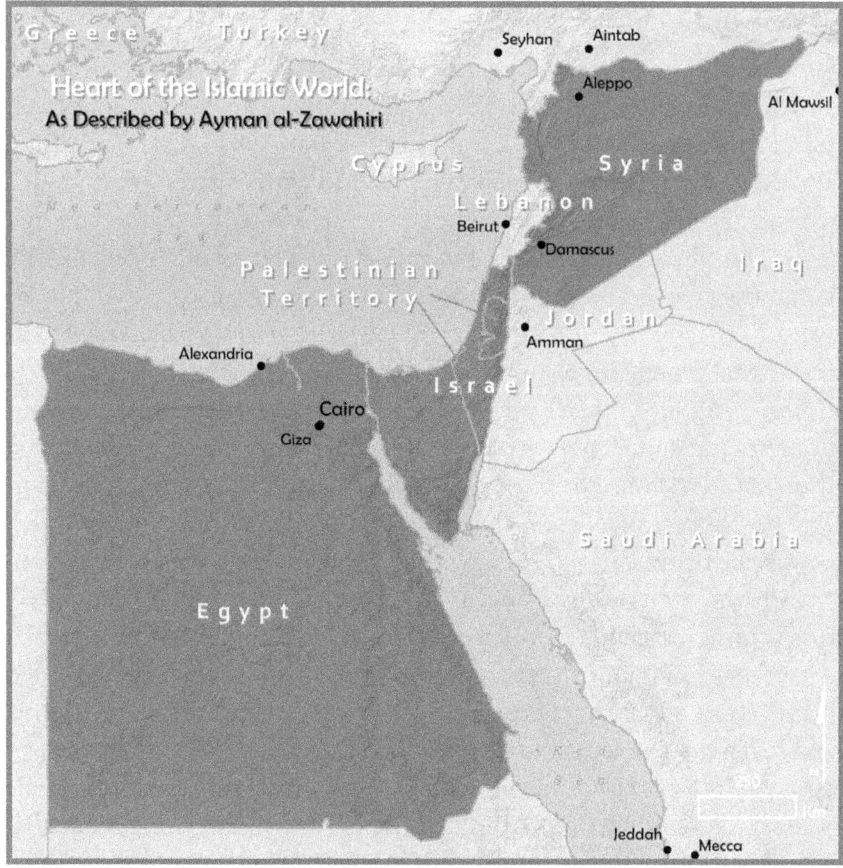

FIGURE 1.10
The heart of the Islamic world as described by Ayman al-Zawahiri. (Data source: political boundaries—ESRI, 2011.)

(see Figure 1.10). He also stated in the same letter "It has always been my belief that the victory of Islam will never take place until a Muslim state is established in the manner of the Prophet in the heart of the Islamic world, specifically in the Levant, Egypt, and the neighboring States of the peninsula and Iraq; however, the center would be in the Levant and Egypt." Both quotes reflect the geographic objectives of al-Qaeda. To the Islamists, this region in the Middle East, also including Lebanon, Jordan, and Saudi Arabia, is much more than a group of countries sectioned off by political boundaries. While the continuing struggle between Israel and Palestine is inherently over territory and the people within it, the people in that and surrounding regions are involved in an added cultural/religious struggle.

Hybrid Space

Humans operate in multiple spaces and, at times, activities occur at the convergence of these spaces within a hybrid space where access in these spaces is necessary, or at least beneficial, for operation (Batty and Miller 2000). For many activities, geographic and virtual spaces are bounded because virtual space attributes, such as accessibility to the Internet depend on physical places. The Internet works to loosen the dependence on location, but does not eliminate it. These spaces are also used in concert such that virtual messages identify physical places, as is the case with terrorist targeting. An example of hybrid space terrorist activities is the strategic placement of cells that may be near a targeted area, but communications and connections to the larger terrorist network are maintained through Internet means. In this example, geographic location, social network topologies, and virtual communications are all equally important.

Cyberterrorism takes place in hybrid space. In the past, some have argued over whether cyberterrorism exists and, especially, whether it exists as terrorism; however, new forms of cyberterrorism initiated online have proven to have real geographic space consequences. Older forms of cyberterrorism focused more on threats to economies and virtual structures. Today's forms have much more potential to incite human threat and violence. In a recent attack on Iran's nuclear capabilities in Natanz, computer hackers were able to attack nuclear centrifuges through use of the cyberworm Stuxnet. The centrifuges were programmed to self-destruct by changing the sensitive operations within the nuclear fuel enrichment plant from the cyberattack, destroying the plant's nuclear capabilities and setting it back years. The attack is suspected by some to be a combined effort between the United States and Israel, though no one claimed responsibility (Rosenbaum 2012).

These capabilities are more alarming considering that al-Qaeda has called for more cyberwarfare activities following the death of bin Laden and has compared the US virtual infrastructure flaws to the vulnerabilities in the transportation network that made 9/11 possible. The levels of preparedness in the face of cyberwarfare that the United States, Europe, and other cyber-dependent nations are unknown but are suspected to be much less than sufficient to fend off attacks.

The implications of hybrid space operations, such as cyberterror, are becoming more threatening as virtual and physical spaces become more integrated. Imagine the loss of the power grid in the middle of summer or the hijacking of military operations. Humans are now much more dependent on virtual space activities. Terrorism in the future will continue to benefit from information age technologies. The increasing dependence on the Internet and social media as global resources will drive the use of cyberterror in the future, taking much of the terrorist activity from physical to virtual spaces. This increasing dependence will integrate human lives with the Internet and World Wide Web much more in the future where direct connections between humans and information networks will put many more at risk from cyberterrorism.

TERRORIST PLACES, MIGRATIONS, AND ACTIVITIES

Havens and Safe Houses

The US Department of State defines terrorist safe havens as "ungoverned, undergoverned, or ill-governed areas of a country and non-physical areas where terrorists that constitute a threat to US national security interests are able to organize, plan, raise funds, communicate, recruit, train, and operate in relative security because of inadequate governance capacity, political will, or both" (2008, p. 196). This definition is very useful for the purpose of this book, as it focuses specifically on terrorists and the security threats they pose.

There are two concepts in this definition that benefit from further explanation. The first is the concept of non-physical areas. By using this definition, it is assumed that havens can be of a virtual nature, including websites and other forums for communication (e.g., blogs, social network sites, chat rooms). The second concept is that the terrorists operate in relative security. This does not imply that they are completely safe from counterterrorist efforts, but rather that they are relatively more secure than they might be in regions of more effective governance.

Types of terrorist residences, temporary or potentially permanent, can be categorized by the level of security a terrorist experiences and the openness with which the terrorist can freely express information on operations, opinions, and intentions. Places that are considered havens may offer state protection, community support, and commodities, such as funding and weapons. Terrorists live in many countries today, but most countries such as the United States and Canada do not offer haven for terrorists; rather, they act only as a place of residence for them.

Terrorist activity originates in geographic havens, which offer advantages of centralized location and security that result in opportunity for training, recruitment, planning, and support (US Department of State 2006; al-Shishani 2009). While havens are typically found to be located in regions of ineffective governance, many other environmental properties are also important in haven selection. Havens must be located where terrorists have access to resources, which may include logistic resources of supplies, funding, and favorable terrain, and general human necessities of food, water, and shelter. Examples of terrorist havens around the world are those located in Somalia, the islands of East Asia, the Afghan–Pakistan border, Iran, Lebanon, Yemen, and the triborder region between Argentina, Brazil, and Paraguay (US Department of State 2006; Hudson 2003).

The triborder region, illustrated in Figure 1.11, has been used as a haven for terrorist organizations including Hezbollah, al-Qaeda, and al-Gama'a al-Islamiyya. This region is not solely a haven for terrorists, but also for organized crime, for which it served initially. The level of criminal operations, weak and corrupt governance, and support from Iran and Lebanon in the region have created a safe location for terrorist activities focused on logistics and fundraising. Other facilitators in the region focus on the people who enter crime and terrorism operations due to unemployment, poor training, and low salaries. Terrorist organizations, such as Hezbollah, work together with crime syndicates including the Hong Kong and Lebanese mafias. It is estimated that between US$300,000,000 and $500,000,000 are sent annually from the tri-border region to Islamist terrorist organizations in the Middle East. Criminal fundraising operations include money laundering (estimated to be US$12,000,000,000 annually in the early 2000s), counterfeiting, and drug and arms trafficking (Hudson 2003).

Within havens, terrorist organizations have the freedom to train and recruit others. In some cases, terrorists can train on an individual basis, which is facilitated by online documents available for individual training. Depending on the size and structure of the terrorist organization, it may operate training camps that train various numbers of potential terrorists. In 2010, there were an estimated 40 terrorist training camps in and around Pakistan. Within these camps, trainees are expected to be led through activities including prayer, specialized training, and indoctrination (Keating 2010). For camps that require weapons training, remote areas where authorities have little to no control are sought. In one account, an al-Qaeda operative, Oussama Abdullah Kassir, was in communications with organization leaders and planning to construct a training

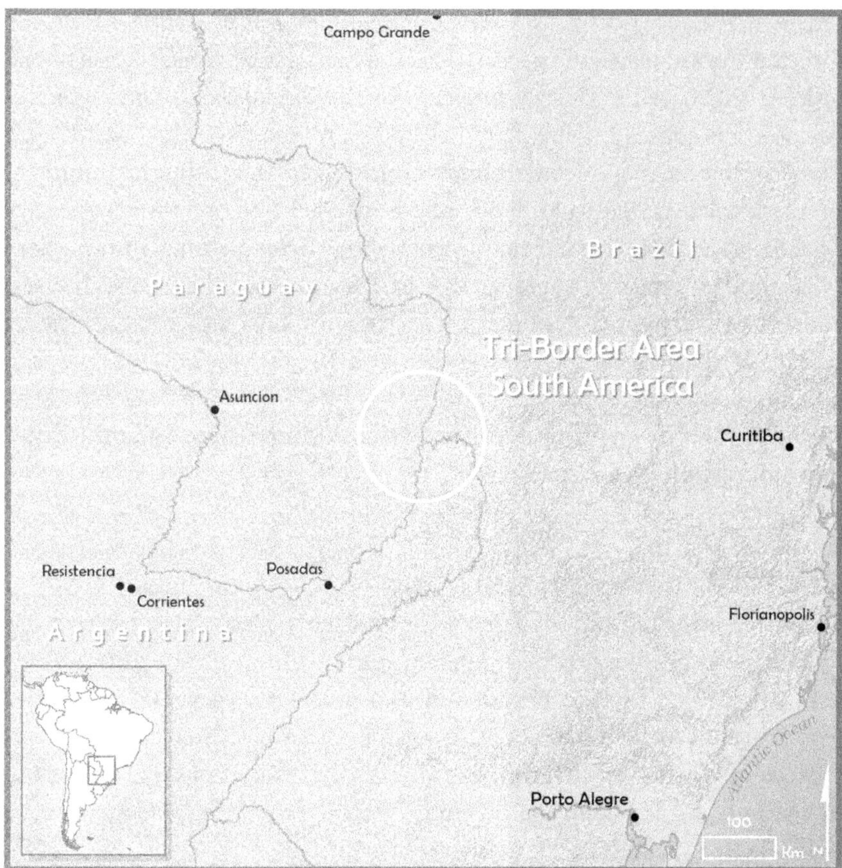

FIGURE 1.11
Triborder region in South America between Argentina, Brazil, and Paraguay. (Data source: ESRI, 2011.)

camp in Bly, Oregon, in the late 1990s. The camp was intended to prepare mujahedin for jihad in Afghanistan or for further training in Middle East training camps. Kassir selected the region as he felt it was similar to Afghanistan. In 2009, Kassir was sentenced to life in prison for multiple charges (Federal Bureau of Investigation 2009).

Safe Houses

Safe houses are intermediate stops between a terrorist's origin and destination. They must be strategically located to offer necessary resources and efficiently move terrorists into and out of regions of interest. These places facilitate temporary residence and secure travel from place to place for a terrorist. They are not meant to be permanent residences. Travel is typically directed toward a specific destination, such as a battle zone, training area, or a terrorist haven. As a brief stop before reaching their destination, terrorists use safe houses to plan activities and gain resources, legal and illegal. These resources may include access to computers and other communication technologies, food and drink, and assistance with obtaining necessary documents, further travel plans, and other logistic/operational information.

Safe houses typically operate covertly. They can take the form of houses, apartments, religious buildings, camps, and business establishments among other places of shelter (Felter and Brachman 2007). Some safe houses, like the al-Qaeda safe house found by US forces in May 2007 near Baghdad, have been suspected to be places of interrogation and torture for information (*Fox News* 2007).

Migrations

Migration is the relocation of people from place to place. It is often referred to as a move of intended permanency, but in this book, the term will be kept simple and used to describe all moves greater than cyclical moves (e.g., travel to work, to the store, to school). There are three main types of migration: voluntary, involuntary, and forced. Migrations are motivated by many factors, though the one main factor is that migrants are leaving to reside in a "perceived" better environment.

Voluntary migrations are those that are completely the motivation of the migrants themselves. Voluntary migrants choose to leave and are happy to do so. They may be moving for a better climate, better job, or education or recreational opportunities. Other migrants are responding to much more dire situations where risk is taken by remaining in their homes. Those in this situation typically have a choice to comply, or stay and die (Adamson 2006; Fellman et al. 2010).

Examples of forced migration are the migration of people to internment camps in World War II, the slave trade of Africans into the West, and the relocation of Native Americans in the United States. Opportunities for individuals or families to migrate safely in these situations would most likely be taken. Those migrants would be considered by the UN definition to be refugees.*

* A refugee is defined by the United Nations as one who "owing to a well-founded fear of being persecuted for reasons of race, religion, nationality, membership of a particular social group or political opinion, is outside the country of his nationality, and is unable to, or owing to such fear, is unwilling to avail himself of the protection of that country" (United Nations 2012, n.p.).

Migrations between voluntary and forced are categorized as involuntary. This type of migration describes those that risk their lives, and possibly the lives of their children, in the process of migration to a perceived better life. Examples of these migrations include ocean-based migrations where travel is made on rafts or other potentially unsafe vessels or those that travel through unsafe environments such as extreme desert conditions (Fellman et al. 2010).

There are varying scales of migration: intercontinental (between continents), intracontinental (within continents), and intraregional (within regions). The majority of migrations occur at relatively short distances, while the longest distance migrations are the most infrequent. The distance of migration is dependent on many factors; for example, motivation, opportunity, mobility, and existence of barriers can all influence this distance.

International migration patterns often follow previous flows to magnet cities or other regions that act as a buffer to the new host society. This is partially why Asian populations are growing on the western coast of the United States and Mexican immigrants are growing in the southwestern states. People tend to prefer migration to regions similar to those of the homeland with respect to cultural/ethnic factors of nationality, language, cuisine, and religion. Patterns of cluster migration, where people of the same ethnicity migrate together, and chain migration, where people of the same ethnicity follow the flow of migration, ensure that some regions maintain a level of ethnic homogeneity (Fellman et al. 2010).

One of the greatest motivations for migration in the future may be environmental threats, which can occur as either forced or involuntary migrations. In some cases of drought or flood, there may be no choice but to migrate or die. Millions have migrated in parts of the Sahel and sub-Saharan Africa because of the risk of starvation (Myers 2002). The potential for rising sea levels and other aspects of climate change threaten to displace millions more in countries such as Bangladesh (Intergovernmental Panel on Climate Change 2007). Environmental refugees may also move more involuntarily as a response to poor agricultural conditions, which has taken place in China and Mexico, or anthropogenic changes to the environment, such as those made for hydroelectric energy (Myers 2002).

Migration is an important geographic process in creating instability leading to terrorism and other forms of conflict. Migrations can change ethnic makeup within regions of destination, which can drive conflict. With respect to terrorism, two types of migration must be considered: migrations that are driving terrorism and migrations that are the result of terrorism.

Migrations Driving Terrorism

Many of the terrorist attacks experienced throughout the world are perpetrated by migrants, including both first- and second-generation immigrants who may or may not be citizens of the target countries. This was the case in the 2004 Madrid bombings and the 2005 London bombings (Adamson 2006). The majority of the 9/11 terrorists originated from Saudi Arabia (National Commission on Terrorist Attacks upon the United States 2004). They were allowed legal entrance into the United States; Mohammed Atta and Marwan Alshehhi were even issued approved student visas post-mortem (Fitzpatrick 2002).

The internationalization responsible for driving global business and culture in the information age is also driving global terrorism. For many, it is much easier and cheaper now to migrate to other countries due to transportation and communications technologies and the presence and strengthening of existing migration networks. These innovations are also responsible for the retention of ethnic roots and strong emotional connections to the homeland that can deter migrants from full assimilation into the host culture. Migrations of one ethnic group into a region of another can drive ethnic conflict and terrorism.

Many are migrating as the result of an oppressive leadership or the threat of harm to oneself or one's family. They are responding to an already violent environment in the homeland by leaving, but may retain a strong emotional connection to the homeland, which is facilitated by active social networks and global information availability. Within these communities may emerge homegrown or foreign fighter terrorists.

Migrations Resulting from Terrorism

Often, those greatly affected by terrorism do not have the resources to migrate far from home. Rather, they move within political boundaries or across them if poor governance is present. With the case of internally displaced persons (IDPs), the migrations are intraregional, within the political borders of the home country, though the borders can sometimes be *fuzzy*, as with the intersection of Pakistan and Afghanistan. In 21 sub-Saharan African countries as of 2011, an estimated 9.7 million people were internally displaced, many resulting from disputes over access to resources, politics, intercommunal violence, and power. The Middle East and North Africa saw an estimated 4.3 million IDPs as of 2011. Many of the IDPs in this region are the result of sectarian violence. While some IDPs are only displaced for short periods and are able to return, many are not and make new homes in settled regions.

Figure 1.12 illustrates the estimated IDPs in 2011, by country, in Africa and surrounding regions. Not all countries were surveyed by the Norwegian Refugee Council, and even for those that were surveyed, some had an undetermined number of IDPs. The accuracy of each country's estimate varies. For example, some countries are given a raw number estimate; others, such as Palestine, are given a number of "about 160,000" (p. 73), which gives less confidence in the estimate. Another designation of reduced confidence gives a maximum number, such as Azerbaijan with "up to 599,000" (p. 63). The estimates with least confidence are those given a minimum number, such as Pakistan with "at least 900,000" (Norwegian Refugee Council 2012, p. 82).

While the potential for error in these estimates is likely high, the data do provide a good view of the global problem of displaced people. In the region shown in Figure 1.12, the two countries with the most IDPs are Iraq, with 2,300,000–2,600,000, and Sudan, with at least 2,200,000. The country with the largest estimated IDP population in 2011 is Colombia with 3,876,000–5,281,000 (not shown in this figure) (Norwegian Refugee Council 2012).

To identify a visual correlation between IDPs and terrorist activity, the reader can compare Figure 1.12 with Figure 1.6 from earlier in the chapter. The authors make no claim of statistical significance for correlation, only that some countries with a relatively large number of IDPs also have had a relatively large number of terrorist attacks. These countries include Afghanistan, Pakistan, India, Iraq, Yemen, Sudan, Somalia, Indonesia, and others. Regions with both terrorism and large numbers of IDPs are unstable and the potential for many forms of conflict is increased.

Diasporas and the Homegrown Threat

Typically, diasporas are conceptualized as migratory groups of people connected through shared sociocultural characteristics, who are a minority in a host land. Assimilation is hindered either by internal controls as a defense mechanism and cultural preservation tactic or by external controls of rejection and subsequent isolation by a host population (Fellman et al. 2010). Residents living in diasporic communities are not necessarily first-generation immigrants, but can be children of immigrants (second

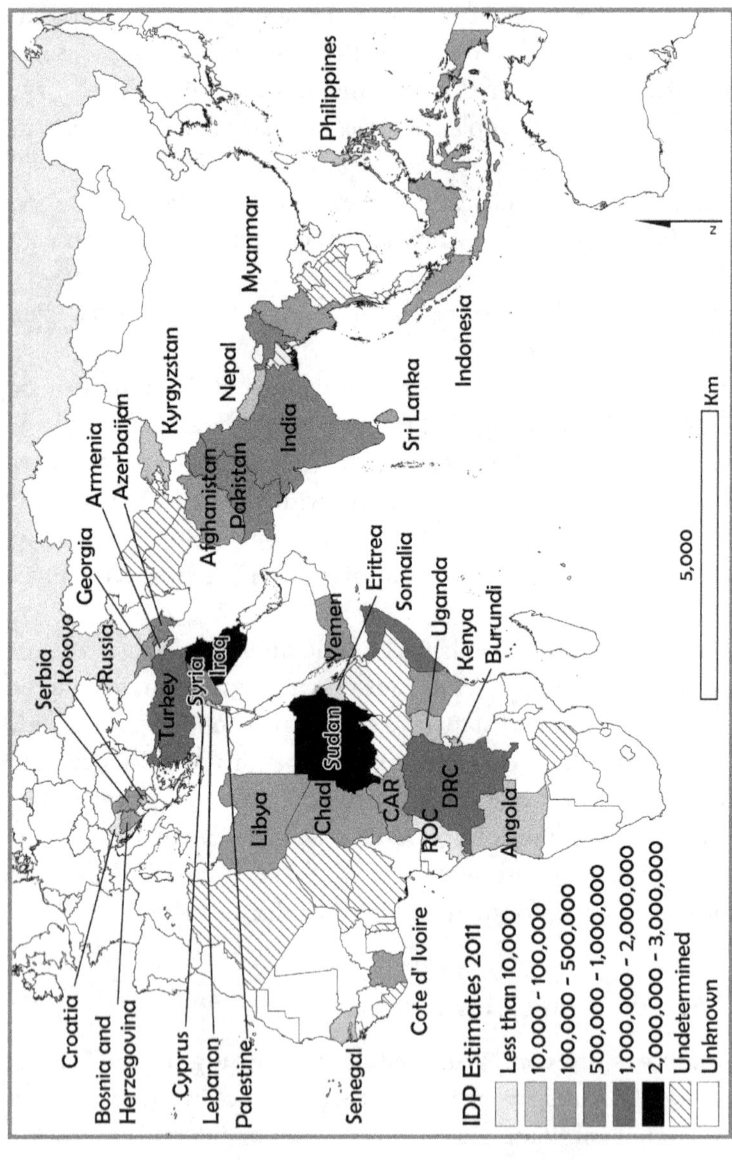

FIGURE 1.12
Estimates of internally displaced persons in and surrounding the African Continent in 2011. (Data sources: IDP estimates—Norwegian Refugee Council, 2012, political boundaries—ESRI, 2011.)

generation), grandchildren (third generation), and so on. The communities can also include converts to diasporic beliefs or ideologies, such as radical Islamists Richard Reid, the "shoe-bomber," and Zachary Chesser, who was responsible for threats to the creators of the *South Park* television program and was apprehended during an attempt to travel to Somalia with suspected attempts to join al-Shabaab (Hoffman 2007; Senate Committee on Homeland Security and Governmental Affairs 2012).

There are different levels of "diasporaness," based on emotional connection to ethnicity, and the homeland and belonging to a specific cultural group (Hoffman et al. 2007, p. 12). The level at which a person or a group of people is diasporic can be said to be based on properties of assimilation and acceptance. It can be difficult to identify levels of diasporaners for people in various stages of assimilation and acceptance by a host population.

Diasporas and national security are a concern, as many Western terrorist attacks and attempts have been carried out by members of diasporic communities (Post and Sheffer 2007). The typical pattern is one of failed assimilation by the immigrant group and a feeling of non-acceptance and alienation. It is this group's feeling of alienation that makes them likely candidates for successful radicalization and the psychological potential for violent activities. This process has led to an estimated 80% of new recruits into the global Islamist terrorist network (Post 2005).

Cultural understanding and tolerance is necessary to avoid these feelings of non-acceptance by immigrants. While moving to identify potential threats to national security, there must also be caution not to alienate people (Hoffman 2007). For example, France's 2011 policy directed toward Muslim women that outlawed the wearing of burqas in public has been met with anger and protest against the French government and many of the French people. Similar bills have been written for Belgium and proposed for the Netherlands (*Al Jazeera* 2011).

Those living in diaspora communities and involved with terrorist activities may be direct participants of attacks, such as with the 2004 Madrid train bombings, which were perpetrated by North African immigrants living in Spain. The diasporic individuals, though, may not be directly involved in attacks, but can still provide other forms of assistance, including tasks of recruitment, funding (legal and illegal), training, and procurement of weapons, as well as other logistical necessities. An example of diasporic assistance to a terrorist organization is the transfer of firearms to the Irish Republican Army (IRA) from the Irish diaspora in the United States. The large majority of weapons confiscated by British officials were traced back to the United States. Mobilized diaspora support communities can pressure governments into political actions through lobbying or other means (Hoffman 2007).

An example of radicalized people within a diaspora is apparent in the Somali diaspora, which in 2012 was estimated to be at least 2,000,000 people residing in North American, European, African, Australian, and Middle Eastern countries. Al-Shabaab, operating in Somalia, has been very effective in recruiting from the global diaspora. While only a small percentage of the 2,000,000 are mobilized and active in terrorism, the number of foreign fighters joining the cause is substantial.

The largest community of Somali migrants in the United States resides in the Minneapolis–St. Paul, Minnesota, area, which was the American origin of approximately 20 foreign fighters in Somalia (Chinn 2009). These fighters were motivated by the US-supported invasion of Somalia by neighboring Ethiopia with the intent to overthrow the Islamic Court Union (ICU), an Islamist government with suspected ties to Islamist terrorist organizations. In 2009 al-Shabaab pledged allegiance to al-Qaeda (Bergen 2009). It is estimated that up to 100 have left the UK for Somalia, about 20 from Sweden, and a suspected, but unknown number from Australia, Denmark, Canada, Germany, and Norway (Shinn 2011). Others within the global diaspora are guilty of funding al-Shabaab from Minnesota and Ohio (Welch 2011; *MSNBC* 2012).

SCALES OF TERRORIST OPERATIONS, ATTACKS, AND INFLUENCE

Terrorist organizations are embedded into regions at various geographic scales. Their operations use a targeted region for operations (e.g., attacks, training, planning, and recruitment), which is chosen for the perceived optimal return. This return can refer to numbers of recruits, amount of money earned, or number of victims. Operations are directly related to the organizational goals. Organizations operate locally, regionally, or globally (Figure 1.13). Locally based activities may or may not cross major national borders, whereas, regionally, an organization is more likely to be focused on a multination area, such as the Middle East or the Maghreb. Global organizations are uncommon, but increasing in number, facilitated by information technologies and globalization. These groups are motivated to influence political activities on a global scale. Some organizations are

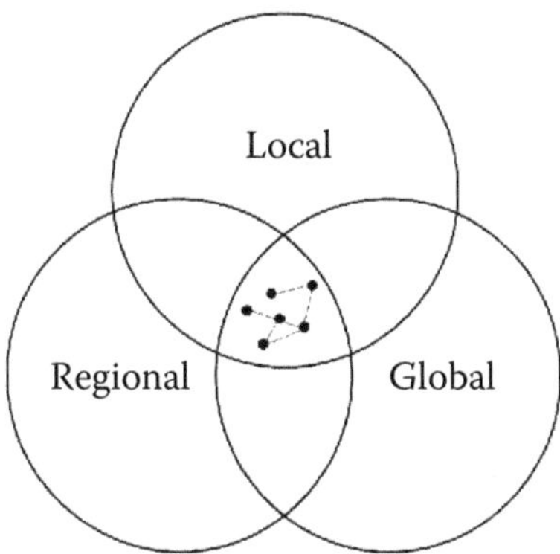

FIGURE 1.13
Terrorist circles of operation and influence.

embedded in all three scales of operations. Decentralized networks such as al-Qaeda have branch and affiliate groups operating within small areas bounded by national borders, and between state borders for operations in a larger region. Also, they focus on global efforts to bring the world under one united political/religious rule.

Al-Qaeda has popularized globalization of terrorism through a franchise model, where terrorists throughout the world are trained, given resources, and sent out to commit terrorist attacks throughout the world. Al-Qaeda's fundraising and recruitment operations also extend to the global scale.

Terrorist Attacks and Impacts on Near and Far Targets

Terrorists are concerned with both attack results and intended influence (i.e., the target audience). For the attacks, "near" and "far" refer to the location of origin of the enemy. The four possibilities for near/far attacks and near/far intended impacts are shown in Figure 1.14. For example, the 1998 US embassy bombings in Dar es Salaam, Tanzania, and Nairobi, Kenya, were attacks on the "far" enemy (the US), even though the attacks were geographically closer to the attackers. This categorization takes into consideration the political and tactical center of the terrorist's origin of operations. The geographic location of the near or far enemy, then, is strategically important, but not used to categorize the activity based on attack or intended impact.

The most common types of attacks are near-enemy and intended near-impact attacks (top left cell in the figure). In this category, attacks

	Near Enemy Attacks	Far Enemy Attacks
Intended Near Impacts	Attack on locally based targets for change in local politics	Attack on foreign targets for change in local politics
Intended Far Impacts	Attack on locally based targets for change in foreign or global politics	Attack on foreign targets for change in foreign or global politics

FIGURE 1.14
Categorizing near and far attacks and intended impacts.

are focused on enemies that are directly affecting the perpetrators or their families and are directed at local changes. This is the most common type of attack and intended impact. Most organizations have local grievances without a global agenda.

Near-enemy attacks and intended far impacts (bottom left cell in the figure) occur when terrorists attack a domestic target to change global policies. This can be seen where organizations target local companies or government entities that are working in cooperation with foreign partners. The attacks are meant to expel foreign involvement, but also to send a message to the foreign entity. Attacks such as these can also be carried out by organizations with goals that are morally or ethically charged. For example, local attacks on abortion clinics or animal study laboratories may have effects on global companies or ideologies that are used in many countries throughout the world.

Terrorists that attack far enemy targets for change in local politics (top right cell in figure) are common where foreign governments or organizations travel to exploit or occupy regions and work together with local governments and politicians. These attacks are typically intended to expel the foreign entity and change local policies. Examples are the terrorist attacks in southern Nigeria against oil corporations and Iraq insurgency attacks against coalition troops.

With far attacks and intended far impacts (bottom right cell in the figure), terrorists may be responding to direct and indirect effects of the enemy actions on them or their families. For example, the spread of Western culture as a factor of a globalized economy is not directly related to policies of Western governments, though parts of Western culture are cited in fundamental Islamist text as being unacceptable. The 9/11 attacks are an example of this category. Al-Qaeda attacked the far enemy and expected policy change on an international scale.

Attack Patterns in Geographic Space

Terrorist attacks are planned with specific goals in mind, which argues for the rationality of terrorism and terrorist operations. Because specific goals are set, attacks tend to have spatial patterns based on strategy. An example of a nationalist/separatist terrorist group that clearly illustrates this concept is seen with Euskadi ta Askatasuna (Basque Homeland and Freedom [ETA]), a nationalist/separatist terrorist organization that operates in Northern Spain and Southern France seeking autonomy for the Basque country and people. This group has shown over time a strategic shift from a control-based focus, characterized by attacks that support control of the people within the region of concern, to an attrition-based focus, characterized by attacks against the enemy state, Spain.

Along with the strategic focus comes a subsequential shift in spatial attack patterns. Control-based attacks tend to be *contagious* in nature (i.e., they occur adjacent in space), while attrition-based attacks tend to be *hierarchical* (i.e., selections for attack targets are made based on some predefined hierarchy of importance) (LaFree et al. 2012). The terms *contagious* and *hierarchical* are essential topics of geographical diffusion, which can be movement of information, goods, people, or, in this case, terrorist activity.

THE FOUR TRADITIONS OF GEOGRAPHY AND THEIR APPLICATIONS TO TERRORISM RESEARCH

The four traditions of geography as defined by Pattison in 1964 are spatial (analysis), area studies, man–land (human–environment interactions) research, and earth science:

- Spatial analysis is the act of separating spatial properties (e.g., distance, pattern, direction) from the "happenings of experience" (Pattison 1964, p. 212). It consists of theories and methods used to identify patterns in spatial phenomena. In terrorism studies, spatial analysis can be used to identify patterns of terrorist activities (e.g., attacks, radicalization, and information diffusion) and unveil aspects of relative location (e.g., nearness to political boundaries, resources, and supportive populations), as well as many other applications.
- The focus of area studies is derived from the term and self-explanatory, as they are studies of areas on the earth and are not limited to either human or physical geography. Area studies are vital to the understanding of terrorist and organization properties of operations as they vary in different places, as well as the regional, cultural, and political properties that facilitate or deter terrorism.
- Man–land (human–environment interactions) research focuses on human use and alteration of the natural environment and the effects of the natural environment on humans. This tradition includes land use and environmental degradation analyses. Some terrorism can be triggered by the use of land and environment in different ways. For example, the MEND terrorists discussed at the beginning of the chapter are responding to land use and pollution from petroleum resources and ultimately would like to see a change in policy such that the profit from resource extraction remains with the local people.
- The earth science tradition is focused on the earth system and its processes including, for example, climate, land cover, and ocean currents. These earth system traits, in many ways, affect conflict, especially in the case of irregular warfare. Earth science, with the help of geospatial technologies, can be used to identify regions of difficult counterterrorism operations based on unfavorable properties of physical terrain. The terrain selected by terrorist groups for combat is believed to be optimal when safety and cover is provided, as well as access to enemy forces. This will always be a trade-off for terrorists and insurgents. Too much safety and cover will not allow enemy forces pathways into areas where attack is possible, and hindering the mobility of the enemy will also hinder the mobility of the terrorist (Taber 2002; Guevara 2007).

GEOGRAPHIC THEORIES OF TERRITORY AND CONFLICT

Many theories and concepts in geography have been developed to help explain and understand conflict-based human activities in geographic space. One historical concept that resonates today was introduced by MacKinder (1904) and discusses an early effort to identify aspects of relative location in the context of geopolitical power on a global scale. The second, developed by McColl (1969), describes spatial characteristics of irregular warfare, including the spatial and organizational evolution of insurgent groups to guerrilla groups to perpetrators of regular warfare. The third is a concept of multiple spaces for interstate conflict termed "ConflictSpace," introduced by Flint et al. (2009). While there are many more geographic contributions to the study of conflict, these three are most relevant to this discussion of terrorism.

Heartland Theory

MacKinder is considered to be the father of modern geopolitics. His heartland theory was introduced in 1904 in his paper, "The Geographical Pivot of History." This theory is an early attempt at recognizing relative location of geographic realities, such as climatic patterns, landscape features, access to oceans, and geopolitics on a global scale. In this article, he states that "man and not nature initiates, but nature in large measure controls" (p. 422). He brings aspects of location, environment, and relative location to the forefront in geopolitical theory. He postulated a global heartland of Eastern Europe and Central Asia surrounded by rimlands of marginal areas ripe for competition and conflict.

Although MacKinder was incorrect in some of his speculations about the aspects of the geopolitical future of Russia and Eastern Europe, his general message that the actual balance of power and control at any given time and place is the product of geographical conditions and the relative numbers, motivation, technology, and organization of the competing peoples has proven out. Political ideas in and of themselves are not sufficient or sustainable over the longer term without the suitable geographic context. While MacKinder was addressing political roles at a global scale, insights into the role of geography have been substantiated at the regional and local geographic scales (MacKinder 1904; Diamond 1997).

The Evolution of the Insurgent State

According to McColl, the progress through the three stages of revolution—"mobile," "guerrilla," and "regular" war—is inherently tied to the control of territory (1969, p. 614). Revolutionary movements necessarily begin in mobile war, as their ideologies are deemed unacceptable by a governing power, and thus have no safe base of operations, only temporary camps. In the next stage of this type of conflict, revolutionary groups are constantly being pursued and eventually realize the need for a territorial base.

An earlier publication by McColl discusses the ideal geographic situation for guerrilla warfare, which includes regions of revolutionary experience; political instability; access to objectives, resources, and services; weak authority, as in border regions; favorable terrain for operations and security; and economic self-sufficiency (McColl 1967).* These criteria are used by revolutionaries for site selection of their base and are indicative of the future success of the base at the specific location (McColl 1969).

Upon selection and population of a fixed area, the area selected becomes the center of the movement. This base is responsible for the military headquarters, supplies, and facilitation of thoughts, ideas, plans, and strategies. Over time, as the movement gains support, it either has to increase the size of the base or move some members to newly established bases. With bases in multiple regions, the movement begins to expand regional control, and revolutionary activities can be more numerous, cover a wider area, and originate from multiple locations. This opens up the potential for coordinated attacks from various directions. Establishing more bases also has implications for propaganda potential and access to new resources, including populations for recruitment purposes, stock and supply areas, and social and health services.

As more bases are formed and the movement continues to expand, strategic selections for expansion are directed at regions with more people. The revolutionary expansion is inherently tied to geography and people as a function of strategy. The new regions of operation are often referred to as *liberated areas*. The expansion of new liberated areas is concurrent with the establishment of guerrilla areas, which are positioned outside heavily populated areas in the *hinterlands*. The guerrilla area activities are

---

* This list of geographical characteristics of ideal guerrilla warfare regions was adapted by McColl from previous publications: Mao, Z. (1953) *Why Can China's Red Political Power Exist?* Peking: Foreign Languages Press; Mao, Z. (1960) *Strategic Problems in the Anti-Japanese Guerrilla War*. Peking: Foreign Languages Press; and Mao, Z. (1968) *The Struggle in the Chingkang Mountains*. Peking: Foreign Languages Press.

directed toward control of infrastructure and are located such that their military and political value is greater than that of the liberated areas.

The shift from guerrilla war to regular war* requires new geographic and political positioning. The guerrillas would now be operating with multiple bases spread out among the warring state and sufficient support from or control of populations in liberated areas. One of the main problems in this stage is the difficulty of communications between those liberated areas. The movement is still not able to operate in one coherent group. Without coherence, parts of the movement can lose direction and structure. Furthermore, the organization that has, up to this point, existed with a mostly military focus, now must shift its energy to political gains, where destruction of government people and property is not enough to sustain the movement.

The natural administrative shift is to structure the organization more like a hierarchical government, where a capital-/province-like structure is formed out of the liberated areas. The bases are more hierarchical in the political structure sense, but individual arms are now able to focus more on local issues, so in some ways, this new structure is a form of decentralization. The movement must also begin to provide services to the people that were once provided by the government. The insurgent base areas continue to increase in number and expand in size with consideration given to key geographic areas including focus on targets, physical terrain, and populations. Assuming that the insurgent state is now at sufficient size, coherence, and political presence, the insurgents are now capable of a sustained war with the government and ready for the final battle for state control (McColl 1969).† The traditional insurgent state's development and function share many properties with the terrorist haven.

ConflictSpace

The idea, or conceptualization, of ConflictSpace is intended to create a multispatial focus for studies of *contentious politics* or conflict (Leitner, Sheppard, and Sziarto 2008; Flint et al. 2009). This is not solely an argument for the inclusion of multiple integrated spaces into studies, but rather a more complex viewpoint of conflict that incorporates multiple space activities and the interactions and interdependence between

* In the stage of regular war, "equilibrium" is also experienced in regard to the military power on both the insurgent and government sides, which can be seen as equal (McColl 1969).

† See this reference for a full and detailed explanation of this process.

them (e.g., how interactions in social space affect geographic location and mobility and vice versa). Leitner et al. (2008) identify five specific spatial traits to consider in contentious politics—scale, place, network, positionality, and mobility—that all seem to be contained in a defined political space.

- Scale refers to the various forms of activities within and between local, regional, or global operating entities.
- Places are conceptualized as locations where people and the interactions between them exist, but also sites of power and meaning. Places are composed of the physical and human environment where boundaries are built, spaces are defined, and interactions and mobilites are shaped.
- Network space bounds interaction between people, where those interactions are necessary for flows of things tangible and intangible.
- Positionality refers to sociospatial location within a network and with respect to new connections outside the network, and the power relations that location provides. This describes geographic centrality and social capital. Varying location will lead to varying perspectives, interactions, and reactions to stimuli and, in general, a different understanding of the world.
- Mobility describes the dynamics of people, ideas, and things over space and time. These five spaces are key to research and understanding contentious politics (Leitner et al. 2008), though there are many other spaces to consider at different levels that will be discussed in this chapter, including social, virtual, perceptual, and activity spaces.

ConflictSpace as a term is introduced by Flint et al. (2009) to "incorporate the analysis of multiple spatialities into the analysis of war" (p. 829). It makes use of the multiple-space theory analysis delineated previously by Leitner et al. (2008). This concept is applied by Flint et al. to conflict on the state-to-state level, but the idea of ConflictSpace can be applied in any warlike situation. Approaching terrorism research from multiple directions with consideration given to multiple spaces and the interactions of activities within those spaces is beneficial. Social network space activities are interdependent with geographic space activities, as are economic, political, and virtual space activities. State and non-state entities in conflict situations are influenced by relative locations and network connections to, and flows between, other actors.

Resident versus Foreign Fighter Terrorists: A Geospatial Concept

Terrorists are either residents of the area they are operating in or fighters operating in foreign lands. Both are discussed in this book, as they are in many other literature. There is an increasing trend to analyze the two groups separately, because the locational intent of violent actors has implications for how the actors should be treated and the locational danger posed by their actions. Members of the two categories can be separated by identifying their place (country) of residence/citizenship and their intended target for violent activity. Those that stay and attack their "homeland" are termed resident terrorists, while those that travel to other countries are termed foreign fighter terrorists. The term "homeland" can also be somewhat ambiguous, because of the effect of perceived spaces, but it is used here to define the place someone is from. Further defining characteristics of foreign fighters are that they join a foreign organization, they lack social connection or citizenship to the warring state, they have no affiliation with a formal military, and that they are unpaid (Hegghammer 2010).

One of the main arguments for separating foreign fighters and resident terrorists into separate groups for research and policy is that their threat is regionally based (i.e., Foreign fighters living in the West and intending to operate in another country are much less threatening to the West than would be terrorists intending to attack their homeland, though the likelihood that they will attack their homeland upon return from their foreign activities is heightened.). This has great implications for what is termed "homegrown terrorism." After one is considered a homegrown terrorist, their future targets are in question. Does one intend to attack the homeland or travel for conflict?

Another argument is that it is easier to identify and predict spatial behavior of conflict and violence if terrorists and foreign fighters are separated into their own categories. By combining the two, the problem is oversimplified, such that attention may not be directed at the right problem. Many detainees at Guantanamo Bay were captured and imprisoned without a full understanding of their activities. Most detainees were foreign fighters that may have posed no direct threat to the United States, although calculating the regional threat in this case can be quite complicated.

The use of foreign fighters in Islamist terrorism is common and has been since the 1980s. Many have left their homes in the West, as well as other parts of the world, to travel to jihad arenas in Bosnia, Chechnya, Pakistan, Afghanistan, and Iraq. This has been a defining property of globally focused terrorist groups such as al-Qaeda that accepts foreign fighters into their ranks.

There are many questions as to why people travel to foreign lands for conflict and many hypotheses that attempt to explain the motivation to become a foreign fighter. Why would someone travel to fight, especially in the jihadist case where much of the focus of Islamist organizations is anti-Western? It seems illogical in cases where those accepting jihadist ideologies travel away from the West, when they can attack without moving at all.

Research has attempted to explain this motivation through factors of opportunity, training, and ideology. Fighting in foreign lands where an insurgency is already underway provides actors with opportunities to train formally and gain real experience in a conflict zone, which may not be available if they plan to attack a Western target. Opportunities to train as an insurgent in the United States are much more limited than in places such as Pakistan, Afghanistan, and Iraq. Also, in the West terrorists often have a one-attack limit before they are caught or killed. Ideology may play a role for those foreign fighters that perceive fighting in insurgencies as being more legitimate than attacking civilians. In this way, they can align their beliefs with those in action already, which is easier than convincing themselves that it is acceptable to kill innocent civilians.

It is shown in research that one is much more likely to be a foreign fighter terrorist than a resident terrorist and that most foreign fighters do not return to their countries with the intent to terrorize the homeland. Some foreign fighters do have plans to attack the homeland, which may have been their own in the first place or may have been heavily influenced by the organization they joined as foreign fighters. For globally minded terrorist organizations, having members within various countries is an asset, especially if the organization is anti-Western and the members are in the West (Hegghammer, in review). These hypotheses, while valuable, are targeted at explaining a complex social system of migrants and it is unlikely that explaining this phenomenon can be done with so few factors.

GEOSPATIAL INFORMATION AND TECHNOLOGIES IN THE CONTEXT OF TERRORISM AND SECURITY

The information revolution is characterized by an infrastructure that can support an increased amount of information and communications, and the technologies to collect, catalogue, and process information. A very important subset of this information is geospatial in nature, meaning that it has some locational or even spatiotemporal component. Geospatial information is everywhere and is available through location-based technologies. Everyone who carries a cell phone is directly or indirectly producing and accessing forms of geospatial information and using geospatial technologies. There are very few societies in the world today that are not affected in some way by these changes, whether socially, economically, or politically. This information and these technologies have been utilized for both terrorism and counterterrorism efforts. Geospatial information and technologies will be introduced here and discussed further in later chapters.

Geospatial Information

Geospatial information is any information with geographical location attributes. It is produced/volunteered by individuals or agencies, collected by various technologies such as satellites, cell phones, and web-based resources, and used in conjunction with a GIS for analysis of spatial attributes and patterns. Most information can have geospatial properties added, as most events and earth features have an absolute and relative location. The information is used by terrorists and counterterrorists for operations and planning. For example, both terrorists and counterterrorists might want to identify urban weaknesses and population vulnerabilities, land use and land cover types for navigation, and locations of resources and supply points.

Global Positioning System

The global positioning system (GPS) is a system of Department of Defense launched satellites that provide locational and navigation information with the combined use of a handheld or transportation-based receiver. GPS allows for users to track locations and navigate through rough terrain or urban areas alike. This technology is available on most cell phones and all smart phones today. It is used by terrorists and counterterrorists for location-based services, such as with operations and planning, as well as targeting.

Remote Sensing

Remote sensing can be defined as the acquisition, processing, and interpreting of reflected electromagnetic radiation and includes tools, such as satellites and sensors, methods, and algorithms for these processes (Sabins 1996). It refers to data and imagery collected from space-borne satellites or airborne sensors, including pan chromatic, true color, infrared, terrain based, thermal, and other forms. Remote sensing has traditionally been an area of research and application for scientists, researchers, and technicians, but today's geospatial technologies have opened up the technologies to the general population. Figure 1.15 shows a screenshot of the Google Earth GIS with a remotely sensed image background viewing the Federally Administered Tribal Areas (FATA) and surrounding regions in Pakistan and Afghanistan. Such information and technologies are used by terrorists and counterterrorists for planning and operations.

Geographic Information Systems (GIS)

A geographic information system (GIS) is defined here as a collection of hardware, software, and data working together with a focus on spatial data storage, processing, analysis, and visualization (see Maguire, 1991, for a discussion on definitions of GIS). Though GIS has traditionally been used by scientists, researchers, and technicians, it has been placed in the hands of the general population without requirements of years of training and thousands of dollars in licensing fees. Programs like Google Earth and Map Quest provide the user with access to valuable information and tools for rudimentary analyses. Any user can now open a free Google Earth application, pan to virtually anywhere in the world, zoom in on a selected location, see a remotely sensed image, and in some places even see a "street view" of the location. This is in large part a visual application for geospatial data, but can provide terrorists with detailed information of potential targets. Those that are more experienced with GIS and have access to more advanced databases and applications to process and analyze the geospatial data to find spatial patterns.

This first chapter provides a conceptual background of the connections between geography and terrorism. Chapters 2–5 will cover in more detail aspects of the geographical dimensions of terrorism and Chapter 6 will attempt to identify areas of interest for terrorist activities in the future.

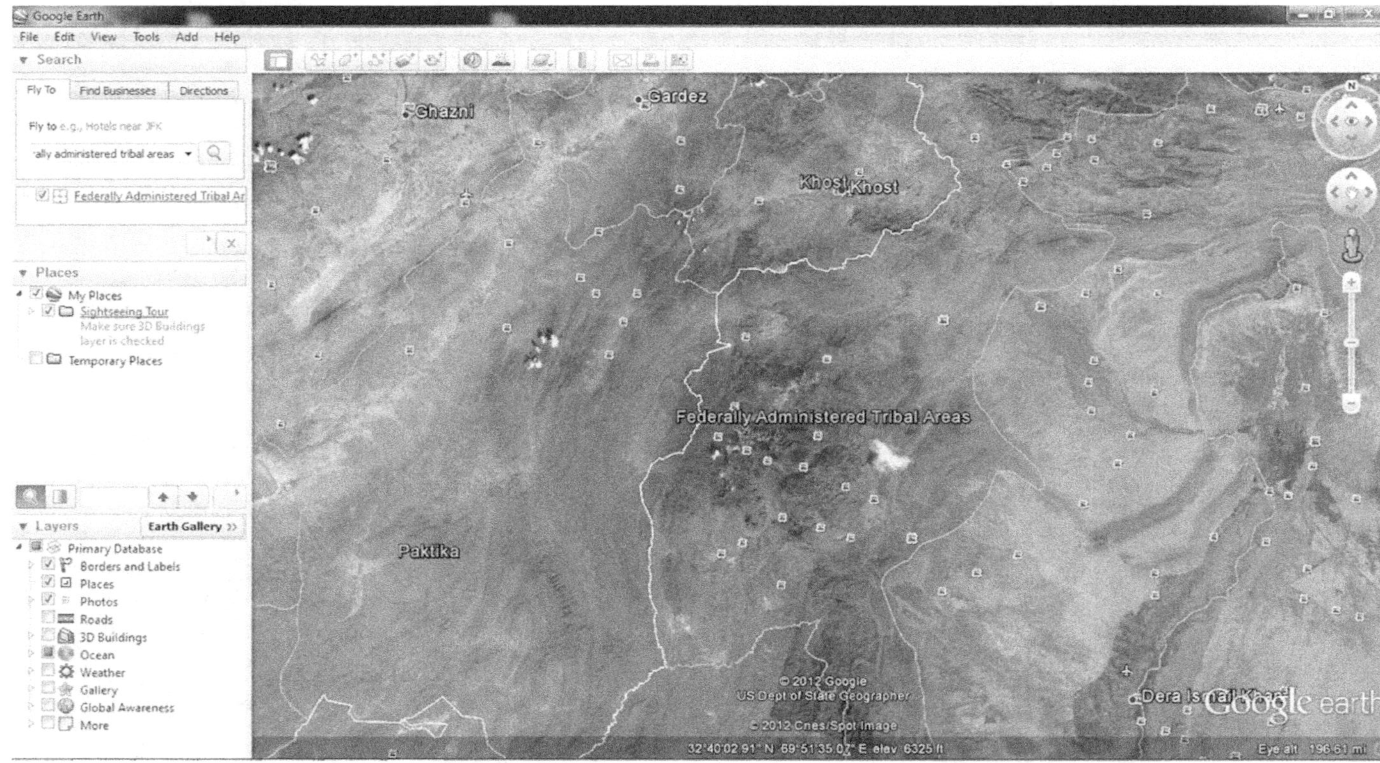

FIGURE 1.15
Screenshot of Google Earth with remotely sensed image background. (Google Earth, 2012; CNES/Spot, 2012. With permission.)

REFERENCES

Adams, P. (1998) Network topologies and virtual place. *Annals of the Association of American Geographers* 88:88–106.

Adamson, F. B. (2006) Crossing borders: International migration and national security. *International Security* 31 (1): 165–199.

Al Jazeera (2011) French face veil ban comes into force. Europe. Last modified November 18, 2011. Available from http://www.aljazeera.com/news/europe/2011/04/20114117646677858.html (last accessed April 29, 2012).

Al-Shishani, M. B. (2009) The concept of safe havens in salafi-jihadi strategy. *Terrorism Monitor: In-Depth Analysis of the War on Terror* 7:6–8.

Arnold, T. W. (1967) *The caliphate.* London: Routledge & Kegan Paul Ltd.

Arquilla, J. and Ronfeldt, D. (2001) The advent of netwar (revisited). In *Networks and netwars: The future of terror, crime, and militancy,* ed. Arquilla, J. and Ronfeldt, D. Santa Monica: RAND Corporation.

Asuni, J. B. (2009) Understanding the armed groups of the Niger Delta. Working paper. Council on Foreign Relations. September. New York.

Barnett, T. P. M. (2004) The Pentagon's new map: War and peace in the twenty-first century. New York: G. P. Putnam's Sons.

Batty, M. and H. J. Miller. (2000) Representing and visualizing physical, virtual and hybrid information spaces. In *Information, place, and cyberspace: Issues in accessibility,* ed. Janelle, D. G. and Hodge, D. C. New York: Springer.

Bergen, P. (2009) Reassessing the evolving al Qaeda threat to the homeland. Testimony presented before the House of Representatives, Committee on Homeland Security, Subcommittee on Intelligence, Information Sharing, and Terrorism Risk Assessment. November 19, 2009.

BBC News (2010) Who are Hezbollah? *BBC News*. July 4, 2010. Available from http://news.bbc.co.uk/2/hi/middle_east/4314423.stm

Center for Religious Freedom. (2002) *The Talibanization of Nigeria: Sharia law and religious freedom*. Washington, DC: Freedom House.

Couclelis, H. (1992) Location, place, region, and space. In *Geography's inner worlds: Pervasive themes in contemporary American geography,* ed. Abler, R. F., Marcus, M. G., and Olson, J. M. New Brunswick, NJ: Rutgers University Press, 215–233.

Crenshaw, M. (1995) *Thoughts on relating terrorism to historical contexts,* Ch. 1. Penn. State University Press.

Cronin, A. K. (2002/2003) Behind the curve: Globalization and international terrorism. *International Security* 23 (3): 30–58.

Diamond, J. (1997) *Guns, germs and steel: The fate of human societies.* New York: W. W. Norton

Energy Information Administration (2011) Niger Delta oil infrastructure. *Country analysis briefs: Nigeria.* Department of Energy. Available from http://www.eia.gov/cabs/Nigeria/Full.html (last accessed August 3, 2012).

ESRI (Environmental Systems Research Institute). (2011) ArcGIS 10. Redlands, CA.

Federal Bureau of Investigation (2009) Al-Qaeda supporter and organizer of jihad training camp in Oregon sentenced in Manhattan Federal Court to life in prison. New York Field Office. Available from http://www.fbi.gov/newyork/press-releases/2009/nyfo091509.htm (last accessed August 7, 2012).

Fellman, J. D., Bjelland, M. D., Getis, A., and Getis, J. (2010) *Human geography: Landscapes of human activities,* ed. 11. New York: McGraw Hill.

Felter, J. and Brachman, J. (2007) An assessment of 516 combatant status review tribunal (CSRT) unclassified summaries. CTC Report. July 25. The Combating Terrorism Center, West Point, NY. Available from http://www.ctc.usma.edu/csrt/CTC-CSRT-Report-072407.pdf

Fitzpatrick, J. (2002) Terrorism and migration. The American Society of International Law, Task Force on Terrorism. Washington, DC.

Flint, C., Diehl, P., Scheffran, J., Vasquez, J., and Sang-hyun, C. (2009) Conceptualizing ConflictSpace: Toward a geography of relational power and embeddedness in the analysis of interstate conflict. *Annals of the Association of American Geographers* 99 (5): 827–835.

Foley, S. (2010) Second U.S. woman swept up in Jihad Jane murder claims: Americans forced to confront reality of possible home-grown extremism. *The Independent*, March 15, 2010. Available from http://www.independent.co.uk/news/world/americas/second-us-women-swept-up-in-jihad-jane-murder-claims-1921435.html

Fox News (2007) How-to manual found in al-Qaeda safe house shows disturbing torture methods. *Fox News*. May 27, 2007. Available from http://www.foxnews.com/story/0,2933,275341,00.html

Garcia, N., Rala, A., Maunahan, A., Wieczorek, J., and Kapoor, J. (2011) GADM Database of Global Administrative Areas. Available from http://www.gadm.org/ (last accessed August 5, 2012).

Harvey, D. (1995) From space to place and back again: Reflections on the condition of postmodernity. In *Mapping the futures: Local cultures, global change*, ed. Bird, J., Curtis, B., Putnam, T., Robertson, G., and Tickner, L. New York: Routledge.

Hegghammer, T. (2010) The rise of Muslim foreign fighters: Islam and the globalization of the jihad. *International Security* 35 (3): 53–94.

——— (In review) Terrorists and foreign fighters: Disaggregating jihadism in the West.

Hoffman, B. (2006a) *Inside terrorism*. New York: Columbia University Press.

———. (2006b) The use of the Internet by Islamist extremists. Testimony presented to the House Permanent Select Committee on Intelligence on May 4, 2006. Santa Monica: RAND.

———. (2007) Radicalization, terrorism, and diasporas. In *The radicalization of diasporas and terrorism: A joint conference by the RAND Corporation and the Center for Security Studies, ETH Zurich*, ed. Hoffman, B., Rosenau, W., Curiel, A. J., and Zimmermann, D. Santa Monica: RAND Corporation.

Hoffman, B., Rosenau, W., Curiel, A. J., and Zimmermann, D. (2007) Discussion. In *The radicalization of diasporas and terrorism: A joint conference by the RAND Corporation and the Center for Security Studies, ETH Zurich*, ed. Hoffman, B., Rosenau, W., Curiel, A. J., and Zimmermann, D. Santa Monica: RAND Corporation.

Hudson, R. (2003, revised in 2010) Terrorist and organized crime groups in the tri-border area (TBA) of South America. Federal Research Division, Library of Congress. Washington, DC.

Hunt, J. and Kahlmeyer, A. (2007) *Islamic law: The Sharia from Muhammad's time to the present*. Jefferson, NC: McFarland & Company, Inc., Publishers.

Intergovernmental Panel on Climate Change (2007) Working group II report: Impacts, adaptation and vulnerability. In *Contribution of working group II to the Fourth Assessment Report of the Intergovernmental Panel on Climate Change*, ed. Parry, M. L., Canziani, O. F., Palutikof, P. J., van der Linden, P. J., and Hanson, C. J. New York: Cambridge.

Israel Ministry of Foreign Affairs (1948) Prevention of terrorism ordinance no. 33 of 5708-1948. Available from http://www.mfa.gov.il/MFA/MFAArchive/1900_1949/Prevention+of+Terrorism+Ordinance+No+33+of+5708-19.htm

Joab-Peterside, S. (2007) On the militarization of Nigeria's Niger Delta: The genesis of ethnic militia in Rivers State, Nigeria. Working paper 21. Center for Advanced Social Science. Port Harcourt, Nigeria.

Johnson, T. and Vriens, L. (2011) Islam: Governing under Sharia. Council on Foreign Relations. Available from http://www.cfr.org/religion/islam-governing-under-sharia/p8034 (last accessed March 14, 2012).

Keating, J. E. (2010) What do you learn at terrorist training camp? *Foreign Policy, FP Explainer.* May 10, 2010. Available from http://www.foreignpolicy.com/articles/2010/05/10/what_do_you_learn_at_terrorist_training_camp (last accessed March 23, 2012).

Kennedy, H. (2005) The caliphate. In *A companion to the history of the Middle East,* ed. Choueiri, Y. M. Malden, MA: Blackwell Publishing, 52–67.

Khan, H., Friedman, E., and Ryan, J. (2010) "Jihad Jane's" arrest raises concerns about home grown terrorists. *ABC News*, March 10, 2010. Available from http://abcnews.go.com/GMA/Politics/jihad-janes-arrest-raises-concern-homegrown-terrorists/story?id=10056187&page=2

Knight, C. G. (1992) Geography's worlds. In *Geography's inner worlds: Pervasive themes in contemporary American geography,* ed. Abler, R. F., Marcus, M. G., and J. M. Olson, J. M. New Brunswick, NJ: Rutgers University Press, 9–26.

Kohlmann, E. F. (2009) Prominent jihad media organizations in Central Asia. The NEFA Foundation. Available from http://www.nefafoundation.org/miscellaneous/FeaturedDocs/nefajihadmedia0309.pdf

Kydd, A. H. and Walter, B. F. (2006) The strategies of terrorism. *International Security* 31:49–80.

LaFree, G., Dugan, L., Xie, M., and Singh, P. (2012) Spatial and temporal patterns of terrorist attacks by ETA 1970 to 2007. *Journal of Quantitative Criminology* 28 (1): 7–29.

Leitner, H., Sheppard, E., and Sziarto, K. M. (2008) The spatialities of contentious politics. *Transactions of the Institute of British Geographers* 22:157–172.

Lloyd-Roberts, S. (2009) Fighting for Nigeria's oil wealth. *BBC News* January 8, 2009. Available from http://news.bbc.co.uk/2/hi/programmes/newsnight/7816654.stm (last accessed August 6, 2012).

MacKinder, H. J. (1904) The geographical pivot of history. *Geographical Journal* 23 (4): 421–437.

Maguire, D. J. (1991) An overview and definition of GIS. In *Geographical Information Systems: Principles and Applications,* Vol. 2. ed. Maguire, D. J., Goodchild, M. F., and Rhind, D. W. London: Longman, pp. 104–114.

Massey, D. (1995) Power-geometry and a progressive sense of place. In *Mapping the futures: Local cultures, global change,* ed. Bird, J., Curtis, B., Putnam, T., Robertson, G., and Tickner, L. New York: Routledge, 59–69.

Masters, J. (2011) Backgrounder: Hamas. Council on Foreign Relations. Available from http://www.cfr.org/israel/hamas/p8968 (last accessed March 14, 2012).

McColl, R. W. (1967) A political geography of revolution: China, Vietnam, and Thailand. *Journal of Conflict Resolution* 11 (2): 153–167.

——— (1969) The insurgent state: Territorial bases of revolution. *Annals of the Association of American Geographers* 59 (4): 613–631.

Medina, R. M. and Hepner, G. F. (2011) Advancing the understanding of sociospatial dependencies in terrorist networks. *Transactions in GIS* 15 (5): 577–597.

Mishal, S. and Sela, A. (2000) *The Palestinian Hamas: Vision, violence, and coexistence.* New York: Columbia University Press.

MSNBC (2012) Ohio man admits fundraising help for Somalia terror group al-Shabaab. Crime and courts. 2-7-12. Available from http://www.msnbc.msn.com/id/46291809/ns/us_news-crime_and_courts/t/ohio-man-admits-fundraising-help-somalia-terror-group-al-shabab/#.T54BaatSTZE (last accessed April 29, 2012.)

Murphy, A. (2003) The space of terror. In *The geographical dimensions of terrorism*, ed. Cutter, S. L., Richardson, D. B. and Wilbanks, T. J. New York: Routledge.

Myers, N. (2002) Environmental refugees: A growing phenomenon of the 21st century. *Philosophical Transactions of the Royal Society* B 357:609–613.

National Commission on Terrorist Attacks upon the United States (2004) *The 9/11 Commission report*. New York: W. W. Norton & Company.

National Consortium for the Study of Terrorism and Responses to Terrorism (2012) Terrorist organization profile: Movement for the emancipation of the Niger Delta (MEND). University of Maryland. Available from http://www.start.umd.edu/start/data_collections/tops/terrorist_organization_profile.asp?id=4692 (last accessed August 5, 2012).

National Counterterrorism Center. (2012) Terrorist groups: Revolutionary Armed Forces of Colombia (FARC). Available from http://www.nctc.gov/site/groups/farc.html (last accessed March 29, 2012).

NEFA Foundation (2007) As-Sahab presents a message from Usama bin Laden: "The solution." Transcript of Usama bin Laden message, September 8, 2007. Available from http://www.nefafoundation.org

——— (2010) Adam Gadahn: "A call to arms" March 7, 2010. Translation of a video released by As-Sahab, official propaganda arm of al-Qaeda. Available from http://www.nefafoundation.org

North Atlantic Treaty Organization (NATO) 2012 NATO's assistance to Iraq. Available from http://www.nato.int/cps/en/natolive/topics_51978.htm. Updated 16 Mar 2012 (last accessed April 18, 2012).

Norwegian Refugee Council. (2012) Global overview 2011: People internally displaced by conflict and violence. Internal Displacement Monitoring Center, Geneva, Switzerland. Available from http://www.nrc.no/arch/_img/9633536.pdf

Onuoha, F. C. (2012) The audacity of the Boko Haram: Background, analysis, and emerging trend. *Security Journal* 25 (2): 134–151.

Pakistani Government (1999) Pakistan anti-terrorism (amendment) ordinance, 1999. Available from http://www.satp.org/satporgtp/countries/pakistan/document/actsandordinences/anti_terrorism.htm

Pattison, W. (1964) The four traditions of geography. *Journal of Geography* 63 (5): 211–216.

Pew Research Center. (2011) The future of the global Muslim population: Projections for 2010–2030. Washington, DC.

Piazza, J. A. (2009) Is Islamist terrorism more dangerous? An empirical study of group ideology, organization, and goal structure. *Terrorism and Political Violence* 21:62–88.

Pillar, P. R. (2009) Who's afraid of a terrorist haven? *The Washington Post*. September 16, 2009. Available from http://www.washingtonpost.com/wp-dyn/content/article/2009/09/15/AR2009091502977.html

Post, J. M. (2005) The psychological and behavioral bases of terrorism: Individual, group and collective contributions. *International Affairs Review* 14 (2): 195–204.

Post, J. M. and Sheffer, G. (2007) The risk of radicalization and terrorism in US Muslim communities. *Brown Journal of World Affairs* 13 (2): 101–112.

Rapoport, D. C. (2002) The four waves of rebel terror and September 11. *Anthropoetics* 8 (1).

Reuters (2011) Shell says Nigeria oil spill contained. 27 December. Available from http://www.reuters.com/article/2011/12/27/us-shell-nigeria-spill-idUSTRE7BQ0M220111227. Accessed14February2012

Rice, S. E. and Patrick, S. (2008) Index of state weakness in the developing world. The Brookings Institution. Washington, DC.

Robb, T. (2012) Welcome to the Ku Klux Clan. Available from http://www.kkk.com/ (last accessed March 29, 2012.

Rock, J. C. (2006) The geographic nature of terrorism. *Pennsylvania Geographer* 44.

Rogan, H. (2006) Jihadism online: A study of how al-Qaeda and radical Islamist groups use the Internet for terrorist purposes. Forsvarets Forskningsinstitutt (FFI) Norweigian Defense Research Establishment.

Rosenbaum, R. (2012) Richard Clark on who was behind the Stuxnet attack. *Smithsonian Magazine.* April.

Sabins, F. F. (1996) *Remote sensing: Principles and interpretation,* 3rd ed. New York: W. H. Freeman and Company.

Sanchez-Cuenca, I. (2007) The dynamics of nationalist terrorism: ETA and the IRA. *Terrorism and Political Violence* 19:289–306.

Senate Committee on Homeland Security and Governmental Affairs (2012) Zachary Chesser: A case study in online Islamist radicalization and its meaning for the threat of homegrown terrorism. Washington, DC: United States Senate.

Shinn, D. (2011) Al-Shabaab's foreign threat to Somalia. *Orbis* Spring: 203–215.

Smith, D. J. (2008) *A culture of corruption.* Princeton, NJ: Princeton University Press.

Smith, S. (2005) The contested concept of security. In *Critical security studies and world politics,* ed. Booth, K. Boulder, CO: L. Reiner.

Taber, R. (2002) *War of the flea: The classic study of guerrilla warfare.* New York: Brassey's Inc.

Tuan, Y.-F. (1996) Space and place: Humanistic perspective. In *Human geography: An essential anthology,* ed. Agnew, J., Livingstone, D. N., and Rogers, A. Oxford: Blackwell Publishers, 444–457.

United Nations (2002) National laws and regulations on the prevention and suppression of international terrorism: Part 1. New York: United Nations.

——— (2005) National laws and regulations on the prevention and suppression of international terrorism: Part 2 (A-L). New York: United Nations.

——— (2012) Refugees. The UN Refugee Agency. Available from http://www.unhcr.org/pages/49c3646c125.html (last accessed: April 26, 2012).

US Department of State (2006) Terrorist safe havens, Ch. 3. In *Country reports on terrorism 2005.* Office of the Coordinator for Counterterrorism, 16–23.

——— (2008) Country reports on terrorism 2008, Ch. 5: Terrorist safe havens (7120 report) 5.1. Terrorist safe havens/strategies, tactics, tools for disrupting or eliminating safe havens. April 30, 2009. Available from http://www.state.gov/documents/organization/122599.pdf

——— (2012) Foreign terrorist organizations, Bureau of Counterterrorism, January 27, 2012. Available from http://www.state.gov/j/ct/rls/other/des/123085.htm (last accessed: March 14, 2012).

US Senate Committee on Homeland Security and Government Affairs (2008) Violent Islamist extremism, the Internet, and the homegrown terrorist threat. Majority & minority staff report. May 8, 2008. Available from http://hsgac.senate.gov/public/_files/IslamistReport.pdf

Vriens, L. (2006) Backgrounder: Armed Islamic group (Algeria Islamists). Council on Foreign Relations. Available from http://www.cfr.org/algeria/armed-islamic-group-algeria-islamists/p9154 (last accessed March 20, 2012).

Wasserman, S. and Faust, K. (1994) *Social network analysis: Methods and applications.* New York: Cambridge University Press.

Weimann, G. (2004) www.terrorism.net: How modern terrorism uses the Internet. Special report 116, ed. United States Institute of Peace. Available from http://www.usip.org/resources/wwwterrornet-how-modern-terrorism-uses-internet

Welch, C. (2011) Minnesota woman guilty of raising money for al-Shabaab. *CNN*. October 20, 2011. Available from: http://articles.cnn.com/2011-10-20/justice/justice_minnesota-al-shabaab_1_al-shabaab-hawo-mohamed-hassan-amina-farah-ali?_s=PM:JUSTICE (last accessed February 29, 2012).

West Point, Combating Terrorism Center (CTC) (2005) Zawahiri's letter to Zarqawi. In CTC's Harmony Document Database. Available from http://www.ctc.usma.edu/wp-content/uploads/2010/08/CTC-Zawahiri-Letter-10-05.pdf

World Bank (2012) Nigeria at a glance. Washington, DC.

Zanini, M. and Edwards, S. J. A. (2001) The networking of terror in the information age. In *Networks and netwars: The future of terror, crime, and militancy: Rand Report MR-1382,* ed. Arquilla, J. and Ronfeldt, D. Santa Monica: RAND Corporation.

2

Terrorist Networks in Geographic-Social Hybrid Space

INTRODUCTION

Mohammed Atta sat in seat 8D in business class on American Airlines Flight 11. It was early morning as the plane was leaving Logan Airport in Boston en route to Los Angeles (National Commission on Terrorist Attacks upon the United States 2004). There were only minutes to sit, think, and reflect on all that would bring him to this place in space and time. He would soon lead his team in one of the most devastating terrorist attacks in history by violently hijacking flight 11 and redirecting it to the North Tower of the World Trade Center (National Transportation Safety Board 2002). Atta was joined on the flight by four other members of the al-Qaeda terrorist cell responsible for the death and destruction on September 11, 2001. The other members were Abdulaziz al-Omari and Satam al-Suqami, near him in business class, and brothers Wail and Waleed al-Shehri in first class. These terrorists were joined in the act by 14 other terrorists on American Airlines flight 77, which would crash into the Pentagon, and United Airlines flights 175 and 93, which would crash into the south World Trade Center tower and a field in Pennsylvania, respectively.

Atta was the leader of operations for the terrorist attacks on September 11, 2001, that would result in the deaths of almost 3,000 people, with numbers still increasing through exposure to hazardous materials at the attack site over a decade later (*Fox News* 2010a). What processes had brought him to this place?

Mohammed Atta was born to a middle class family in Egypt in 1968. In 1990, he graduated with a degree in architectural engineering from Cairo University. In 1992, after a couple years of work as an urban planner,

TABLE 2.1

9/11 Flights and Hijackers

	American Airlines Flight 11	American Airlines Flight 77	United Airlines Flight 175	United Airlines Flight 93
Hijackers	Mohammed Atta	Khalid al-Mihdhar	Marwan al-Shehhi	Ziad Jarrah
	Waleed M. al-Shehri	Majed Moqed	Fayez Ahmed	Admed Alhaznawi
	Wail Alshehri	Salem Alhamzi	Ahmed Alghamdi	Ahmed Alnami
	Satam al-Suqami	Nawaf Alhamzi	Hamza Alghamdi	Saeed Alghamdi
	Abdulaziz al-Omari	Hani Hanjour	Mohald Alshehri	

he moved to Hamburg, Germany, to continue his education in engineering and planning, where he graduated from the Technical University of Hamburg-Harburg. He was thought at the time to be a pleasant and intelligent student. It is believed that his shift to radical Islam occurred during his initial stay in Hamburg. While there, he joined a working group intent on bridging the Muslim/Christian gap at the al-Quds Mosque. At al-Quds he became more radical in his thinking and began to express anti-Semitic and anti-American opinions.

While at the mosque, Atta and others were influenced by the radical Islamist Mohammed Haydar Zammar, who had fought in the Afghan-Russo war in the 1980s and preached the importance of jihad. In the late 1990s, Atta and others formed what was to be known as the Hamburg cell, a group of anti-American, radical Islamists ready for violent jihad. The core members of this cell were Atta, Ramzi bin al-Shibh, Marwan al-Shehhi, and Ziad Jarrah. Each of the core members became an important component of the 9/11 attacks (see Table 2.1 for their placement on the 9/11 flights). Three of the four—Atta, al-Shehhi, and Jarrah—were hijackers on three different planes, while bin al-Shibh was unable to obtain a visa in to the United States. He supported operations and network connectivity from outside the United States through assistance with communications between the hijackers and core al-Qaeda members, and by transferring money.

Other members of the Hamburg cell included Said Bahaji, Zakariya Essabar, Mounir el Motassadeq, and Abdelghani Mzoudi. The social network necessary to carry out the 9/11 attacks was beginning to form in a geographic location that gave the members access to security, information, sources of radicalization, and support of each other.

In late 1999, the four core members of the Hamburg cell had decided to fight jihad in Chechnya. In a case of being at the right place at the right time,

Atta and the others met Khalid al-Masri on a train in Germany and discussed jihad. Al-Masri connected them to al-Qaeda operative Mohamedou Ould Slahi, who was operating in Germany. Slahi convinced them to travel to Afghanistan for training rather than traveling to Chechnya.

The Hamburg cell members' trip to Afghanistan stopped at Karachi and then Quetta, both in Pakistan. In Quetta, they were to stop at a Taliban office. With a code name given to them by Slahi, they were quickly escorted from Quetta to Kandahar, Afghanistan. Upon arrival in Afghanistan, al-Shehhi was sent to the United Arab Emirates for training and Ramzi bin al-Shibh met with Osama bin Laden. All four members had pledged their allegiance to bin Laden. The members of the Hamburg cell, with their newly formed connections to a much larger network, began to resemble a group capable of orchestrating the largest terror attacks on American soil.

The three remaining members in Afghanistan met with Mohammed Atef, a senior al-Qaeda member, who gave them some details about their "highly secret mission" and instructed them to go back to Germany and enroll in flight training classes. Atta, who had been chosen to be the leader of operations by Osama bin Laden, was informed of potential targets, which included the US Capitol, the Pentagon, and the World Trade Center. While they were away from Germany, the activities of the core Hamburg cell members were covered up and kept secret by the members that remained in Germany.

By mid-2000 the four members of the 9/11 team were back together in Hamburg following some brief detours. Atta and bin al-Shibh stopped in Karachi where they met with Khalid Sheikh Mohammed (KSM), the mastermind of the 9/11 attacks. He gave them further instruction on the mission that would assist the terrorists to operate securely in the United States. KSM would continue to be active in planning the 9/11 attack and remained in close contact with the other terrorists. Upon researching flight schools in multiple countries, it was determined that they would have to enroll in flight schools in the United States. By the end of 2000, three of the four core Hamburg cell members had traveled to the United States.

Figure 2.1 shows Atta's path of radicalization and attack potential before reaching the United States. The path is delineated in lines of varying shade and width to emphasize advancement through levels of radicalization and potential. At each step in the space–time path, Atta becomes more capable of leading the most destructive terrorist attack on US soil. Some key points of Atta's radicalization may have occurred in the 1992–1999 period, when his motivation for jihad began. However, the potential to execute an attack

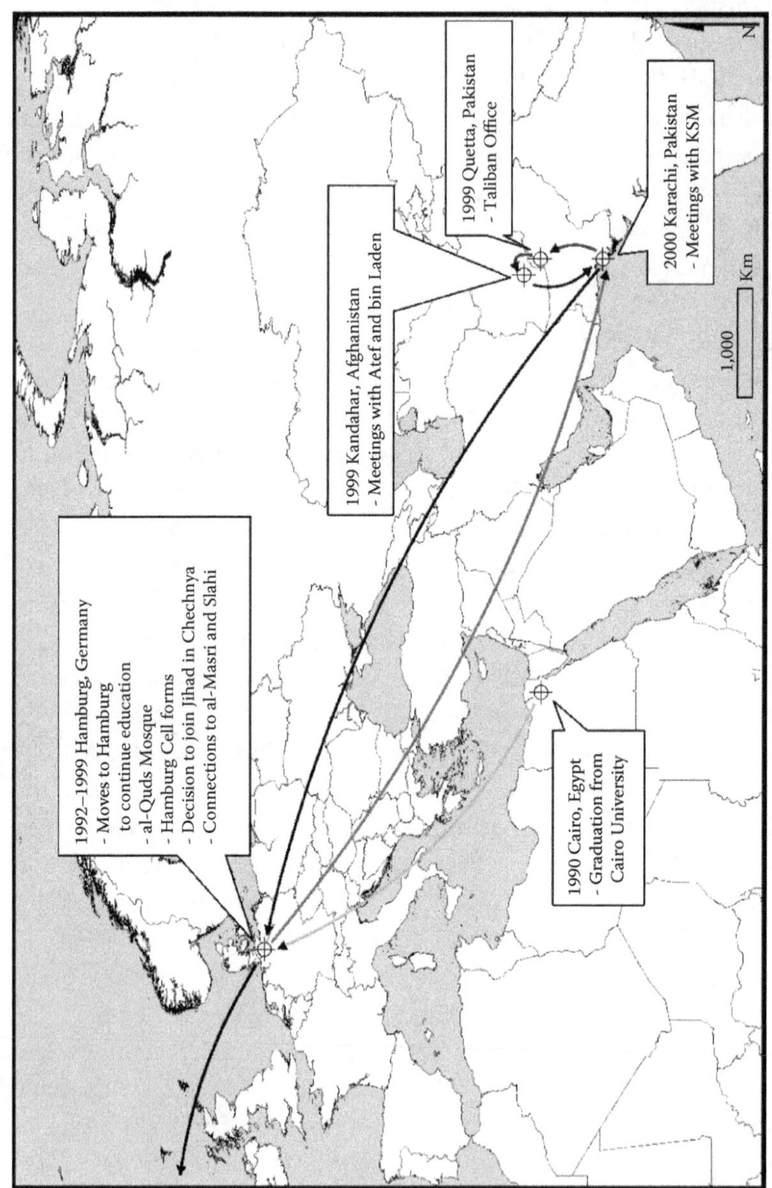

FIGURE 2.1
Mohammed Atta's path of radicalization and potential.

the size of the 9/11 attack did not exist until connections to al-Qaeda were in place. That potential grew through additional meetings with al-Qaeda operatives and senior members of the organization.

This figure illustrates the importance of places, people, and connections in terrorist networks. In Hamburg, Atta found others to share his radical views. Also, he built preliminary connections to al-Qaeda. In Quetta, he had to pass through the Taliban office, a gateway to senior members of al-Qaeda in Afghanistan, members that would instruct him on his mission and provide the know-how and other resources. In Karachi, Atta met with KSM, who instructed him further on operations in the United States. By the time Atta returned to Hamburg, approximately 1–2 years after he left, he was a much larger threat as a terrorist. This example, over such a short period of time, is a testament to the value of networks operating in key locations.

The 9/11 attacks would require the networks for personnel and finances that included many more people than the Hamburg cell and al-Qaeda leadership. Bin Laden and others had already selected other terrorists that would take part in the attacks. These terrorists would travel to the United States in 2000. Some, including Nawaf al-Hazmi and Khalid al-Mihdhar, would find supportive communities, such as those at the King Fahd mosque in Los Angeles and the San Diego Islamic Center. These places act as cultural sanctuaries for terrorists among the resident Islamic population. Hazmi received $5,000 from the Islamic Center's account, turning the center into a node in their financial network. The money was wired by Ali Abdul Aziz Ali, KSM's nephew, in Dubai, UAE. Ali would continue to be a vital connection in the financial network by wiring money to other 9/11 terrorists.

In the United States, some of the 9/11 terrorists would begin their flight training in multiple states, including Arizona and Florida. Other members were recruited as "muscle hijackers" and were not trained as pilots, but had other training in areas such as firearms and topography (National Commission on Terrorist Attacks upon the United States 2004). The terrorists would continue to prepare for their mission within and outside the United States. Mohammed Atta and others practiced flying. They took long flights on commercial airlines to understand air operations, while some of the muscle hijackers traveled outside the United States for further training. The necessary network connections were in place for the remaining training, planning, and coordination to make the operation a success.

Atta was the leader of operations and effectively coordinated the 9/11 attacks (National Commission on Terrorist Attacks upon the United States 2004). He sat in seat 8D on American Airlines flight 11 for a few minutes after take-off and then, with help from the four other terrorists on the flight, violently hijacked the plane, redirected it, and flew it into the North Tower of the World Trade Center. The passengers on the plane were told to stay quiet and that their plane was returning to the airport. None of them knew the terrorists' intentions.

This brief summary of events that led to the 9/11 attacks illustrates the importance of social networks and geographic location for meeting, motivation, and planning. The members of the Hamburg cell needed connections to the core of al-Qaeda. This network was built over time from family, clan, and friendship connections, as well as strong connections built in training camps and on the battlefield in Afghanistan (Krebs 2002a). While the terrorists on the four planes may not have fought in Afghanistan in the 1980s, they relied on an international network of radicals, some of whom did. Much of the training occurred in camps such as al Farouq near Kandahar, Afghanistan. Financial transfers and other assistance originated in places like Dubai, which acted as a transit hub. Terrorist travel and planning utilized safe houses, such as the one managed by KSM in Karachi, Afghanistan. Upon arrival in the United States, the terrorists were provided with culturally supportive communities to assist with smooth entry, movement and final operation.

This recitation describes very important properties of the Islamist network that still operate today. Redundancy exists among the network members and their capabilities, such that replacement is possible. Another important property of the network is connection control, which was exercised very efficiently in the 9/11 case. For security and resilience purposes, many of the terrorists involved did not know each other. Even some on the same hijacked flight did not know each other. With this lack of social connectivity, capturing a few terrorists would not place the remaining parts of the mission in jeopardy (Krebs 2002a). Mohammed Atta was an agent in a complex social, financial, and geographical network that was dynamic in space and time. Much of this network still operates today.

Terrorist organizations, like human societal structures in general, are organized into social networks of various forms of structure and connectivity. The structure of each organization influences resilience, flows, and efficiency. The network structures are influenced by internal as well as external drivers and in many cases are adaptable to their environments.

HYBRID SPACE: THE INTERSECTION OF SPACES

Hybrid space, as defined in the first chapter, is the conceptual domain where organizations and individuals operate at the intersection of geographic, social, and virtual activity spaces. Social networks are embedded within geographic spaces where access to "things" and people is necessary. The intersection of social and geographic spaces is a conceptual hybrid, geographic-social hybrid space, or "geosocial" space. This space contains properties of geography/environment and social structure/connections that are of crucial importance for network connectivity, accessibility, and activities.

The combination of hybrid space with the virtual space domain is the deployment area for terrorist network structures, flows, and network typologies in the information age. Many operations of the globalization process, such as decentralized functional responsibilities and increased communications, take place in hybrid spaces. These operations are facilitated by the Internet and other forms of virtual communications technologies. These hybrid spaces are the environment in which various forms of terrorist network structures function across the globe.

The process of activity space hybridization revolves around accessibility to resources in all forms. For example, Internet businesses are able to reach many people online. The sales message must adapt to the new areas and cultures in which sales are targeted. Expansion of product sales requires that the company warehouses be strategically located for an efficient flow of product deliveries. Efficiency can be defined by close proximity to the customers ordering products, configuration of the transportation networks to provide access, and/or minimization of the total costs of shipping (Batty and Miller 2000).

Present-day global terrorism takes place on geographic and virtual battlefields. Geographic and virtual spaces share similarities when considering them as terrorist activity spaces. In the way of maintaining network connectivity, they both facilitate many of the same terrorist necessities of accessibility such as havens, training, radicalization, and flows (Table 2.2). However, face-to-face interactions seem, at this point in time, to be most effective. The degree and quality of training is much greater when an individual enters a training camp, rather than taking lessons from an online manual. The way a terrorist is trained translates directly to his or her potential for attack intensity. There is no substitute for the amount of knowledge and experience of training camp leaders.

TABLE 2.2

Operational Similarity in Geographic and Virtual Spaces

Geographic Space		Virtual Space
Exist in places where terrorists are able to live and operate in a secure manner	Havens	Exist in virtual places where terrorists and supporters are able to conduct virtual jihad in a secure manner
Occurs in places where terrorists train and effectively learn to be "professional" terrorists	Training	Occurs in virtual places where terrorists have access to instructional and training materials
Occurs in places where potential terrorists are exposed to and accepting of radical ideas	Radicalization	Can begin in virtual places where potential terrorists have access to radical ideas
Occur over material networks of people in support of terrorism	Flows	Occur over virtual networks composed of computers, servers, and data lines

Many geographic terrorist activities can exist without their virtual space counterparts, but are assisted by virtual space communications and become less vulnerable to counterterrorist operations. Virtual space activities often rely on geographic places. For example, many of the ideas, messages, and instructions originate at specific geographic locations that act as terrorist havens. At times, virtual space activities such as Internet posts refer to geographic places as attack targets. Examples of these might be large social events, such as the Olympics and the World Cup; countries including Iraq, the United States, and Pakistan; and specific targets of government and commercial buildings.

The Internet has provided a forum for sympathizers, an important resource for funding, and an outlet for propaganda. Ideological and logistical messages are distributed to the general public through the Internet in hopes of recruitment and seemingly random attacks, and psychological warfare spreads in the form of videos and recorded speeches. This is in itself a form of terrorism, as many of these messages threaten violence.

Before the Internet, the majority of places where terrorists congregated were located in geographic space. Today's communication technologies allow for those meeting places to be extended to virtual spaces, where virtual communities are created and not bound by traditional geographic borders. The Internet has been theorized to be most beneficial in supporting previously built social connections, rather than creating new social networks (Hampton and Wellman 2003); however, the virtual spaces inhabited by terrorists and other radical thinkers may facilitate violence and the joining of new terrorists to an already established network that is constructed as much by choice as it is by recruitment (Cronin 2006).

It is believed that most active terrorist organizations have an Internet presence, although Islamist organizations are the most prevalent (Hoffman 2006). Many of these organizations publish web pages in multiple languages in order to reach out to people of different cultures and ethnicities. By using other languages it is easier to break down cultural and ethnic barriers in pursuit of support and sympathy. Some may support the cause because of similar sentiment or a shared enemy.

Twenty-first century terrorism is analogous in many ways to the Internet sales example. Even with terrorist use of the virtual domain, the geographic expansion and likely decentralization of terrorist networks is a necessary strategic move to influence more area, gain a larger recruiting pool, develop new logistical havens, and increase attack spaces. Correspondingly, the social space networks of allegiances must remain intact as virtual and geographic expansion takes place, or the organizations risk the chance of fragmenting.

For terrorist organizations to exist as networks there must be specific social topologies to define the network structures, as well as locational attributes and activities that foster growth, strength, and safety. The social aspects of the networks are, more often than not, dependent on geographic space. For example, recruitment, in many cases, is based on closeness in geographic space, while the closeness in social space can come later through activities of training, attacking, etc. On the other hand, terrorists can move in geographic space to be closer to nodes in their social networks. For an attack to occur, terrorists will most likely rely on previously built social connections, but the attack requires planning and placement in geographic space. Social, virtual, and geographic spaces are interdependent when considering terrorist network activities.

International terrorist networks are affected by changes in their environments in a process termed coevolution that drives systemic adaptation in the network. Coevolution is the process, whereby, systems dynamically adapt with other systems and agents that are active in a shared environment (Kauffman 1995; Manson 2001). The networks respond to external and internal forces. One such force might be an effective counterterrorism effort within a region. In such a case, the adaptation might be a strategic alliance with another organization (Koza and Lewin 1998). A major feature of coevolution is that the actual structure of the terrorist network evolves when faced with changes in its geographic, social, and virtual environment.

TERRORIST NETWORKS AND THEIR ORGANIZATIONAL STRUCTURES

Terrorist groups operate within the convergence of social, network, and geographic spaces with various networked organizational structures. The two main organizational structures of terrorist networks are hierarchical and decentralized. However, the networks can range along the spectrum from totally hierarchical to fully decentralized.

Figure 2.2 shows the conceptualized forms of hierarchical and decentralized terrorist network structures and the processes involved in evolving to a decentralized structure. At the very top of this figure is the hierarchical,

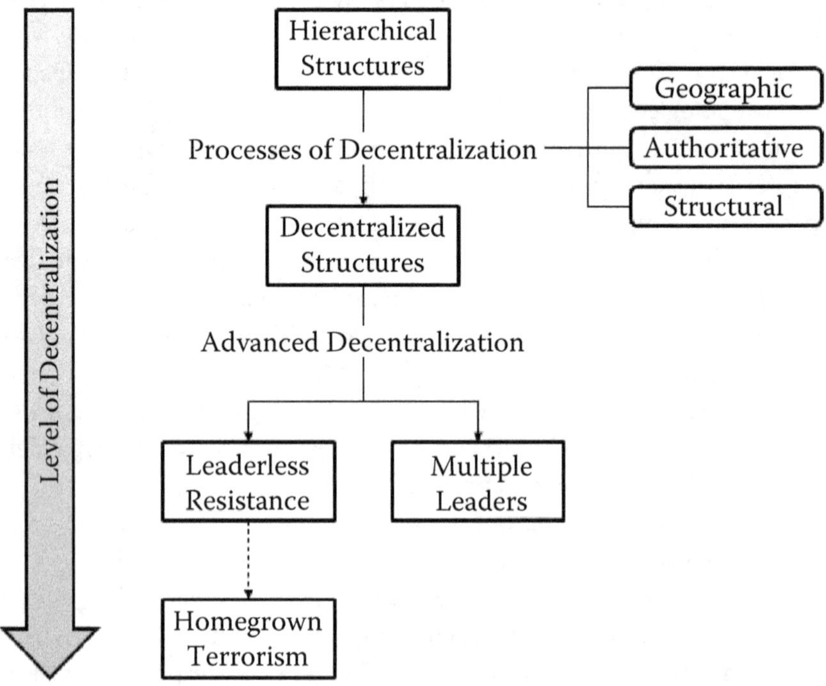

FIGURE 2.2
Network structure and level of decentralization.

or pyramidal, structure where authoritative responsibilities flow downward through the organization from the leaders to other members of the network. At the bottom of the figure is homegrown terrorism, a phenomenon where no formal structure exists and actors follow messages distributed by media and/or other sources.

A hierarchical terrorist network structure is one that is formed with well-defined levels of leadership control. In hierarchical organizations, a leader manages organizational activities by delegating tasks to lower levels. Lower level terrorists answer to upper level leaders and act only when they are instructed to do so. The authority flows from the top and then down through the ranks, typically in a pyramidal shape.

Ideological organizations, including Leninist, Maoist, and many other political groups, tend to have hierarchical structures. This is because coordinated activities toward a specific target are required. The target often is a government entity, and such attacks necessitate strict control of operations, which is more likely in a hierarchical setting (US Army 2007).

Benefits of hierarchical organization include firm control over the network, people, planning, and direction of the organization. With this type of structure, it is easier to command fighters, plan operations, and keep all activities within the focus of the leadership. Once an organization decentralizes, much of the control is lost.

One of the major downfalls of the hierarchical structure is that it is less resilient and relatively vulnerable to damage or destruction by capturing or killing leaders in the organization and effectively "decapitating" it (Tucker 2001). Next are two examples of relatively hierarchical terrorist organizations: the PIRA and Hezbollah.

Hierarchical Terrorist Network Structure

The Provisional Irish Republican Army

The Provisional Irish Republican Army (PIRA) was a nationalist terrorist organization active mostly in Northern Ireland (shown in Figure 2.3). It formed in 1969. As a nationalist organization, its main goal was the liberation of northern Irish territory from British rule. The PIRA split from the Irish Republican Army (IRA) and was composed of members who supported the continued use of violence in the path to a free Irish state. The IRA, also known as the Official IRA, wanted an end to the violence and, upon division and splintering, disappeared from existence (Gregory 2010).

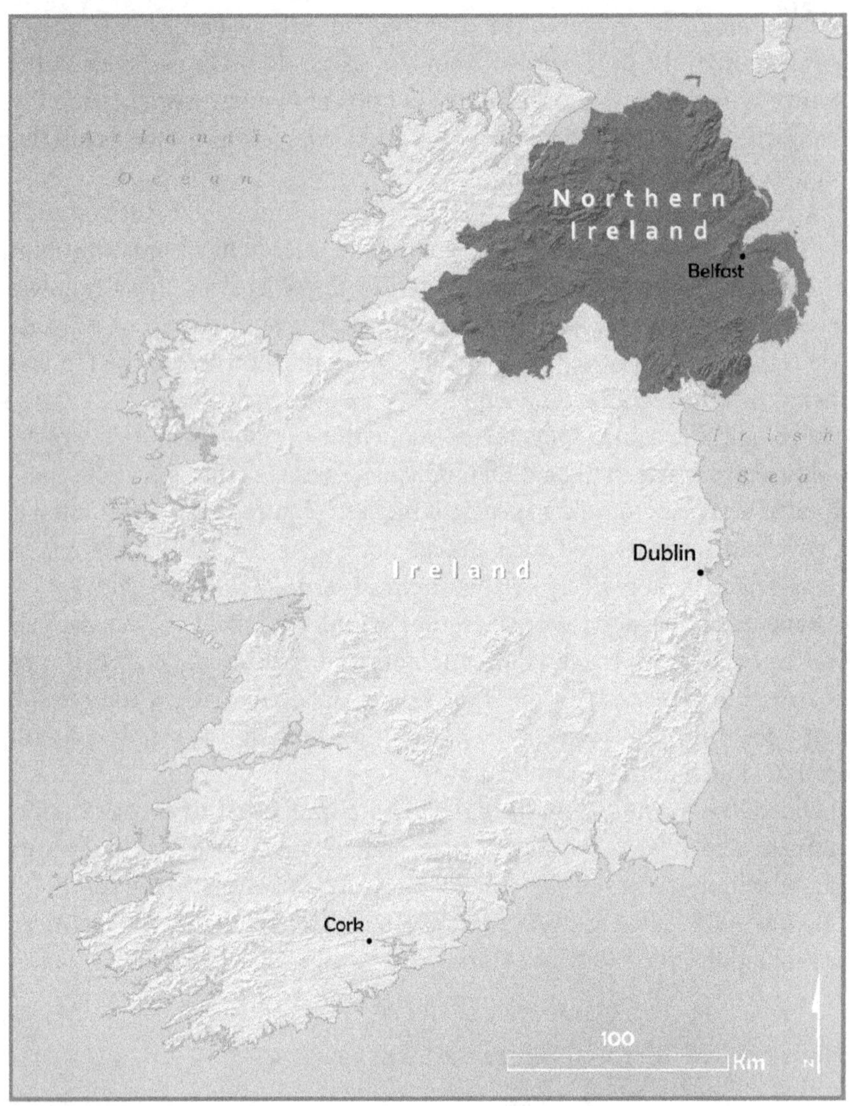

FIGURE 2.3
Ireland and Northern Ireland. (Data source: ESRI, 2011.)

The PIRA maintained assaults against mainly British targets from 1969, when it formed, to 1994 when the organization declared a cease-fire. The slow progress of talks prompted renewed attacks in 1996 and 1997, but another ceasefire was restored in 1997. The Belfast Agreement, also known as the Good Friday Agreement, was accepted in 1998; this included Sinn Fein, the PIRA's political wing, as an official entity, along with the British and Irish governments. A decommissioning of the PIRA's weapons, which truly marked an end to violence, began in 2001 (Gregory 2010).

Since the beginning of the PIRA in 1969, it has been responsible for approximately 1,800 deaths, about 650 of which were civilian. On July 28, 2005, the PIRA issued an official announcement that claimed an end to any further violent operations. The goals of the organization would be approached strictly through political means (*The Guardian* 2005). However, two splinter groups of the PIRA still practice terrorism: the Real IRA and the Continuity IRA. The aggression against the British by these splinter groups remains focused on a "united Ireland free of British rule" (Gregory 2010).

The PIRA operated as a hierarchical organization with a pyramid-shaped structure. Authority in the PIRA began with the Army Council, which determines all military policy. It then flowed downward from the Army Council to the General Headquarters (GHQ). The GHQ contained the operational departments: Quartermaster, Security, Operations, Foreign Operations, Finance, Training, Engineering, Intelligence, Education, and Publicity. The flow then moved downward to the Northern and Southern Commands. The Northern Command oversaw the provinces of Northern Ireland, as well as their five bordering counties, while the Southern Command oversaw the other 21 counties. Below the Northern and Southern Commands were brigades. The brigades were those active in attacks and were composed of brigadiers, operations commanders (OCs), and active service units (ASUs). All entities mentioned here are termed the "operational members." Working outside the operational membership are the "non-operational members," who make up the support network offering assistance in funding, safe houses, hiding weapons, and other types of logistic support (Horgan and Taylor 1997).

Hezbollah (The Party of God)

Hezbollah formed in 1982 and operates primarily in southern Lebanon. The organization's control areas are shown in Figure 2.4. It is a nationalist, Shia Muslim-based terrorist organization that has fought for the removal of Israeli forces from southern Lebanon and Palestine. Hezbollah shifted its operations to include a political organization working in Palestine, as well as continuing as a direct action terrorist group (Azani 2006). In 1992, the organization gained seats in parliament and has remained a legal political

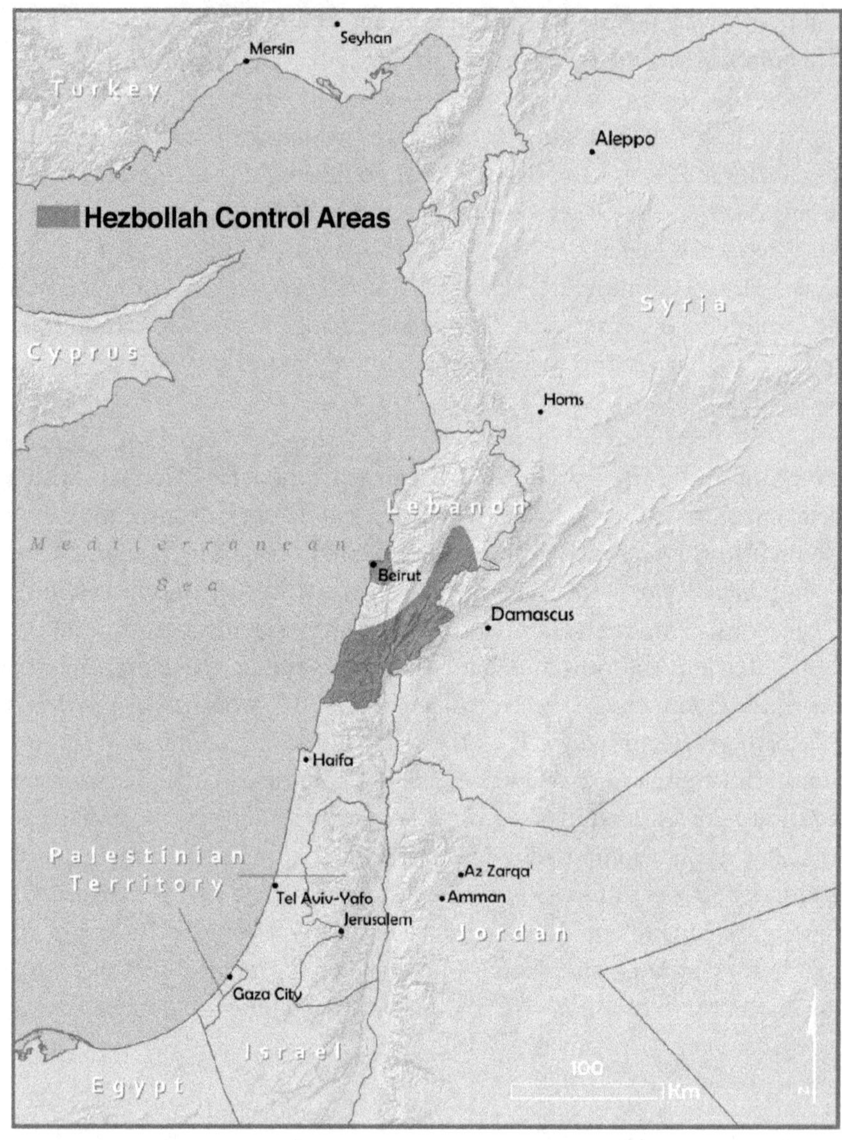

FIGURE 2.4
Hezbollah control areas in Lebanon. (Data source: National Counterterrorism Center (n.d.), political boundaries—ESRI, 2011.)

force since (Cragin 2005). In the 2009 elections, Hezbollah lost the majority of seats in the Lebanese parliament to a pro-Western coalition (*VOA News* 2009). They remain active in violence and terrorist activity and are still considered a terrorist organization by the United States (Council on Foreign Relations 2010).

Hezbollah can be classified as a hierarchical organization. Its unified leadership is in control of all decision making and organizational operations in both political and military areas (Azani 2006). This leadership is heavily influenced by state sponsors Iran and Syria. In recent years, the Shia rulers of Iran have become very influential on Hezbollah as Syria has moved toward civil war.

Hezbollah, like the PIRA, has a pyramidal structure to its hierarchy. At its apex is the secretary general. There have only been two leaders in the organization's history: Abbas al-Musawi, who was assassinated by Israeli's security forces in 1992, and Hassan Nasrallah. Below the secretary general is a deputy secretary general. The generals lead a Shura Council that controls military, political, and social operations. Below the Shura Council are secondary councils/committees, the number of which differs by source. Those that typically appear in literature are the political, executive, jihad, and judicial councils. Below the secondary councils are financial, social affairs, education, health, information, military, and security units. Again, these vary based on source, but all accounts investigated delineate a pyramid structure. Operations are broken down into three geographical regional commands: Beirut and southern suburbs, Bekka Valley, and South Lebanon (Cragin 2005).

Hezbollah has expanded its international network for operations beyond Lebanon. It has operations in over 40 countries (Azani 2006). Illegal activities are used to raise funds and include money laundering, smuggling, and weapons and drug trafficking. It is believed that these activities are a result of an attempt to strengthen the group's black-market infrastructure for increased independence from the aid of the state sponsors, Syria and Iran. Black market Hezbollah cells have been discovered in the US cities of Charlotte, North Carolina, and Detroit, Michigan. In the early 1990s the organization strengthened its intelligence network. Many believe that Hezbollah's intelligence and direct action capabilities are being employed as a surrogate for Iranian agents in attacks on Israeli targets across the globe.

Recruitment efforts in Southern Lebanon include use of non-military activities such as summer camps and soccer leagues. This allows Hezbollah to select new recruits from the most intelligent and/or athletic of each group. Another form of recruitment effort involves charity donations by the organization in Lebanon. Charitable tasks lead to greater support from the public and have helped the dual identity of the group as both a terrorist organization and a political organization (Cragin 2005).

Hezbollah claims to have the direct support of over 20,000 people; its fighting force is much smaller—in a range of 500 to 4,000. Currently, task forces of 50 members are used for selected operations, such as money laundering or intelligence-gathering. They are selected based on proficiency, experience, and location relative to the needed skill sets. Using these task forces, a compartmentalized robust network structure is maintained (Cragin 2005).

Decentralized Terrorist Network Structure

The process of decentralization for terrorist networks occurs in three forms: geographic, authoritative, and structural. Geographic decentralization occurs as terrorists migrate away from a central location to various places throughout the globe. It occurs as ideas spread and people in various locations join the network.

Authoritative decentralization occurs when decision-making power within an organization is shifted from the core and shared by many within the organization. While the core leadership of many terrorist organizations still controls much of their direction, some have distributed their management power throughout the network and, in extreme cases, to branches and affiliates in remote geographical locations. This is the most widely discussed form of decentralization.

Finally, structural decentralization occurs when redundant connections are added to the network. The number of functional connections for each node in the network becomes more uniform and structural connectivity of members is distributed across the network, such that more nodes have higher connectivity traits.

Terrorist networks that conform to decentralized structures can advance further to leaderless resistance (i.e., terrorists have no real connection to the organization in question) and multiple leaders (i.e., rather than one core leadership, more are created that operate typically in different regions) models (Medina and Hepner 2008). These advanced decentralization structures can be seen in today's Islamist terrorist network.

One of the main processes fostering terrorist network decentralization is the creation of operational cells that are linked to authority, but operate autonomously. In a cellular system, the pyramidal structure is flattened and may only exist for the leadership in the network, if at all. The terrorist network structured in cells has security benefits resulting in greater resiliency. Losing members of a network cell to capture or death will not jeopardize members of the network outside the cell, allowing other planned operations to remain intact (US Army 2007). In some cases, such as with al-Qaeda, a cell leader leads the operation and is in contact with an agent handler who is assigned to the cell. The handler is in charge of the mission and can be either near the cell or at a safer remote location (Gunaratna 2002). Members of the cell may not come into contact until soon before an attack is about to take place (Krebs 2002b), as was the case in the 9/11 attacks.

Successful terrorist cells have been responsible for the September 11, 2001, attacks in New York; the July 7, 2005, London bombings (*BBC News* 2008); the March 11, 2004, Madrid train attacks (*BBC News* 2007a); the November 26–29, 2008, Mumbai attacks (*BBC News* 2010); and the October 12, 2002, bombings in Bali (*BBC News* 2009). Cell attacks that have been thwarted since 9/11 include a train bombing in New York (Crosson et al. 2009), attacks in China (Demick 2010), and attacks on American facilities in Germany (*BBC News* 2007b), as well as many others.

Terrorist cells operate in a clandestine manner and exist sometimes as "sleeper cells," where they remain hidden until they are called to action. Sleeper cells are placed in strategic locations throughout the world for purposes of carrying out attacks at a later date. At least one member of the cell is connected to the terrorist network directly. Each cell remains covert and waits for its call to act in some way for the organization. Multiple Islamist sleeper cells within the United States and other countries have been discovered prior to attacks. While there have been fears in the past that an "army of 'sleepers'" exists within the United States, there is no evidence to support this fear (Jenkins 2010, p. 4).

Globalization and Terrorist Network Decentralization

The most recent trends in terrorist networks are toward increased social, virtual, and geographic decentralization. The decentralization of terrorist networks is facilitated by the unceasing movement toward globalization. Through rapid air travel, communications, financial linkages, and cultural transfer of the information age, terrorist communities have become "glocalized." This is the situation where strong ethnic, family, and clan relationships between individuals and communities can be maintained at longer distances with much of the same intensity previously available only through communal residence in a clan area or homeland (Mok, Carrasco, and Wellman 2010). In this glocalized existence, many terrorist organizations operate in a geographically distributed manner, but maintain traditional local rule sets and allegiances (Marret 2008).

Globalization facilitates the spread of international terrorist organizations and support communities (Cronin 2006). The effects of globalization, such as economic marginalization and cultural intrusion, provide perceived justifications for terrorist activities. One of the impacts of globalization, termed time–space compression, threatens traditional cultures and their sense of place (Harvey 1995). Cultural/religious terrorists feel threatened by the loss of cultural identity as they and, particularly, their children are displaced from a home-cultural place, which has great significance to their religion, culture, and traditions.

The impact of globalization is furthered by increasingly available and accessible transportation technologies that lower the "cost" for the migration of individuals from their traditional places and communities. In turn diaspora communities may provide remittance support and sanctuary destinations for terrorist decentralization across the globe.

Benefits and Disadvantages of Decentralization

Decentralization provides benefits and disadvantages to terrorist networks. In a decentralized terrorist network, leadership is distributed throughout the network. Resilience is the primary advantage. Removal of leaders does not destroy a decentralized network. Multiple key leaders must be removed before they can be replaced to damage the terrorist network significantly (Sageman 2004). Another benefit is that a decentralized organization has a better opportunity to grow to a size and geographic distribution capable of sustaining activities within many nations. Decentralized terrorist network structures operating today are highly connected and clustered, and can adapt to a changing enemy and environment and quickly repair damages (Medina and Hepner 2008).

Decentralization is not without its disadvantages. Decision making and operational control are redistributed from the original core leadership of the organization to other members. When loosely connected or unconnected groups and individuals act on behalf of the movement, unwelcome activities or an unwanted narrative may result. A good example of this disadvantage occurred in Iraq when Abu Mussab al-Zarqawi, leader of al-Qaeda in Iraq, was publicizing images and video of hostage beheadings, often of other Muslims. Al-Qaeda central realized the public relations damage the media releases were causing to their narrative of assisting fellow Muslim Iraqi people. Ayman al-Zawahiri, second in command for al-Qaeda, subsequently sent al-Zarqawi a letter stating the public relations threat and a request for those types of media releases to halt—but in no way stating that the violence should halt (West Point, Combating Terrorism Center 2005). The following sections provide examples of organizations that decentralized for increased security and efficiency.

Euskadi Ta Askatasuna (ETA) (Basque Fatherland and Freedom)

The ETA is a nationalist terrorist organization that operates mostly in Spain. It is also known to have socialist and Marxist motivations (Sanchez-Cuenca 2007). The goals of this group are to create an autonomous state for the Basque people, who are based in northern Spain/southern France as shown in Figure 2.5 (National Consortium for the Study of Terrorism and Responses to Terrorism 2010). The region marked in dark gray is the area claimed by the organization called Basque Country.

The ETA began its use of violence in 1968, 9 years after the organization formed in 1959 (Stewart 2009; US Department of State 2012). In the years since its inception, the ETA has been blamed for multiple attacks and at least 800 deaths. A cease-fire in 1998 lasted 14 months and ended with the breakdown of peace talks and recommenced attacks in 2000. The ETA announced a permanent ceasefire on March 24, 2006 (Shahar 2006); however, a wave of attacks after the cease-fire, including the bombing at the Barajas International Airport in Madrid, indicates a possible resurgence of the organization (*CNN* 2009).

The ETA organization conformed to a hierarchical structure in the past, but evolved into a decentralized network over the years (US Army 2007). They have traditionally been led by a committee, which is still in place. The Zuzendaritza Batzordea (Zuba), or leadership committee, is composed of 7–11 individuals and acts as the supreme political and operational council for planning and direction of the organization. There is also an advisory committee, Zuba-Hitu, which is composed of 15 members of the organization, most of whom are now imprisoned in Spain and France.

In the past it only had three compartments below the Zuba: logistic, military, and political. After 2000, changes divided the compartments into 11 subgroups: logistic, political, military, information, recruitment, international relations, reserves, negotiation, treasury, prisoner support, and extortion (elcorreodigital 2006).* This compartmentalization of operations is an attempt to decentralize operations by reducing the vulnerability of

* The number of subgroups and their titles and tasks, as well as other details of the ETA's structure, differ by source.

FIGURE 2.5
The Basque country region in Spain and France. (Data source: ESRI, 2011.)

the central leadership, increasing the resilience to counterterrorist actions. The subgroups operate autonomously, such that each of the groups knows nothing about the others' operations. The capture of members from one subgroup will not affect the operations of any others. One of the main outcomes of this structure is excessive specialization, where each subgroup only performs specific tasks.

After some time, the ETA realized the disadvantages of highly specialized subgroups, including coordination difficulties between subgroups resulting in less effective and unresponsive operations. ETA reorganized these subgroups into cells where members specialize in multiple activities. This created cells that are truly autonomous and much more functional. With this transformation, the slowness and inefficiency of the previous network structures were removed. However, the reduction in specialization of individual cell members reduced the effectiveness of attacks. Overall, the improved coordination and quickness to action benefits outweigh the disadvantages (Alexander, Swetnam, and Levine 2001).

ETA used its Basque homeland operational area on the border between France and Spain to decentralize command, control, and operational units geographically. France was used as a planning, financial sourcing, and decision-making base for the leadership of ETA. Operations were, for the most part, undertaken in Spain or other parts of the world. Thus, ETA members were not sought by French authorities and had relatively free movement in southern France. The international border, extradition treaties, and jurisdictional issues thwarted Spanish counterterrorism efforts against ETA members in France. This is a strategy used by several other terrorist groups to great advantage.

Al-Qaeda (The Base) and the Decentralized Islamist Terrorist System

Al-Qaeda and the greater Islamist terrorist network have their foundations in the 1980s when a Mujahideen force joined to fight against the Russian occupation of Afghanistan. The initial organization of Mujahedeen was the Mekhtab al-Khadamat (MaK) (Services Office) and was co-led by Abdullah Azzam, a Palestinian, and Osama bin Laden from Saudi Arabia. The MaK was a center for recruitment of fighters for the Afghan jihad. The majority of the Mujahedeen in Afghanistan originated from Saudi Arabia, Yemen, and Algeria, but included fighters from all over the world. Following the defeat of the Russians, a lengthy process of structural evolution turned the MaK into al-Qaeda and then into the global Islamist terrorist system of the twenty-first century. The links that connected these terrorists were the jihadist narrative of those who had trained together in the many terrorist training camps and had experienced jihad firsthand in Afghanistan (Bergen 2001).

Al-Qaeda is a radical Sunni Islamist organization with primarily cultural/religious motivations focused on global jihad. Their initial main goal as stated by Osama bin Laden in 1996, and again by al-Qaeda in 1998, is freedom from "Zionist-Crusaders" (i.e., the Western world and its allies) (*PBS* 2010a, 2010b). As stated by bin Laden, "There is no more important duty than pushing the American enemy out of the holy land" (*PBS* 2010a). This goal includes the removal of the physical, economic, and political presence of Israel, the United States, and allies from the Middle East, who are accused of "corrupting life and religion" (*PBS* 2010a).

Specific countries of interest discussed as lands of Islam by Osama bin Laden and al-Qaeda are Iraq, Saudi Arabia, Israel, Egypt, and the Sudan. It is forecast by al-Qaeda that less American influence in the Middle East will lead to an Islamist takeover of the holy lands, including Jerusalem (*PBS* 2010a, 2010b). Israel and Palestine have been a continuing topic of multiple audio recordings by bin Laden (see NEFA Foundation 2008a, 2009a, 2009b), and he stated in 2008, "I would like to reassure you that the Palestinian issue is the primary central issue of our movement" (NEFA Foundation 2008d, p. 1). The strategic succession on the path to the "liberation" of Palestine is to gain control of surrounding countries and regions such as Somalia, the Islamic Maghreb, Afghanistan and Pakistan, the Levant, Yemen, and especially Iraq and organize them in an attack to acquire control of Israel (Mozaffari 2007; NEFA Foundation 2009b; Shayea 2010).

Al-Qaeda's foundation in the 1980s was created as a network with a hierarchical core. The organization has evolved drastically since its formation during the Russo-Afghan War. At present it exists as a relatively decentralized organization geographically, authoritatively, and structurally. It resembles the network dynamics of a social movement more than those of a conventional terrorist organization (Medina and Hepner 2008). This system has grown much larger than the al-Qaeda network and can be referred to as the global Islamist network; it includes multiple branches of al-Qaeda, affiliate organizations, and leaderless individuals that share the Sunni Islamist ideology.

The al-Qaeda core hierarchical structure has an emir-general (Osama bin Laden until his death in 2012) at the apex. Below the emir general is the Shura Majlis, which includes the most experienced members who serve as a consultative council. Directly below the Shura Majlis are four compartmentalized committees that are in charge of military, finance and business, fatwa and Islamic study, and media and publicity. Each of these committees is led by an emir. The tasks are carried out by a large network of terrorists organized into cells, allied groups, and affiliated organizations (Gunaratna 2002).

The al-Qaeda network has been in the process of decentralizing for years. As the leaders of al-Qaeda were targeted and hunted, decision making necessarily became more decentralized for resiliency. Members trained to fight in Afghanistan and Iraq returned to their home nations with the inspiration for jihad. This created a geographic diffusion of ideology, committed individuals, and terrorist tactical knowledge. The decentralization has created a global jihad movement, which is much more advanced than the foundational al-Qaeda network that began in the aftermath of the Russo-Afghan war (Bergen 2001). Al-Qaeda has become a nebulous network organization, still with a core leadership, but characterized by "franchises" in regions of the world. These franchise groups maintain a very loose linkage with the core for ideological guidance and financial and logistical assistance, but maintain their own command and control structure and operational decisions.

The result is a global social network of Islamists with sparsely located leaders. For example, al-Qaeda in the Arabian Peninsula (AQAP) includes Yemeni members who were recruited by al-Qaeda for the Afghan jihad, in which some were bin Laden's personal bodyguards. Members of Jemaah Islamiyah operating in Indonesia and Malaysia, the Chechen insurgency in Chechnya, and Abu Sayyaf, operating in the Philippines, also fought in the 1980s Russo-Afghan war. Sharing activities such as training has worked to the benefit of the Islamist movement, because of the similarities of terrorist ideologies and goals. Similar situations, such as Euskadi Ta Askatasuna's (ETA) training of Fuerzas Armadas Revolucionarias de Colombia's (FARC) forces has not led to an extended geographic network for either of the organizations.

While al-Qaeda's focus is on the Middle East and southwest Asia, the global jihad is the underlying next step for the group. Countries of primary concern for al-Qaeda were defined by bin Laden as "all states of the Islamic world from Indonesia to Mauritania without exception [as they] fall into one of two categories: crooked states and even more crooked states" (NEFA Foundation, 2009b p. 6). Only Sunni Muslims are accepted into the al-Qaeda organization (Shayea 2010), with other Muslim sects being viewed as having been exposed to the proper word of God, but made a conscious choice not to follow. To Muslims, "crooked" means Muslims that do not adhere to fundamental Sunni Islamist ideologies and governments that do not rule by Sharia law. Figure 2.6 shows the Muslim world, mapped by the national percentage of Muslims. Areas of higher Muslim populations will be areas of focus for al-Qaeda's global jihad to restore the caliphate.

The global caliphate, a part of fundamental Islamic prophecy, is a political/religious entity based on Islam that governs all people in the

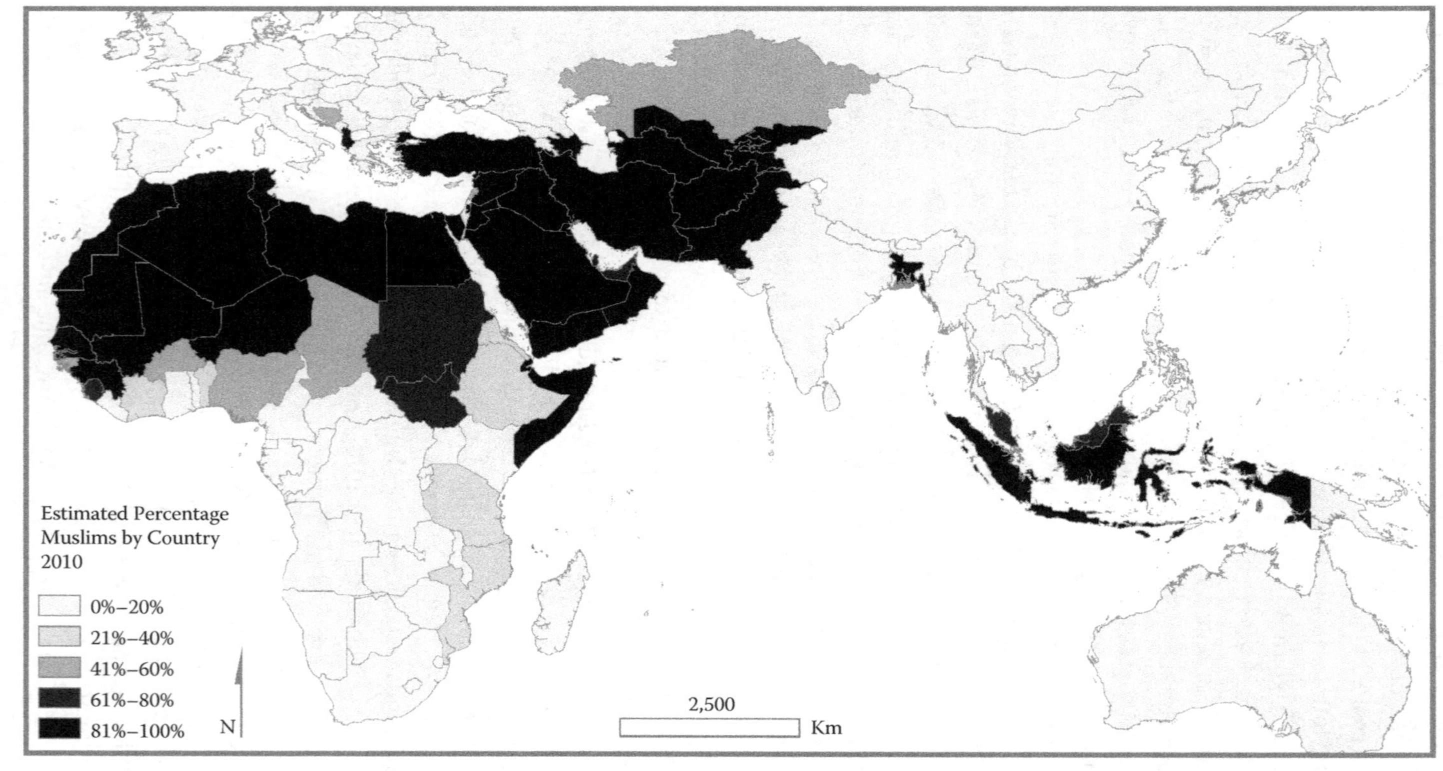

FIGURE 2.6
The Muslim world. (Data source: Pew Research Center, 2010.)

Ummah, or the collective Muslim body of the world (*Asharq Alawsat* 2001; NEFA Foundation 2008b, 2008c; Lia 2008).

Leaderless Resistance and Multiple Leaders: Models of Advanced Decentralization

The evolution of terrorist organizations into flat, decentralized organizations is becoming much more common. Terrorist networks are evolving toward leaderless resistance and multiple leader models, both of which are advanced forms of decentralization. In the leaderless resistance model, terrorists are unconnected to any terrorist network and act completely autonomously. The necessary ingredient is a message or narrative that compels this type of terrorism from a charismatic person or larger organization. In 1983, Louis Beam, a white supremacist and radical nationalist ideologist, wrote an essay, titled "Leaderless Resistance," describing the structure of "non-organization" as a system where "all individuals and groups operate independently of each other, and never report to a central headquarters or single leader for direction or instruction, as would those who belong to a typical pyramid organization" (Southern Poverty Law Center 2002; Beam 1992).

Leaderless resistance is described by Beam to be a variant of the cellular organization system with no hierarchical control over actions, where operatives receive information from widely available sources such as media, computers, and other forms of distributed information (Beam 1992). The application of leaderless resistance is much easier with the advent of the Internet and the increased availability of messages. The terrorist acts violently in his or her own way or as suggested by the outside person or organization. This type of terrorism has increased and is potentially more dangerous now that terrorist instructions on weapons, tactics, and targets are available in the media and over the Internet.

The multiple leaders model maintains social structure and at least regionally based, loose hierarchies. Leaders in this model typically represent a region and may or may not be in contact with each other. Each leader and his or her corresponding terrorists follow the message, as do leaderless terrorists; however, the terrorists act based on a local hierarchy, which makes the overall movement more regionally adaptive. The leaders in this model can also promote leaderless resistance. A regional leader can excite leaderless operatives by disseminating ideologies and ideas.

TABLE 2.3

Differences between Leaderless Resistance and Multiple-Leader Terrorist Structures

	Leaderless Resistance	Multiple Leaders
Social connectivity	No	Yes
Hierarchy	None	Can be minimal, but some hierarchy must exist
Can include aspects of the other	No	Yes
Major benefits	Geographic reach for attack is unhindered	Control
	No resources required from organization	Coordination
	Organization seems ubiquitous	Attacks can be more effective because of organizational resources

The main difference between these two models is connectivity. With leaderless resistance there is no formal social connectivity between operatives and leaders, but the multiple leaders model infers structure and hierarchy, which requires social connections. Table 2.3 shows differences between these two decentralized terrorist network models.

Hybrids of these two models exist and may be more prevalent than a pure form of either. Acting on the "message" or narrative of the group, both leaderless resistance and multiple leaders can respond to meet the goals defined in the message. Sections of the network can attack in a directed manner with resources coordinated by the multiple leaders; at the same time leaderless operatives can attack on their own to create confusion and increase the impacts.

Figure 2.7 shows conceptualizations of leaderless resistance and multiple leaders models. Hierarchical and cellular structures are delineated by pyramidal and non-pyramidal networks, respectively. Social connections that should exist are drawn in solid lines, and those that may or may not exist are shown in dashed lines. In this figure, the leaderless resistance model shows the dissemination of a message (symbol of electric bolt) that influences "lone wolf" terrorists (terrorists working alone), cells, and hierarchically structured organizations to act. The multiple leaders model shows groups of regional, hierarchical terrorists that may or may not be connected to each other. The hybrid model shows aspects of both. Leaders in hierarchical organizations influence others by disseminating a message and coordinating action; hierarchies are connected to cells and leaderless units, which can operate as ideologists with a message or direct action operatives.

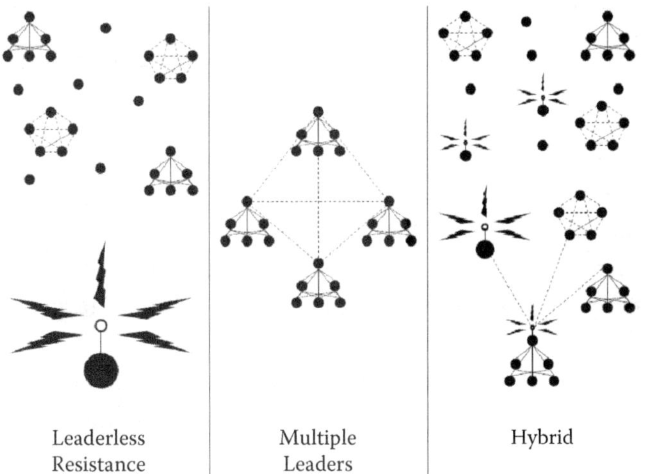

FIGURE 2.7
Conceptual visualizations of leaderless resistance, multiple leaders, and hybrid models.

Leaderless resistance strategies have been used by radical Americans on both the ultraconservative and the ultraliberal sides. Organizations such as the Army of God, an antiabortion-focused group; the Earth Liberation Front (ELF), an environmentally focused group; and the Animal Liberation Front (ALF), an anti-animal-cruelty focused group, are known to deliver messages and tools for actors in leaderless resistance. The threat from leaderless terrorists in the West is increasing in both Islamist and non-Islamist arenas. Recent reports suggest that there has been a large increase in the number of autonomous, antigovernment militias within the United States (Kelleher and Stoddard 2010).

One of the most infamous events of leaderless, lone-wolf terrorism is the Oklahoma City bombing of the Murrah federal building, which killed 168 people. Timothy McVeigh, who was executed for his crime in 2001, stated his motivation for the bombing was to "put a check on government abuse of power."

Both leaderless and multiple leaders structures are utilized by international terrorist groups, including the larger Islamist network (i.e., al-Qaeda and affiliates). The Islamist network is geographically, authoritatively, and structurally spread over regions throughout the globe. Since counterterrorism monitoring of the Internet, financial transactions, and other communications networks is very high in Europe and the United States, these groups are increasingly dependent on more autonomous units to convey messages and undertake actions.

THE CONNECTION BETWEEN THE GLOBAL JIHAD AND LEADERLESS RESISTANCE

The term jihad has two meanings. The "great jihad" refers to the war against inner demons that all humans face, while the "little jihad" refers to external war (Bergen 2001). The emphasis on jihad for external war against enemies of Islam attracts Muslims throughout the world and directs them toward specific political and geographic targets. The fundamental Islamic interpretation of little jihad promotes decentralization. According to the al-Qaeda narrative, it should be the action for every able bodied Muslim regardless of geographic location, financial situation, or social stature (Raufer 2003). This was the intent of the 1998 fatwa that initialized the "World Islamic Front" and stated that murdering Americans is the "individual duty for every Muslim who can do it in any country in which it is possible to do it" (National Commission on Terrorist Attacks upon the United States 2004, p. 47).

The advanced decentralization of Islamist terrorism was conceptualized by ideological leaders in the network and formerly outlined by Abu Mus'ab al-Suri in *The Call for Global Islamic Resistance,* published online in 2004 (Lia 2008, p. 443). In this work was the specific call for assistance from those that have no connection to the terrorist organization. Figure 2.8 illustrates the conceptual structure of the global jihad with core al-Qaeda at the center.

The circle of guidance is responsible for leadership and planning of the direction of the Islamist movement. The members in this circle are at the top of the loose leadership hierarchy. They design the ideological, strategic, and logistic principles of the global jihad and disseminate them using social networks and media outlets.

The circle of coordination is composed of members of the global jihad who are committed followers of the leadership and narrative provided by the circle of guidance. The circle of guidance is specifically designed for planning and dissemination of information, while the circle of coordination is composed of brigades designed to carry out jihadist activities per direct instruction.

The circle of the call is composed of members of the global Jihad with no direct command connection to the Islamist network. They are expected to carry out acts of jihad by peripheral instruction through word of mouth or virtual/media outlet communication (the call). Operations by the members in this circle are facilitated by the many documents (e.g., training manuals, fatwas, religious and ideological texts) widely available online.

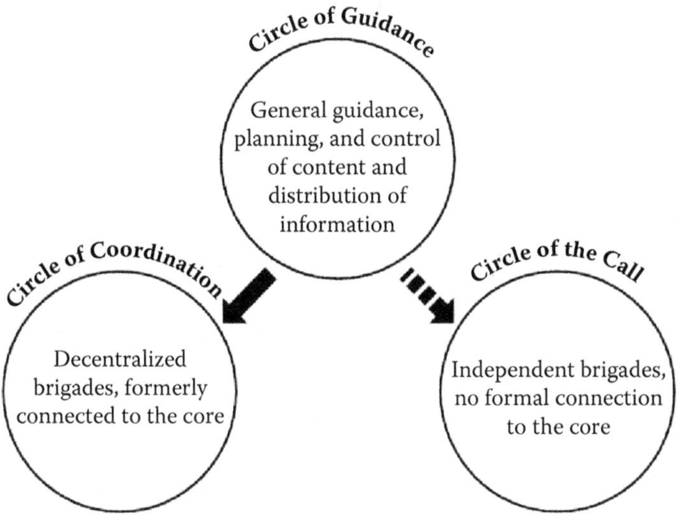

FIGURE 2.8
Organizational circles of the global Islamic resistance brigades.

The Islamist terrorist system is structured such that it poses two main threats of violence. The first is the Islamist terrorist network, which includes al-Qaeda at the ideological center with its core (circle of guidance) and multiple branches and affiliates (circle of coordination). Second are individuals that answer "the call" with no direct and therefore traceable connection to the network.

Homegrown Terrorism

The advanced decentralization of the global Islamist network in the late 1990s to early 2000s has driven the popularization of the term "homegrown terrorism." Homegrown terrorism can be defined as any act or planned act of terrorism perpetrated by a person or persons operating within the country of their birth or long-time residence. The term is used to describe terrorists that are indoctrinated and further radicalized to the stage of violent activities from within their "homeland." Processes of indoctrination and radicalization can originate from anywhere. The concept of homegrown terrorism has its foundations in geography. It differentiates between terrorists that operate within their country of primary residence and those that operate based in foreign countries.

The definition provided here does not differentiate between terrorist motivations or the locational origin of the "message," and it does not categorize terrorists as leaderless. Homegrown terrorists can be structured in hierarchical or decentralized networks. The authoritative structure of the organization does not limit the use of homegrown terrorism. A hierarchically structured terrorist organization can influence populations to act in its favor through the use of propaganda. However, the use of homegrown terrorism by a hierarchically structured organization outside the homeland will be an act of decentralization and may drive the system into continued decentralization processes. The information age makes homegrown terrorism that originating from a foreign ideology more likely, as more foreign radical ideas are available for sympathizers. It becomes a more powerful concept when the guiding message originates from a foreign land, because it implies that foreign terrorists have penetrated another nation's borders strictly through disseminating information. It can be a powerful tool of any terrorist organization that has the means of diffusing information.

Homegrown terrorism is presently a threat throughout the world. Homegrown terrorists become much more dangerous when a connection is made to the larger terrorist system. Most large Islamist terrorist attacks are carried out by individuals who have formal, face-to-face interactions with members of the terrorist network. This was the case with the Madrid bombings in 2004 (Gunaratna 2004), the London bombings in 2005, and the airline bombing plot in 2006 (Hoffman 2009), which were all identified as homegrown terrorist attacks, and were found to be conducted by individuals connected to the Islamist terrorist network.

Large attacks require materials, social resources, and know-how that are most effectively transferred through direct communications and formal training that are available with established terrorist organizations. However, many terrorists who join the terrorist network today are "answering a call" and may soon prove to be as dangerous as those that have made the real connection to the network for training and further radicalization (Kohlmann 2008; Bergen and Hoffman 2010).

TERRORIST NETWORKS FLOWS

Up to this point, focus has been on the structure of terrorist networks with discussion of their implementations in various regions and under varying conditions. The ultimate reason for a network is to facilitate the flow and dissemination of information and materials to support the terrorist group's mission. Flows can include ideas and ideologies from leaders in the network to active and potential terrorists, information, weapons, money or items that represent money, such as drugs and diamonds, field operatives for strikes, and recruits through migration channels to training camps.

The Flow of Ideas and Information and Principles of Communication in the Information Age

The flow of ideas and information for terrorist networks is vital for support, recruitment, and group operations. Communication technologies have facilitated the geographic decentralization of terrorist networks by extending the flow of information. Not only does today's technology allow for contact between people over much of the globe, but also access to powerful computers, wireless technologies, and locational technologies of global positioning systems (GPS) are all available within a mobile phone. Spreading information, ideas, and ideologies is a strategy used by terrorist organizations to build communities of sympathizers, contact and radicalize potential recruits, and instruct potential homegrown terrorists. Within the Internet are virtual "places" terrorists can go to receive information anytime. This allows potential terrorists to gain information and instructions that are operationally relevant. Access to people has been greatly extended with the advancement of communications technologies that allow for greater opportunities for those who send and receive information.

There are several forms of communication and ways to disseminate information. Major principles of present-day communication focus on (1) spatial, (2) temporal, and (3) distributional aspects. These principles make communication much more powerful and are widely used in the information age.

The spatial aspects of communication can be conceptualized as presence and telepresence forms. These forms can be simply stated as communications that occur with people "here" and "there." The presence form describes communications that take place through face-to-face contact versus the telepresence form, where the presence of both parties is not required. Telepresence communications are much more available within twenty-first century technologies.

The temporal aspects of communication refer to the synchronous and asynchronous forms. Simply stated, these types of communications between people are those that occur "now" and "later." Synchronous communications take place between two people coincident in time versus those that can be distributed at one time and reached at another (Miller 2004). Asynchronous communications are also much more available with information age technologies. These temporal characteristics of communication have also been referred to in terrorism research as active and passive communications (Cozzens 2005).

The distribution aspects of communication refer to the number of people receiving and distributing information. This phenomenon can be conceptualized in a similar way as data model applications. In the most simple form, the transfer of data or information can occur from one to one (1:1), one to many (1:M), and many to many (M:N) (Shekhar and Chawla 2003). In the 1:1 and 1:M cases, messages can be intended for one or many recipients. In the M:N case, the same or a similar message can be distributed from many people to many people. In many terrorist situations, this is the intent for documents that travel online.

Terrorists' Use of the Internet and the World Wide Web

Terrorists use the modern media, communications technologies, the World Wide Web (WWW), and the Internet to provide information about the organization and its goals, psychological warfare, propaganda, transfer of information data collection, fundraising, recruitment and mobilization, and maintaining togetherness and social structure.

Many terrorist websites include information about the organization, its goals, profiles of leaders, news reports, and other pertinent information. Often, in nationalist/separatist cases, the organizations offer maps of the territory of concern. This is the case for Hamas in Palestine, FARC in Colombia, and the Liberation Tigers of Tamil Eelam (LTTE) in Sri Lanka (Weimann 2004). By offering information of the organization, the members can publish their opinion of the organization and other information, which will often not identify with "terrorism." Organization websites may also attempt to draw readers in by constructing a community setting to which others feel they can belong.

In a terrorist network, the social connections and structure of the network are vital to its survival. The Internet is used by terrorists and supporters, as it is among non-terrorists, as a forum to maintain social network connections. It allows sympathizers and supporters to feel that they are part of the "movement." In the Islamist case, one of the main principles of Islamism is the oneness of the Ummah (Mozaffari 2007). The communications facilitated by the Internet are vital to maintaining connections within the global Ummah. The Islamist network is more than just a group of connected terrorists and organizations. The Internet brings like-minded people together. In mid-2010, a support group for "Sharia Law and Restoration of the Caliphate" was found on the popular social networking website Facebook.

Psychological Warfare

Al-Qaeda and other organizations are responsible for the use of psychological warfare in the form of posted videos of attacks, hostages, and other forms of violence; however, most terrorist organizations do not publicize their violent activities (Weimann 2004). There are many videos of Islamist attacks posted online, as well as attack claims by various organizations, Islamist and non-Islamist. These and messages of impending threats from attacks are meant to create fear in the population.

Much of the flow of ideas to impact the beliefs and emotional state of both followers and the greater population occurs as propaganda. Propaganda efforts include leader interviews and eulogies for martyrs. Many leaders in the Islamist network have been interviewed by the media and the interviews have been printed or posted online. In some cases, videos are also available. In 2010, a post including the German language memoirs of Eric Breininger, a German convert to Islam who became a member of the Islamic Jihad Union, was available online. He was also congratulated as a martyr and a short eulogy was provided (NEFA Foundation 2010a).

Bin Laden had reached out in propaganda efforts to US President Barack Obama, as well as to the American and European people. A 2010 audio recording of bin Laden titled "From Usama to Obama" threatened America with violence until peace is "a reality in Palestine" (NEFA Foundation 2010b). Two other recordings by bin Laden released in 2009, titled "Statement to the American People" and "Message to the People of Europe," attempted to reach out to the people of the United States and Europe by explaining the terrorist organization's sentiment on perceived Western government injustices (NEFA Foundation 2009c, 2009d).

One of the many benefits of terrorist organizations posting their own information on the Internet and in the mass media is that they can paint their activities in a favorable and justifiable context. Terrorists become freedom fighters; attacks can become defensive necessities, and murderers can be heroes. The Internet provides terrorist organizations with an outlet to post interpretive news on battles and movements. This is the case for the LTTE group, who used the Internet as an alternative news source to the government-controlled media for Tamils throughout the world (Hoffman 2006). Propaganda provides the pro-organizational information to gain public opinion, recruits, financial donations, and other types of support.

Some propaganda focuses on moral support. In the Islamist case, this often includes religious reasoning for violent activities. The duty of Muslims to participate in jihad and the importance of jihad are common topics for posts. Moral support originates from both terrorists and the public. Islamist ideologists often discuss the wrongdoings of enemies and the Muslim obligations of jihad. They also sometimes give some strategic direction. Public supporters offer their gratitude for the Mujahedeen and enter into pro-jihadi discussions, which may be transmitted to the Mujahedeen in the field to promote purpose. Islamists are fully aware of the nature of this war and the importance of information and propaganda.

Transfer of Information and Data Collection

There is a great amount of terrorist training resources available online, much of it published by terrorist organizations. These resources include documents and videos on topics such as military and guerrilla warfare training, making bombs and dirty bombs, martial arts training, making poison, and instructions on maintenance of computer and information privacy. These materials are meant to reach people at all levels of the terrorist network—observers, supporters, potential terrorists, and active terrorists. A resource posted online titled "44 Ways of Supporting Jihad," written by American-born terrorist Anwar al Awlaki, discusses ways to support jihad, such as "financing a mujahid," "taking care of the family of a mujahid," "fighting the lies of the Western media," and "following the news of the jihad and spreading it" (NEFA Foundation 2009e). Another document published online titled "How Can I Train Myself for Jihad?" directs those looking for military training to publications of the US Army that are available for a low price or on the Internet for free. Any useful information, even that published by their enemies, is fair game.

A large part of terrorist data and information available for mining is information for attack planning, coordination, and other logistic activities. Information for attacks such as transportation routes, weak points, and building structures can be found online. Terrorists have also been found to use geospatial technologies such as Google Earth for planning purposes. Google images of British military bases in Basra, Iraq, were confiscated at insurgents' homes, which elevated concern over the use of high-resolution satellite images by terrorists for targeting of government buildings and other secure installations (Hearn 2007). This is not the only case of terrorists using freely available high-resolution imagery for strategic or attack-based purposes. Palestinian militants affiliated with the Al-Aqsa Martyrs Brigade also used Google Earth to attack specific targets in Israel (Chassay and Johnson 2007). The Internet and other information technologies were used to coordinate much of the September 11 attacks (Weimann 2004).

Fundraising

Fundraising for terrorist organizations and operations occurs online. Many supporters of terrorism, who are not radicalized to the point of committing violence, contribute to violent activities in the name of shared opinions. In the Islamist case, much of online financing effort contains propaganda that showcases the strength of jihadist organizations through attack and operations footage. This is meant to impress potential funders. Organizations have openly posted bank account numbers online for donations (Rogan 2006). An account number posted on a Chechen insurgency website was tied to a bank account in Sacramento, California, and a link found on an IRA website allowed supporters to make credit card donations to the organization (Weimann 2004).

Al-Qaeda has used charity organizations as a front for funding (Thomas 2003). Some of these organizations were operating inside the United States and have since been shut down (Soloway, Nordland, and Nadeau 2002). Many other online sources of terrorist funding such as Azzam Publications, an Islamist publishing house that is no longer operating, are presently participating or have participated in the past in online fundraising for al-Qaeda (US Senate Committee on Homeland Security and Government Affairs 2008).

Recruitment and Mobilization

The Internet and the World Wide Web are used by terrorist organizations for recruitment and mobilization. Terrorist groups that are decentralized or in the process of decentralizing—especially those that plan to take advantage of a leaderless resistance organization—use the Internet to recruit, mobilize, and direct members toward targets in geographic places. The messages are intended to reach many potential jihadists. For example, a message posted on a website affiliated with al-Qaeda in 2007 states that it is acceptable in Islam to use arson as a warfare method to cause casualties, exhaust resources, and create economic problems. This type of warfare was termed the "forest jihad" (Fighel 2009). As well as the other purposes discussed here, a great benefit of using the Internet for purposes of mobilization is that there are no geographical barriers or distance constraints (Thomas 2003).

Material Flows

The most important spatial concerns in terrorist network research are the geographic spaces where terrorists reside, act, and interact, and virtual spaces where connections are maintained to construct global terrorist systems. Superimposed on these spaces are communication and transportation links to facilitate material flows of food, weapons, and supplies (Castells 2000).

Flows of Goods and Money

One of the most important flows for a terrorist network is the flow of supplies and money, which flow through various legal channels, such as postal and parcel delivery services. In many cases illegal channels are used, such as smuggling routes, fraudulent shipping documentation, and couriers to transport weapons, attack plans, and money. Terrorist organizations become involved with the production and trade of commodities such as drugs, weapons, cigarettes, diamonds, and gold (US General Accounting Office 2003). The income from these activities is used to finance terrorist operations around the world. These goods typically move through an illicit network, while money moves through both illicit and legal financial networks.

The flow of goods and money is dependent on other structural networks. The improving infrastructure network in Afghanistan benefits the drug trade network. New roads are used for terrorist transport of drugs, fighters, weapons, and other goods (Braun 2005). Goods and money are many times most securely and efficiently transferred in a face-to-face manner. Al-Qaeda uses this technique, which is most dependent on geographically based social networks of clan or family membership (Basile 2004).

The Hawala System of Money Transfer

The use of diaspora or migrant populations is an important component of terrorist flow of materials. The most well known of these systems is the hawala system. It is a trust-based money transfer system that is available for people to send or receive money anywhere in the world, as long as a hawaladar (financial network agent) can be reached. There are two types of hawala, "white hawala" and "black hawala." The former used to describe legal activities, and the latter used to describe illegal activities. Hawala is used for money laundering as dirty money can come in, and clean money can be paid out (Basile 2004). This is an attractive property for terrorists who are involved in criminal activities. Other similar financial networks exist; one is the "flying money" system of China, which is also used internationally (Jost and Sandhu 2000).

The basis of the hawala system resides in Dubai, because it is a free-trade zone. There are many benefits for those that send and receive money from using the hawala system, especially for illicit activities:

- Cost effectiveness
- Efficiency
- Reliability
- Lack of bureaucracy
- Lack of a paper trail
- Tax evasion

It has low overhead and exchange rates, and can be integrated with existing business activities. The system is efficient in that the transfer is much quicker than other options, only taking 1 or 2 days, and will not delay transfer due to non-working days and time differences. International transfers that may be problematic with other transfer options are much simpler in this system. Because there is much less bureaucracy in the hawala system, individuals need not have a bank account, social security number, or other attributes that other systems require.

Hawala is reliable in its simplicity. The nature of this money transfer system allows it to be paperless, such that there is no paper trail for authorities to track people and transfers. Hawaladars often keep no records. Transfers are not recorded, so tax authorities have no opportunity to scrutinize those that send or receive money (Jost and Sandhu 2000). This may be the single most important aspect of this money transfer network for terrorism and other criminal activities.

This system has been used extensively by Kashmiri terrorists (Ganguly 2001). The money transfer system has been tied to an assassination of an Indian politician, where the terrorists used it to transfer drug sale profits to arms dealers for weapons that would be used in the assassination. Bombings in India in 1993 were also traced to money transferred by the system used to buy explosives and pay operatives (Jost and Sandhu 2000). The hawala system has also been used frequently by al-Qaeda and is increasingly used by other terrorist organizations (Rabasa et al. 2006; National Commission on Terrorist Attacks upon the United States 2004).

Drug Production and Trafficking

Drug production, distribution, and sales are a primary source of income for the FARC in Colombia and the Shining Path in Peru (Basile 2004; Kleiman 2004). Hezbollah and Hamas, who utilize the triborder area between Argentina, Brazil, and Paraguay as a haven, have been found to support their activities in Lebanon and the West Bank with income generated from illicit activities and drug trade in South America (Kleiman 2004). One of the main financing sources of the Taliban is drug production and trade (Mount 2009). The Taliban banned the growth of the poppy, the plant used to make opium, in 1997 and again in 2000. However, when faced with the need for money, they failed to enforce the restrictions and have levied high tax rates and participated in the opium trade since that time (Perl 2001). They have used drug-based earnings to purchase weapons, finance military operations, and fund terrorist organizations in neighboring countries, including the Islamic Movement of Uzbekistan and the Chechen insurgency.

Flows of People and Geographic Paths to Radicalization

Many terrorist organizations, such as those that have nationalist/separatist motivations, focus on local regions and territories. For them, most movement and migration are local, as they move to attack, retreat, and populate territories. The Islamist terrorist network is more global in scope. Many agents of this network travel often and over great distances. Movement of people takes place to and from training opportunities in havens and attack opportunities in jihad arenas.

Much of this relocation occurs in continuous flows. Examples include the flows of terrorist migration to Afghanistan in the 1980s (Bergen 2001), Bosnia in the 1990s (Kohlmann 2006), and the present insurgency in Iraq (PJ Sage Inc. 2008a). There are many "arenas of jihad" including, as stated by al-Qaeda ideologist Abu Musab al-Suri, the "Arab lands of Al Sham to Egypt, North Africa and Yemen to the Arabian Peninsula, [and] also various places such as Afghanistan and Bosnia, Chechnya, Eritrea and Somalia, the Philippines, Burma, India and Kashmir and all other places tormented by Jews, Crusaders, apostates and their hypocrite allies" (Al-Suri 1999).

Specific cases of migration reported by media sources are those of Adam Gadahn, who left the United States to join al-Qaeda in Pakistan; Eric Breininger, who left Germany to join the Islamic Jihad Union in Pakistan; John Walker Lindh, who left the United States to join the Taliban in Afghanistan; and Anwar al Awlaki, who migrated from the United States to the UK, and then to Yemen with connections to al-Qaeda and other Islamist organizations.

In 2007, documents were captured in Sinjar, Iraq, that provided information on jihadist migrations into Iraq (PJ Sage, Inc. 2008a). The resulting database compiled by PJ Sage, Inc. in 2008 includes information on origins of foreign fighters, dates of movement, and coordination activities (PJ Sage, Inc. 2008b). Figure 2.9 shows the geographic origins of foreign fighters in Iraq that traveled from summer 2006 to fall 2007. This is a small sample of the actual number of jihadist migrants, but it highlights problem areas such as Saudi Arabia, Libya, and Syria.

The present-day Islamist terrorist network was built in great part by migrant jihadists (Bergen 2001). Many of the top members in the Islamist network fought together in the Russo-Afghan war that brought many terrorists—leaders and non-leaders—together (Medina 2012). The scale of present day migrations for jihad and the connectivity of terrorist network structures provide great implications about future world stability.

Jihadists that migrate to jihad arenas are typically either at a physically radicalized stage of terrorism (i.e., having the skill and motivation to conduct violent actions) or in the process of reaching that stage from a mentally and potentially active radicalized stage (i.e., accepting of violent terrorist actions and motivated to be active themselves). There are geographic places that help facilitate the radicalization of potential terrorists and supporters. Some may become radicalized at home, others in schools or at religious institutions. Some Islamists, like Kevin James, become

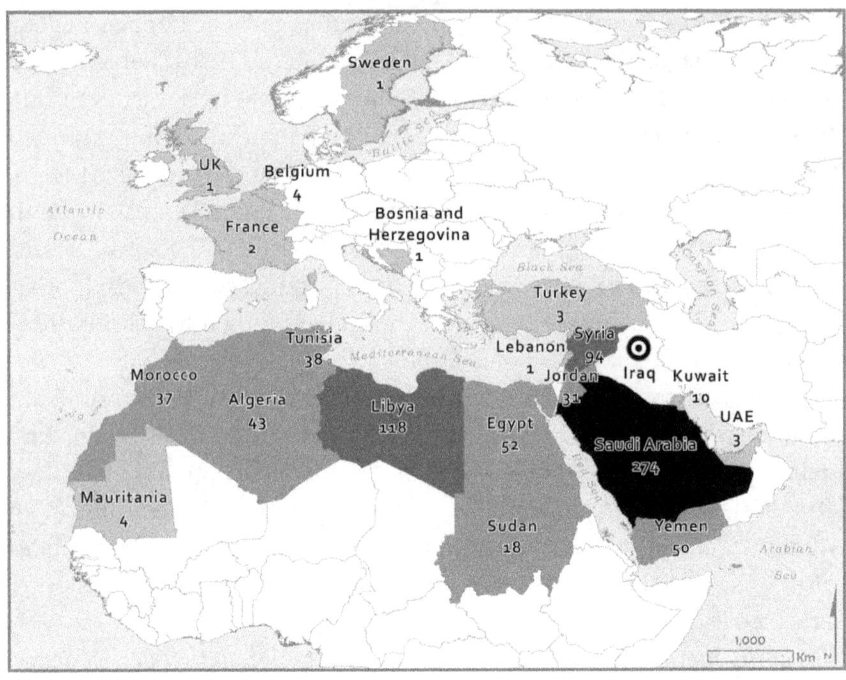

FIGURE 2.9
Countries of origin of 1,119 jihadist foreign fighters in Iraq. (Data sources: PJ Sage Inc., 2008b, political boundaries—ESRI, 2011.)

radicalized in prison. While in prison, James founded an Islamist organization and converted other prisoners. When he was released, his organization committed 11 robberies, of which the proceeds were to be used for terrorist attacks in California (US Senate Committee on Homeland Security and Government Affairs 2008).

There are many mosques that have preached or now preach radical ideas and/or are attended by radical Islamists. These may act as safe houses for jihadists in transit. Some mosques found to be purveyors of radical ideas in the past are the Farouq Mosque in Brooklyn, New York, led by radical ideologist Sheikh Omar Abdel Rahman; the Dar al Hijrah mosque in Falls Church, Virginia, attended by Fort Collins shooter Nidal Hasan and 9/11 bombers Nawaq Alhazmi and Hani Hanjour; the Islamic Center in San Diego, California, attended by 9/11 bombers Khalid al-Midhar and Nawaq Alhazmi; and many more (Watkins 2009; National Commission on Terrorist Attacks upon the United States 2004; Esposito, Cole, and Ross 2009). Anwar al-Awlaki, American-born al-Qaeda ideologist in Yemen, had a presence at the Dar al-Hijrah mosque in Virginia and the San Diego Islamic Center (Shane and Mekhennet 2010).

The radicalization process can be seen as a geographic "path" as well as a psychological one. A hypothetical example is one where an individual begins the radicalization process through information online and then begins attending a radical mosque. Through social connections at the mosque he or she finds a path to a jihadist training camp in Pakistan and from there travels to one of the many jihad arenas to fight.

REFERENCES

Alexander, Y., Swetnam, M. S., and Levine, H. M. (2001) *ETA: Profile of a terrorist group.* Ardsley: Transnational Publishers, Inc.

Al-Suri, A. M. (1999) Muslims in Central Asia and the coming battle of Islam. Available from www.archive.org

Asharq Alawsat (2001) Excerpts from Knights Under the Prophet's Banner by Ayman al-Zawahiti. December 2, 2001. London.

Azani, E. (2006) Hezbollah, a global terrorist organization. Hearing of the House Committee on International Relations, Subcommittee on International Terrorism and Nonproliferation, September 2006. International Institute for Counter-Terrorism. Available from http://www.ict.org.il/Articles/tabid/66/Articlsid/231/currentpage/10/Default.aspx

Basile, M. (2004) Going to the source: Why al Qaeda's financial network is likely to withstand the current war on terrorist financing. *Studies in Conflict and Terrorism* 27:169–185.

Batty, M. and Miller, H. J. (2000) Representing and visualizing physical, virtual and hybrid information spaces. In *Information, place, and cyberspace: Issues in accessibility,* ed. Janelle, D. G. and Hodge, D. C. New York: Springer.

Beam, L. (1992) Leaderless resistance. *The Seditionist* 12.

Bergen, P. (2001) *Holy War Inc.: Inside the secret world of Osama bin Laden.* New York: The Free Press.

Bergen, P. L. and Hoffman, B. (2010) *Assessing the terrorist threat: A report of the Bipartisan Policy Center's National Security Preparedness Group*. Bipartisan Policy Center.

Braun, M. A. (2005) US counternarcotics policy in Afghanistan: Time for leadership. Prepared statement, hearing before the Committee on International Relations House of Representatives, March 17, 2005.

BBC News (2007a) Madrid train attacks. *BBC News.* February 14, 2007. Available from http://news.bbc.co.uk/2/hi/in_depth/europe/2004/madrid_train_attacks/default.stm

——— (2007b) Germany foils 'massive' bomb plot. *BBC News*. September 5, 2007. Available from http://news.bbc.co.uk/2/hi/6979295.stm

——— (2008) London attacks. *BBC News.* July 8, 2008. Available from http://news.bbc.co.uk/2/hi/in_depth/uk/2005/london_explosions/default.stm

——— (2009) Bali terror attack. *BBC News*. March 5, 2009. Available from http://news.bbc.co.uk/2/hi/in_depth/asia_pacific/2002/bali/default.stm

——— (2010) Mumbai attacks. *BBC News*. May 3, 2010. Available from http://news.bbc.co.uk/2/hi/in_depth/south_asia/2008/mumbai_attacks/default.stm

Castells, M. (2000) *The rise of the network society*. Malden, MA: Blackwell Publishing.

Chassay, C. and Johnson, B. (2007) Google Earth used to target Israel. *The Guardian* October 25, 2007. Available at http://www.guardian.co.uk/technology/2007/oct/25/google.israel

CNN (2009) Bombing wave marks ERA campaign's 50th year. August 10, 2009. Available from http://www.cnn.com/2009/WORLD/europe/08/10/spain.eta.background/index.html#cnnSTCText

Council on Foreign Relations (2010) Hezbollah (a.k.a. Hizbollah, Hizbu'llah). Updated July 15, 2010. Available from http://www.cfr.org/publication/9155/hezbollah_aka_hizbollah_hizbullah.html

Cozzens, J. (2005) Islamist groups develop new recruiting strategies. *Jane's Intelligence Review* February: 22–25.

Cragin, K. (2005) *Hizballah, the party of god*. In *Aptitude for destruction—Volume 2: case studies of organizational learning in five terrorist groups*. Santa Monica: Rand Corporation, 37–55.

Cronin, A. K. (2006) How al-Qaeda ends: The decline and demise of terrorist groups. *International Security*, 31 (1): 7–48.

Crosson, J., Parascandola, R., Gendar, A., Pearson, J., Moore, T., and Mcshane, L. (2009) Reputed al Qaeda terror cell operative Najibullah Zazi arrested by FBI. *New York Daily News*, September 20, 2010. Available from http://www.nydailynews.com/news/world/2009/09/19/2009-09-19_zazi_cuffed_after_qaeda_canary_sings_li_secret_code_used_to_inform_plotters_li.html

Demick, B. (2010) China says terrorist cell broken up; 10 arrested. *Los Angeles Times*, June 24, 2010. Available from http://articles.latimes.com/2010/jun/24/world/la-fg-china-terror-arrests-20100625/2

elcorreodigital. (2006) ETA ha modificado su estructura interna por motives de seguridad. Política. March 23, 2006. Available from http://www.elcorreo.com/vizcaya/pg060323/actualidad/politica/200603/23/ECD_eta_funcionamiento.html

ESRI (Environmental Systems Research Institute) (2011) ArcGIS 10. Redlands, CA.

Esposito, R., Cole, M., and Ross, B. (2009) Officials: US Army told of Hasan's contacts with al-Qaeda. *ABC News*, November 9, 2009. Available from: http://abcnews.go.com/Blotter/fort-hood-shooter-contact-al-qaeda-terrorists-officials/story?id=9030873&page=2

Fighel, J. (2009) The "forest jihad." *Studies in Conflict and Terrorism* 32:802–810.

Fox News (2010a) 9 Years later, nearly 900 9/11 responders have died, survivors fight for compensation. Politics. September 11. Available from http://www.foxnews.com/politics/2010/09/09/report-responders-died-ground-zero-illnesses/

——— (2010b) Raw data: Joseph Stack suicide manifesto. US February 18. Available from http://www.foxnews.com/story/0,2933,586627,00.html. Last Accessed 6-2-2012

Ganguly, M. A. (2001) Banking system built for terrorism. *Time* Oct. 5.

Graduate Institute, Geneva and the Program on Humanitarian Policy and Conflict Research, Harvard University (2008) Euskadi Ta Askatasuna (ETA) (Basque Fatherland and Liberty). Available from http://www.armed-groups.org/6/section.aspx/ViewGroup?id=56-

Gregory, K. (2010) *Provisional Irish Republican Army (U.K., Separatists)*, Available from http://www.cfr.org/publication/9240/

Guardian, The (2005) Full text: IRA statement. London. Available from http://www.guardian.co.uk/politics/2005/jul/28/northernireland.devolution

Gunaratna, R. (2002) *Inside al Qaeda: Global network of terror.* New York: Berkeley Publishing Group.

——— (2004) The post-Madrid face of Al Qaeda. *Washington Quarterly* 27:91–100.

Hampton, K. and Wellman, B. (2003) Neighboring in netville: How the Internet supports community and social capital in a wired suburb. *City and Community* 2 (4): 277–311.

Harvey, D. (1995) From space to place and back again: Reflections on the condition of post-modernity. In *Mapping the futures: Local cultures, global change,* ed. Bird, J., Curtis, B., Putnam, T., Robertson, G., and Tickner, L. New York: Routledge.

Hearn, K. (2007) Terrorist use of Google Earth raises security fears. *National Geographic News* March 12, 2007.

Hoffman, B. (2006) *Inside terrorism.* New York: Columbia University Press.

——— (2009) Radicalization and subversion: Al Qaeda and the 7 July 2005 bombings and the 2006 airline bombing plot. *Studies in Conflict and Terrorism* 32:1100–1116.

Horgan, J. and Taylor, M. (1997) The Provisional Irish Republican Army: Command and Functional Structure. *Terrorism and Political Violence* 9:1–32.

Jenkins, B. M. (2010) Would-be warriors: Incidents of jihadist terrorist radicalization in the United States since September 11, 2001. RAND Corporation: Santa Monica.

Jost, P. M. and Sandhu, H. S. (2000) The hawala alternative remittance system and its role in money laundering. INTERPOL. Available from http://www.interpol.int/public/financialcrime/moneylaundering/hawala/default.asp

Kauffman, S. A. (1995) *At home in the universe: The search for laws of self-organization and complexity.* New York: Oxford University Press.

Kelleher, J. B. and Stoddard, E. (2010) Special report: Rapid growth of militias feeds off politics. *Reuters* April 28, 2010. Available from http://www.reuters.com/article/idUSTRE63R2O020100428

Kleiman, M. A. R. (2004) Illicit drugs and the terrorist threat: Causal links and implications for domestic drug control policy. CRS Report for Congress. Congressional Research Service, Library of Congress.

Kohlmann, E. F. (2006) The Afghan-Bosnian mujahideen network in Europe. Presented at the Center for Asymmetric Threat Studies (CATS) Workshop at the Swedish Emergency Management Agency (SEMA) Conference, Swedish National Defence College, Stockholm, Sweden, May 4–5, 2006. Available from http://www.fhs.se/en/Research/Centers-and-Research-Programmes/CATS/News/Workshop-4-Cooperating-against-terrorism-EU-US-relations-post-September-11th/

——— (2008) "Homegrown" terrorists: Theory and cases in the war on terror's newest front. *Annals of the American Academy of Political and Social Science* 618:95–109.

Koza, M. P. and Lewin, A. Y. (1998) The co-evolution of strategic alliances. *Organization Science* 9 (3): 255–264.

Krebs, V. (2002a) Mapping networks of terrorist cells. *Connections* 24 (3): 43–52.

——— (2002b) Uncloaking Terrorist Networks. *First Monday,* 7.

Lia, B. (2008) *Architect of global jihad: The life of al-Qaida strategist Abu Mus'ab al-Suri.* New York: Columbia University Press.

Manson, S. M. (2001) Simplifying complexity: A review of complexity theory. *Geoforum* 32:405–414.

Marret, J.-L. (2008) Al-Qaeda in Islamic Maghreb: A "glocal" organization. *Studies in Conflict and Terrorism* 31:541–552.

Medina, R. M. (2012) Social network analysis: A case study of the Islamist terrorist network. *Security Journal,* published online on May 28, 2012. To be printed in 2014.

Medina, R. M. and Hepner, F. G. (2008) Geospatial analysis of dynamic terrorist networks. In *Values and violence: Intangible aspects of terrorism,* ed. Karawan, I. A., McCormack, W., and Reynolds, S. E. Berlin: Springer.

Miller, H. J. (2004) Tobler's first law and spatial analysis. *Annals of the Association of American Geographers* 94:284–289.

Mok, D., Carrasco, J.-A., and Wellman, B. (2010) Does distance still matter in the age of the Internet? *Urban Studies* 47 (13): 2747–2783.

Mount, M. (2009) Taliban with drug ties now in US cross-hairs. CNN. August 10, 2009. Available from http://www.cnn.com/2009/WORLD/asiapcf/08/10/afghanistan.drugs/index.html

Mozaffari, M. (2007) What is Islamism? History and definition of a concept. *Totalitarian Movements and Political Religions* 8:17–33.

National Commission on Terrorist Attacks upon the United States (2004) *The 9/11 Commission report.* New York: W. W. Norton & Company.

National Consortium for the Study of Terrorism and Responses to Terrorism (START). 2010. Terrorist organization profile: Basque fatherland and freedom (ETA). University of Maryland. Data managed by the Memorial Institute for the Prevention of Terrorism (MIPT) until 2008. Available from http://www.start.umd.edu/start/data/tops/terrorist_organization_profile.asp?id=31

National Counterterrorism Center (n.d.) Terrorist groups: Hezbollah. Available from http://www.nctc.gov/site/groups/hizballah.html (last accessed August 2, 2012).

National Transportation Safety Board (2002) *Flight path study—American Airlines flight 11.* February 19. Office of Research and Engineering. Washington, DC. Available from www.ntsb.gov/info/Flight_%20Path_%20Study_AA11.pdf

NEFA Foundation. (2008a) Transcript of Usama Bin Laden audio recording produced by the As Sahab Media Foundation: "The way for the salvation of Palestine." Released March 20, 2008. Available from www.nefafoundation.org

——— (2008b) Selected questions and answers from Dr. Ayman al-Zawahiri—Part 1. Released on April 17, 2008. Available from http://www.nefafoundation.org/miscellaneous/FeaturedDocs/nefazawahiri0508.pdf

——— (2008c) Transcript of Usama Bin Laden audio recording produced by the As-Sahab Media Foundation: "A message to the Islamic nation." Released May 18, 2008. Available from http://www.nefafoundation.org/miscellaneous/FeaturedDocs/nefabinladen0508-2.pdf

——— (2008d) Usama Bin Laden: "Message to people of the West on 60th anniversary of Israel" May 15, 2008. Available from www.nefafoundation.org

——— (2009a) Transcript of Usama Bin Laden audio recording produced by the As Sahab Media Foundation: "A call for jihad to stop the Gaza assault." Released January 14, 2009. Available from www.nefafoundation.org

——— (2009b) Usama Bin Laden: "Practical steps to liberate Palestine." Released on March 14, 2009. Available from www.nefafoundation.org

——— (2009c) Usama Bin Laden: "Message to the people of Europe." September 25, 2009. Available from www.nefafoundation.org

——— (2009d) Usama Bin Laden: "Statement to the American people." September 13, 2009. Available from www.nefafoundation.org

——— (2009e) Anwar al Awlaki: "44 Ways to support jihad." Released: February 5, 2009.

——— (2010a) German Islamic jihad union member Eric Breininger reportedly killed in Pakistan, originally released May 4, 2010. Available from www.nefafoundation.org

——— (2010b) Usama Bin Laden: "From Usama to Obama." January 24, 2010. Available from www.nefafoundation.org

Perl, R. F. (2001) Taliban and the drug trade. CRS Report for Congress. Congressional Research Service, Library of Congress.

Pew Research Center. (2010) The future of the global Muslim population. Washington, DC. Available from http://features.pewforum.org/muslim-population/ (last accessed July 23, 2012).

PJ Sage Inc. (2008a) Where are they coming from? Beyond Iraq and Afghanistan: What foreign fighter data reveals about the future of terrorism. Available from http://www.pjsage.com/Beyond_PJSAGE_v1.pdf

PJ Sage Inc. (2008b) Foreign fighter database. Available from http://www.pjsage.com/products.htm

PBS. (2010a) Transcription of Bin Laden's fatwa, 1996. Accessed March 10, 2010. Available from http://www.pbs.org/newshour/terrorism/international/fatwa_1996.html

——— (2010b) Transcription of al Qaeda's Fatwa, 1998. Accessed March 10, 2010. Available from http://www.pbs.org/newshour/terrorism/international/fatwa_1998.html

Rabasa, A., Chalk, P., Cragin, K., Daly, S. A., Gregg, H. S., Karasik, T. W., O'Brien, K. A., and Rosenau, W. (2006) Beyond al-Qaeda: Part 1. The global jihadist movement. Santa Monica, CA: RAND Corporation.

Raufer, X. (2003) Al-Qaeda: A different diagnosis. *Studies in Conflict and Terrorism* 26 (6): 391–398.

Rogan, H. (2006) Jihadism online: A study of how al-Qaida and radical Islamist groups use the Internet for terrorist purposes. Forsvarets Forskningsinstitutt (FFI) Norweigian Defence Research Establishment. Available from http://rapporter.ffi.no/rapporter/2006/00915.pdf

Sageman, M. (2004) *Understanding terror networks*. Philadelphia: University of Pennsylvania Press.

Sanchez-Cuenca, I. (2007) The dynamics of nationalist terrorism: ETA and the IRA. *Terrorism and Political Violence* 19:289–306.

Shahar, Y. (2006) Basque separatist group ETA declares "permanent ceasefire." International Institute for Counter-Terrorism. Available from http://www.ict.org.il/NewsCommentaries/Commentaries/tabid/69/Articlsid/125/Default.aspx

Shane, S. and Mekhennet, S. (2010) Imam's path from condemning terror to preaching Jihad. *The New York Times,* May 8, 2010. Available from www.nytimes.com/2010/05/09/world/09alwaki.html

Shayea, A. E. H. (2010) Reviving the dead: The Yemeni government and al-Qaeda's resurgence. *Arab Insight* 2:67–77.

Shekhar, S. and Chawla, S. (2003) *Spatial databases: A tour.* Upper Saddle River, NJ: Prentice Hall.

Soloway, C., Nordland, R., and Nadeau, B. (2002) Hiding (and seeking) messages on the web. *Newsweek* June 17.

Southern Poverty Law Center (2002) From push to shove: Radical environmental and animal-rights groups have always drawn the line at targeting humans. Not anymore. *Intelligence Report* 107. Available from http://www.splcenter.org/get-informed/intelligence-report/browse-all-issues/2002/fall/from-push-to-shove

Stewart, J. (2009) Europe's oldest terrorist organization: The Basque ETA marks 50 years of operations. The Jamestown Foundation, *Terrorism Monitor* 7 (14): 5–7.

Thomas, T. L. (2003) Al Qaeda and the Internet: The danger of "cyberplanning." *Parameters* Spring: 112–123.

Tucker, D. (2001) What's new about the new terrorism and how dangerous is it? *Terrorism and Political Violence* 13:1–14.

US Army (2007) A military guide to terrorism in the twenty-first century. *US Army Training and Doctrine Command, DCSINT handbook no. 1.* Available from http://www.au.af.mil/au/awc/awcgate/army/gidterr/

US Department of State (2012) Chapter 6. Foreign Terrorist Organizations. Basque Fatherland and Liberty (ETA). July 31, 2012. Available from http://www.state.gov/j/ct/ris/crt/2011/195553.htm#eta

US General Accounting Office (2003) Terrorist financing: US Agencies should systematically assess terrorists' use of alternative financing mechanisms. Report to Congressional Requesters, November 2003.

US Government. (2007) H.R. 1955, Violent Radicalization and Homegrown Terrorism Prevention Act of 2007. Read in the Senate of the United States, October 24, 2007. Available from http://www.govtrack.us/congress/bills/110/hr1955/text (last accessed July 23, 2012).

US Senate Committee on Homeland Security and Government Affairs (2008) Violent Islamist extremism, the Internet, and the homegrown terrorist threat. Majority and Minority Starr Report. May 8, 2008. Available from http://hsgac.senate.gov/public/_files/IslamistReport.pdf

VOA News (2009) Official results show Lebanon's pro-Western coalition wins vote. June 8, 2009. Available from http://www.voanews.com/english/news/a-13-2009-06-07-voa19-68826702.html

Watkins, F. (2009) Alleged Fort Hood shooter tied to mosque of 9/11 hijackers. *USA Today,* November 8, 2009. Available from http://www.usatoday.com/news/nation/2009-11-08-fort-hood-mosque_N.htm

Weimann, G. (2004) www.terrorism.net: How modern terrorism uses the Internet. Special report 116. ed. United States Institute of Peace. Available from http://www.usip.org/resources/wwwterrornet-how-modern-terrorism-uses-Internet

West Point, Combating Terrorism Center (CTC) (2005) Zawahiri's letter to Zarqawi. In *CTC's harmony document database*. Available from http://ctc.usma.edu/harmony/harmony_docs.asp

3

The Geography of Terrorism, Aspirational Geography, and Safe Havens

INTRODUCTION

In the late 1800s and, especially, after World War I, Western diplomats partitioned many areas across the world, denying the geographic and cultural complexity of these places. Friedrich Nietzsche's quote, "All things are subject to interpretation, whichever interpretation prevails at a given time is a function of power and not truth," seems a very appropriate characterization of this process. The goal of the partitioning of land and national boundary delineation was distribution of control to various European nations and their complicit local regimes. The political boundaries were redrawn across Eastern Europe, southwest Asia, and the Middle East, largely by Western European men with minimal cultural understanding of the human geography of these regions. These decisions laid the foundation for the tribal and ethnic conflicts leading to the insurgencies and terrorist groups of the twenty-first century.

Perhaps even more so today, many in the diplomatic, media, and military worlds view terrorist groups and their geographies through the lens of their own political philosophies, theories, and short-term strategic goals. Thus, their motivations and approaches toward preemption of terrorism and counterterrorism are distorted by the colonial legacy, ulterior motives, and their simplistic perceptions about the goals of the terrorist groups. In many cases, terrorist groups are much more grounded in their core beliefs and historical narratives as motivations for actions than abstract political theories. Western diplomats continue to ignore many of the core beliefs, economic disparities, homeland aspirations, and on-the-ground realities of the people, clans, tribes, and cultures of the areas (Kaplan 2009).

Identification and comprehension of the philosophies, cultural organization, and landscape realities that compose the fabric of terrorist groups from a geographical perspective are imperative. This comprehension will assist in understanding the activities of the group, its potential targets, and its endgame goals. The communities of support on which all groups depend and countermeasures to diminish the groups' terroristic potential are linked to these dimensions of the group as well. These cultural and economic realities of various groups have geographic manifestation in aspirational homelands, insurgent state creation, and the quest for safe havens—all of which are crucial to understanding and countering terrorists in the future.

The literature of different disciplines uses different terminology, such as geographic havens, safe havens, sanctuaries, or black holes (Korteweg and Ehrhardt 2005). The primary factors involved in their establishment are similar; the difference is the emphasis given to individual factors by one discipline over another. For this treatment, the concepts will be described for a comprehensive view and the terms will be used interchangeably, but the emphasis will be on the relevancy of physical and human geographic factors.

GEOGRAPHY OF ASPIRATIONAL HOMELANDS

An aspirational goal is one that a group desires to obtain, but cannot due to specific factors. This group is termed an aspirational audience. In terms of the geography of terrorism, the aspirational audience is the small group of active terrorists and the much larger group of community supporters for the terrorist faction. Control of geographic space most often means control over a land area, a homeland, or a resurrected, historical cultural region that has an extreme intrinsic meaning to the terrorist group and its communities of support. The aspirational homeland for many terrorist groups, whether they are nationalistic, cultural, or ideological, is a geographic area to control, or homeland. Knowledge of the geography of the actual land area aspired to by terrorist groups is key to countering these groups.

Terrorists' goals can be intellectual, philosophical, or cultural and often vague or ill-defined in nature. However, the desire for control over geographic space is a more fundamental and concrete goal likely linked to the primal need to establish a home territory for sustenance and security. Creation of this territory often signifies victory to most terrorist groups whether they are nationalistic, ideological, or cultural/religious in their general motivation. Wallensteen and Sollenberg's (1997) research determined that the vast majority of all conflicts have a basis in ethnic differences and disputes. Virtually all ethnic conflicts have control of territory as a primary issue in the conflict. Certainly, by definition, nationalist groups seeking to create a homeland as their primary goal regard possession and control of land over the long term as primary, above all other political and social goals.

In addition, control of geographic territory is important to most cultural and some ideological terrorist groups due to the historical linkage of a place or area with cultural practice, history, and ethnicity. Osama bin Laden declared the al-Qaeda goal of a caliphate composed of the Levant, Iraq, Palestine, the Arabian Peninsula, and Egypt. This aspirational geography reflects the historical geography of Islam, the relevant battleground of Iraq, and Egypt, the home nation of al-Qaeda leader Ayman al Zawahiri. This is the geographic nucleus to create the global caliphate.

Over 80% of nation-states are composed of two or more ethnic groups. In some nations, these groups have developed a social structure fostering integration and consolidation. In other nations, internal friction due to historical events, basic differences in cultural practice, devotion to tribal and clan governance, and/or marginalization of one group by another results in the desire for a group to have autonomy or separation.

In many situations, the political, religious, or ethnic minority or marginalized group is prone to violent response if two conditions are met (Toft 2003): 1) the group demands sovereignty over the territory that it occupies and 2) the nation-state views the territory as indivisible from the remainder of the nation. Groups demand control of areas in which they are geographically concentrated and have historical claim. Their right to claim and their interest in doing so tend to diminish as distance increases from this concentration.

Kurdistan

Large numbers of the estimated 30 million Kurds populating areas of Turkey, Syria, Iraq, and Iran are on a quest for homeland—a quest that remains an active issue for the Kurds and the nations comprising their desired homeland nation (Figure 3.1). Kurdistan is referred to as the

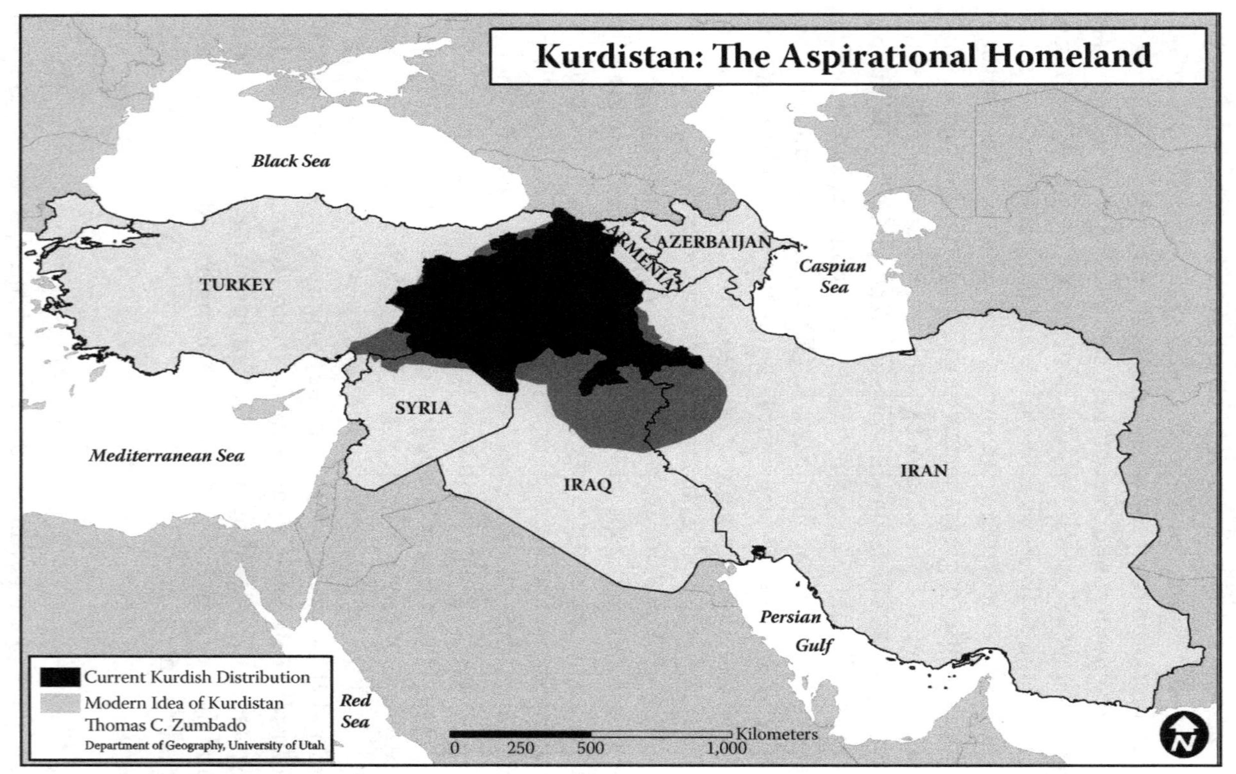

FIGURE 3.1
Kurdistan: the aspirational homeland.

largest nation without a state (i.e., an aspirational geographic construct for a Kurdish homeland). While the boundaries of Kurdistan are ill defined, the desire for a sovereign homeland is very real among the Kurdish residents of Turkey, Iraq, Syria, and Iran. The area around the Zagros and Taurus Mountains of Anatolia has been inhabited by Kurds for several thousand years before the current era (CE). The Islamic control of the region, which began in the seventh century, led to most Kurds becoming non-Arab Sunni Muslims.

As early as the late 1500s, written records indicate a desire for Kurdish political and ethnic consolidation (Izady 1992). During the 1919 Paris Peace Conference and the 1920 Treaty of Sevres, an area of Turkey was delineated as an autonomous Kurdistan. However, by 1923 the Treaty of Lausanne partitioned the former Ottoman Empire into independent Turkey, Iraq, Transjordan, Palestine, and Syria. The European powers eliminated the proposed Kurdistan in the final settlements of land control in southwest Asia and the Middle East. Culcasi (2010) states that even though Kurdistan never gained sovereignty or recognized borders, it does exist. While the lack of recognized borders has meant that Kurdistan does not exist as a sovereign nation, this lack of borders—or, rather, the overlay of several nations upon Kurdistan—has perpetuated the movement for the creation of Kurdistan centered in Turkey. Figure 3.1 shows a comparison of the historical range of Kurdish settlement, the current concentration of Kurds, and one concept of a twenty-first century Kurdistan.

Ergil (2007) contends that the basic Turkish conception of nation building requires a standardized cultural conformity that is in direct opposition to the cultural geographic reality of Turkey. Turkey has numerous non-Turkish ethnic groups of which the Kurds are the largest, comprising approximately 20% of the population. The Kurdish aspirational homeland is an ill-defined region of over 20 million Kurds making up a large percentage of the area's population. As is often the case, denial of economic opportunities and cultural identity to Kurds has helped to solidify community opposition at all levels to Turkish policy and actions. The result has led to the rise of Kurdish insurgency and terrorist groups. As many as 10 separate Kurdish terrorist groups are operating in pursuit of an independent Kurdistan (National Consortium for the Study of Terrorism and Responses to Terrorism [START] 2012), of which the Kurdistan Workers Party (PKK) is the best known.

At the height of the PKK activities against the central government in the late 1980s and 1990s, Ergil (2007) estimates that the active PKK militia numbered 10,000 with 500,000 active supporters and over one million sympathizers among the Turkish and diaspora Kurdish populations. Currently, the Turkish army is fighting a counterinsurgency campaign against Kurds in Turkey and across the border in northern Iraq, where the downfall of Saddam Hussein has led to a greater degree of Kurdish autonomy in Iraq. The Kurds use the international border as a means of providing a safe haven from the Turkish army. The lack of unity among Kurds and some beneficial responses from the central governments, primarily Turkey, have diminished terrorist group support and lessened the demand for a sovereign nation of Kurdistan (Culcasi 2010).

Whether it be an aspirational homeland or insurgent state, the terrorist group uses the area under its control to further its cultural, nationalistic, and/or ideological goals. The nation-state resists demands from the groups, not wanting to set a precedent that will foster claims from other groups leading to devolution of the existing nation. Numerous examples of this theory of indivisible territory (Toft 2003) exist across the globe. This conflict is demonstrated in the devolution of the USSR to the many separate nations formed from the former republics. At some point in the disintegration of the former Russian empire, the Russian leaders had to set a counter-precedent of resisting further separation by ethnic regions. This was the basis for the rise of the Chechen terrorist groups in the Russian Federation Republic of Chechnya during the post-Soviet era, made infamous with the 2004 Beslan school massacre and the 2010 Moscow metro bombing in response to Russian army intervention. These relatively homogenous groups under control of another group or central government view the instantiation of a homeland under their control as the defining measure of their cultural and ideological identity.

POLITICAL AND GEOGRAPHICAL BORDERS

A primary geographic issue in the group's vision of a homeland is where the borders of the homeland area are to be delineated. A border, as a concept, has a multitude of meanings—as functional barriers of sovereignty and as symbolic and perceptual barriers to human interaction (Bauder 2011). Political borders are lines on the landscape (walls, fences) and maps to demarcate boundaries of political and military control between two nations. Geographical borders are the physical features, such as valleys, rivers, and mountain ranges, that are natural demarcations of the landscape. Geographical borders include the cultural area demarcations, such as areas of transition in ethnicity, language, tribe or clan, and other social cultural features. In most cases, clan and tribal allegiance is a stronger influence than economic, political, or even religious affiliations (Kaplan 2009). Across the globe, the concentration of members of the clan or tribe, and historical claims on a perceived homeland are used to delineate geographical borders.

In many situations, the borders of the aspirational homeland do not correspond with the national border demarcations, or they cross one or more national political borders. Further complicating the situation, the formation of the caliphate of fundamentalist Islam essentially does not recognize national political governments, and therefore political borders have no legitimacy.

The Conference of Berlin in 1884 epitomizes the ineptness of political border designation when it does not consider the physical and cultural geographies of the areas to be bounded. The political borders delineated by the European colonial powers in this conference did not respect the physical geographic boundaries that the tribal groups had used for centuries to delineate homelands of control. For much of Africa, the result is that modern nations contain tribal groups that are historical enemies. Groups are severed from their migratory areas of subsistence and the destruction of the social fabric of tribal groups being split into different nations.

A more current example of the non-alignment of political and geographical borders resulting in acrimony, insurgency, and terrorism is Afghanistan. The prevalent Western media theme on the Taliban is that they are Islamic fundamentalists with the goal of establishing an Islamic state in Afghanistan. The goals of the Afghanistan Taliban and the newer organization, the Pakistan Taliban, are different. The former is focused on control of Afghanistan and the latter has a Pakistan focus with more inclination to support regional actions (Shane 2009).

Underlying this situation is the Taliban as the latest incarnation of Pashtun nationalism. Forty-two percent of the Afghanistan population is Pashtun. Their area, combined with the Pashtun areas of Pakistan, create a potential unified ethnic homeland termed Pashtunistan (Kaplan 2009). Looking at the map of Pashtun dominance (Figure 3.2) across western Pakistan and southern and eastern Afghanistan, one sees the

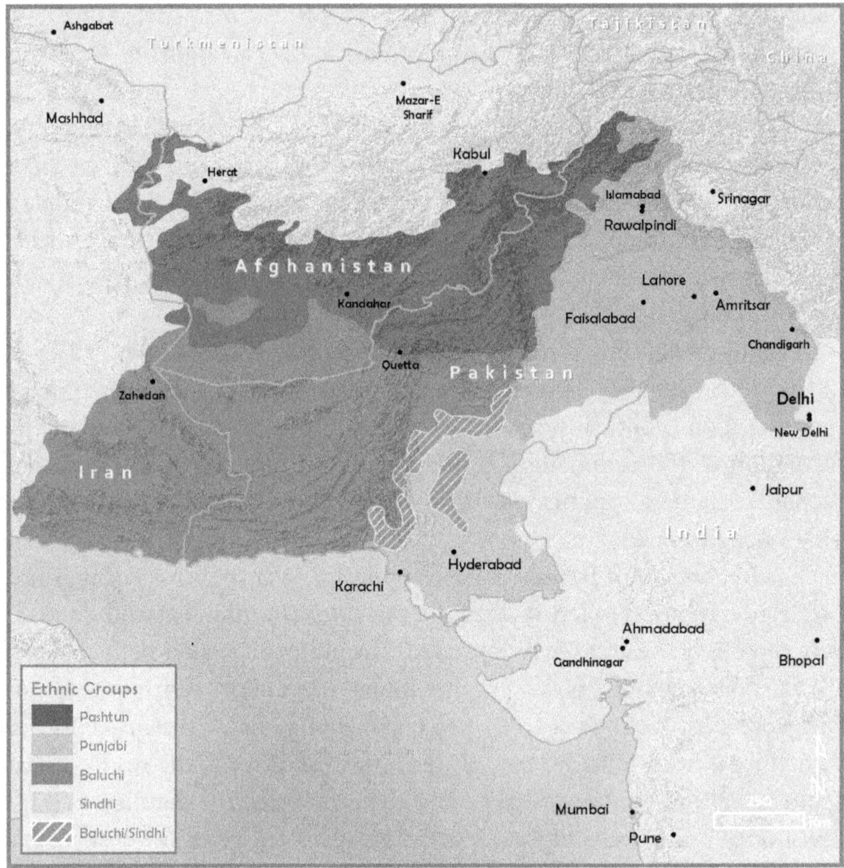

FIGURE 3.2
Pashtunistan.

political border established in British colonial times bisecting the Pashtun home territory into both nations. The ethnic convergence of Pashtuns in Afghanistan, Pakistan, and the Taliban is further reinforced by the ethical code and laws of behavior termed Pashtunwali.

Pashtunwali dates back to before the cultural overlay of Islam and political borders. The primary components include hospitality (*melmastia*), asylum (*nanawatai*) and loyalty (*sabat*). These aspects of the Pashtunwali provide more understanding as to why Pashtuns from Pakistan and members of the Haqqani network or the Taliban are welcomed, provided refuge, and shown loyalty based on a common Pashtun and tribal heritage. Attempts to sever these linkages between Pashtun terrorists and the community of support in Pashtunistan with political borders, alternative ideologies, such as democracy, and other enticements face significant historical resistance based on ethnic aspirations for a Pashtun nation.

A geographic correspondence of Pashtun areas with Taliban activities is shown by comparing Figure 3.2 and Figure 3.3. Figure 3.3 was compiled by the International Council on Security and Development (ICOS). ICOS is a non-governmental organization that operates local data gathering and analysis in Afghanistan. The area of "permanent presence" of the Taliban is defined by one or more attack per week. The percentages are calculated by dividing the Taliban attack areas by the total area of Afghanistan. Taliban attacks are difficult to verify, and the calculation of the percentages (80%, 17%, and 3%) using the relative areas defined by attack point data is less than optimal. Although one must be skeptical of the map implication that this much territory of Afghanistan is controlled directly by the Taliban, the map does indicate substantial Taliban activity and relatively more Taliban activity in ethnic Pashtun areas.

Contrasting the area of Pashtun dominance in Afghanistan are the concentrations of other groups of Tajiks (27%), Hazaras (9%), and Uzbeks (9%) (CIA 2012). These areas are much less supportive of Taliban activities and have oriented themselves to linkages to similar ethnic nations from the former Soviet republics in Central Asia. This mismatch of ethnic and political borders accounts in large part for the intractable problems of creation of a unified Afghanistan controlled by a central government in Kabul.

THE INSURGENT STATE AS A HOME FOR TERRORISTS

Related concepts for explanation of geographical areas as a physical base for terrorist groups involve quasi-states and insurgent states (Jackson 1990). In a quasi-state, postcolonial positions of power within national and local institutions are occupied and used to the benefit of the individuals in power: corrupt governmental officials and their corporate allies. The average citizen receives little in terms of public goods and services associated with the independent nation, a condition often more pronounced in this age of globalization. This form of a political economy can lead to the insurgent state.

The traditional embodiment of the geographic area physically maintained by insurgents and terrorists is the insurgent state. The insurgent

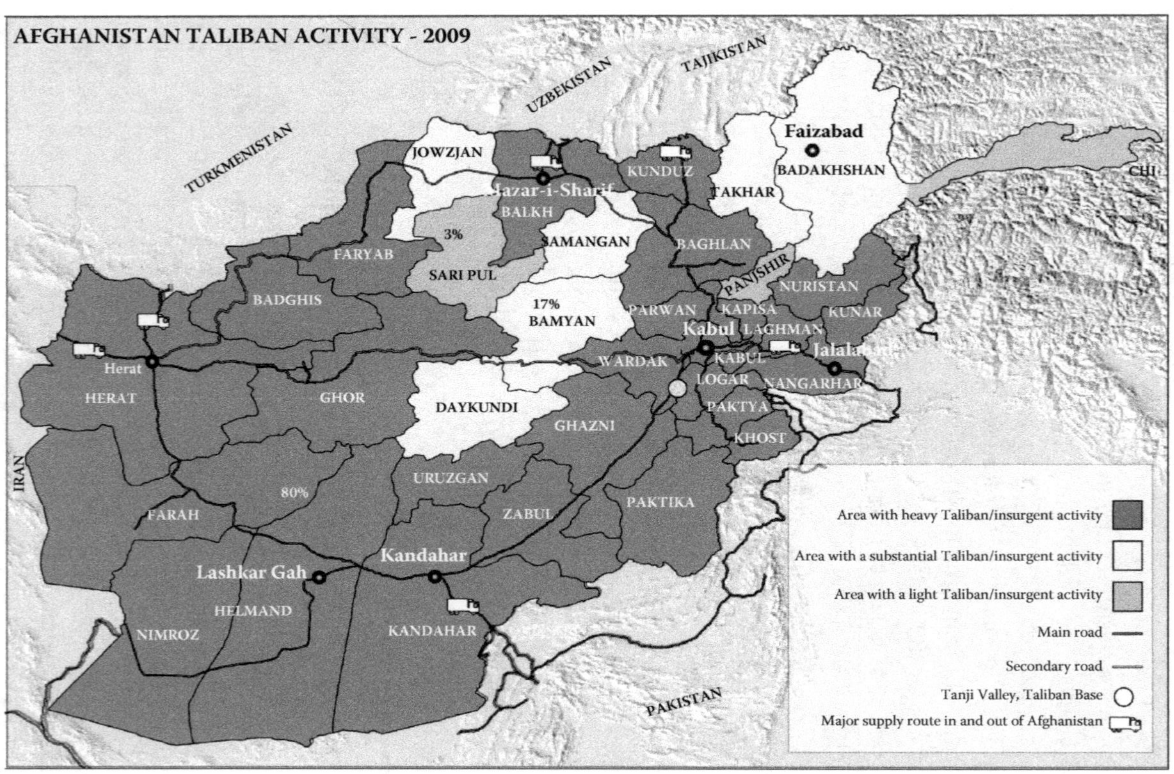

FIGURE 3.3
Taliban activity in Afghanistan, 2009. (The International Council on Security and Development [ICOS]. With permission.)

state becomes a reality inside a sovereign nation as central governmental control diminishes in an area and terrorist groups fill in the local populace's need for security, governance, and basic social and educational services (Lohman 2000). Areas that become insurgent states are geographically inaccessible because of mountains or jungles. More problematic are areas that are ethnically inaccessible—virtually all tribally governed areas of the world. Cross-cultural mediators are rare as they are suspect by both locals and central government personnel (Simons and Tucker 2007). Those areas that are inaccessible due to both physical and social geographic factors have very significant potential as insurgent states. Chechnya and the FATA region of Pakistan are examples.

McColl (1969) identified several factors conducive to the formation of an insurgent state: previous political opposition to the central government; political instability; access to important military, economic, and political facilities; and confused lines of authority and jurisdiction, such as proximity to international borders. In addition, the insurgent state requires a landscape conducive to concealment and security of insurgent forces.

Naxalites in India

Naxalite is a general characterization of several militant leftist ideological terrorist groups active in a corridor from Nepal to southeastern India. The name is derived from the village Naxalbari in the state of West Bengal, India. The Naxalites are ideological terrorists responsible for numerous attacks; the most deadly was the April 2010 killing of approximately 80 Indian security personnel. The Naxalite movement began in West Bengal, but has spread along a north–south corridor including the rural and remote jungle areas in the states of Chhattisgarh and Andhra Pradesh. The map in Figure 3.4 indicates the range of the Naxalite movement area in which the members operate training camps, plan and mount operations, and rely on support from networks of operatives and supporters in the local villages.

Most of the community of support comprises tribal groups and local villagers displaced from land ownership and economic opportunities by governmental officials and programs, as well as private corporations intent on accessing land and natural resources. The Naxalites have established an insurgent state in which they operate with relative impunity. They influence both the formal and informal economies of their area. They provide

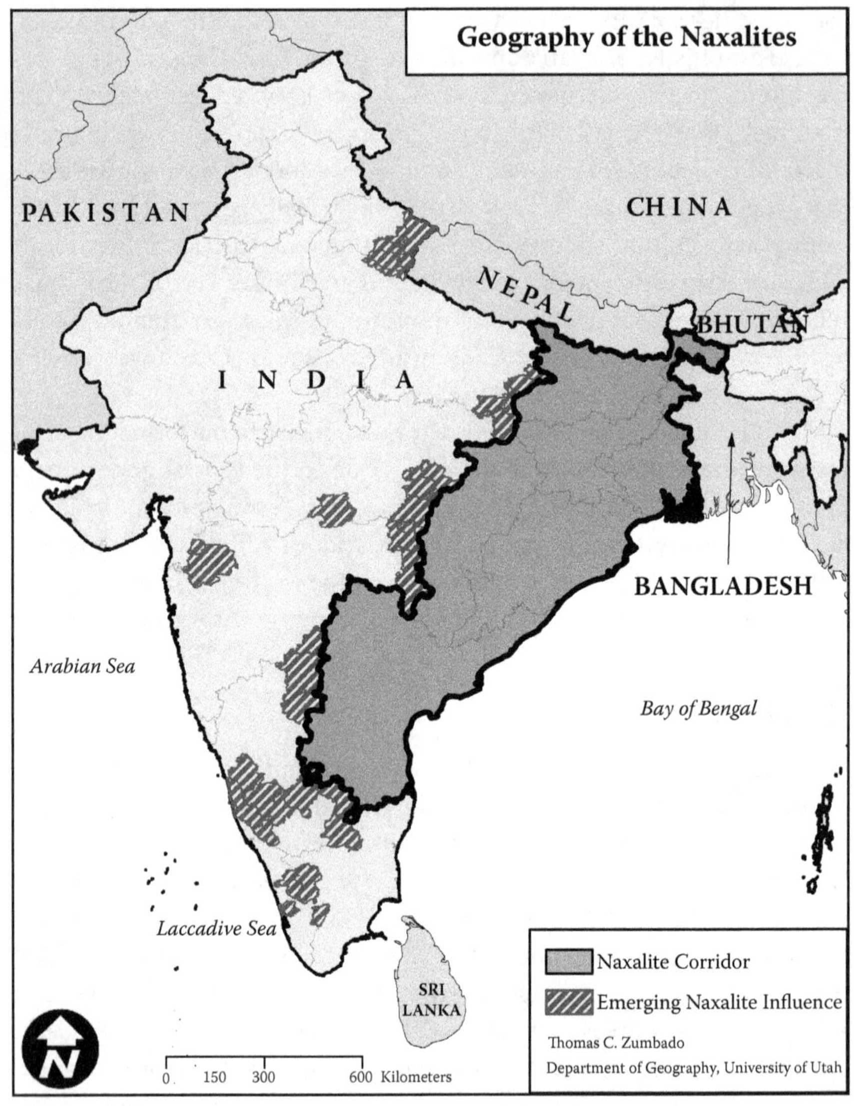

FIGURE 3.4
The geography of the Naxalites.

security and levy taxes on the opium and cannabis grown by local farmers, who can earn more growing drug crops than traditional crops. While the Naxalites are a confederation of Maoist and Communist groups based in India, they have globalized linkages to leftist supporters all over the world, including Nepalese leftist insurgents and, possibly, Chinese communists who would like to undermine the Indian government.

HAVENS FOR TERRORIST GROUPS

A terrorist safe haven has traditionally been a physical geographic area of relative security used by terrorists to indoctrinate, recruit, train, regroup, and prepare and support their operations. Physical safe havens provide security for terrorist leadership, allowing them to plan and to facilitate terrorist activities with relative safety. The presence of terrorist safe havens in a nation or region is not necessarily related to state sponsorship of terrorism. Physical safe havens are often found in undergoverned territories or associated with unrestricted crossing of international boundaries. Denying terrorists physical safe havens has been a primary goal in undermining terrorists' capacity to operate effectively. The focus on havens has been a key element of US counterterrorism policy and practice.

Global communications and financial infrastructure, such as the Internet, global media, and unregulated economic activities, supplement the capabilities offered by a physical safe haven (US State Department 2009). Terrorists use these globalized technology systems for recruitment, training, planning, funds transfer, and intelligence collection between and among terrorists and terrorist groups. These "virtual" havens are highly mobile, difficult to track, and difficult to control. The use of virtual space by terrorists was discussed in Chapter 2.

The role and importance of the physical area of haven as a necessity for a terrorist group, in the age of virtual space, is a topic of much debate. Two related issues are central to the debate. The first is whether a geographic haven comprising a physical area is necessary as a safe haven for twenty-first century terrorists. The second concerns whether making physical havens the primary target of counterterrorism efforts is an effective and productive strategy to combat international terrorism.

Conventional views are that a geographic haven is essential for a group's security, training, and planning efforts and to project a concrete image of achievable victory by control of territory. Recent developments in the use of virtual space by terrorist groups for some of these activities have suggested that focus on geographic havens is overstated and even counterproductive. One of the major arguments minimizing the importance of geographic havens questions whether a localized focus on specific areas is sufficiently relevant to the battle against globalized, international terrorist movements. Innes (2007) states that terrorists have used advanced communications technology to create virtual refuges for their activities and do not have to rely on real physical space.

Some have postulated that the counterterrorism focus on safe havens actually impedes a global approach to diminishing terrorism (Pillar 2009). The use of modern technology does provide new means for recruiting using websites and video on the Internet. Financing is no longer a matter of collection of cash from the population of an area or external communities of support. Electronic transfers allow the collection and storage of concealed funds to finance a group's operations all over the world. Some training in intelligence tradecraft, weapons production and use, and security measures is being done over the Internet as well.

In spite of a changing technology picture, the need for a physical safe haven for terrorist groups such as al-Qaeda is still the dominant view (US State Department 2009; Korteweg and Ehrhardt 2005; Cragin 2011). The role of a geographic area for fundamental terrorist group activities is vital and, in many cases where nationalism or establishment of a homeland is a primary goal, part of the group's reason for existence.

Geographic Haven

A geographic haven is a physical area of relative security exploited by terrorists to indoctrinate, recruit, train, and regroup, as well as prepare and support their operations. Physical safe havens provide security for many senior terrorist leaders, allowing them to plan and to inspire acts of terrorism around the world. The presence of terrorist safe havens in a nation or region is not necessarily related to state sponsorship of terrorism. In most instances, areas or communities serve as terrorist safe havens despite the government's best efforts to prevent this. The elimination of terrorist safe havens is a primary component of counterterrorism strategy (UN Security Council Resolution 1373).

The geographical aspects of a haven include the physical landscape that provides shelter, concealment, and sustenance for terrorist activities; relative location of an area to national borders, coastlines, and communities of support; location within an aspirational cultural or homeland, thus surrounded by people on a similar ethnic and cultural quest for a land to call their own, albeit without the terrorism tactics.

Lohman (2000) discussed the geographic factors essential for an insurgency. Many of these same factors are necessary for a terrorist group to establish and maintain a safe haven. Geography alone does not make the conditions requisite for a safe haven. The factors most often cited leading to the creation of a terrorist haven are comparable to those for an insurgent state: weak governance, alienation of the citizens of an area from the central government, history of instability and corruption, social and economic disenfranchisement from the rest of the nation, and favorable physical and human geographic features in an area (Kittner 2007; Abbott 2004). In addition, a haven often must provide economic sanctuary for terrorists, meaning a readily available means to provide income for the group, such as cocaine production and the FARC in Colombia and the opium production of Afghanistan for the Taliban.

Korteweg and Ehrhardt (2005) studied 41 havens (black holes) within sovereign nations. They identified five categories of factors that contribute to a lack of centralized governmental control that seem to be a necessary but not sufficient condition to lead to the formation of a haven:

- Societal tensions
- Legacy from civil conflict
- Geography
- Corruption and policy failure
- External interference

Additionally, they identified factors that provide a comparative advantage for that area then to be utilized by non-state terrorists:

- Religion and ethnicity (community of support)
- Legacy of civil conflict
- Geography
- Economic opportunities and underdevelopment
- Regional stimuli

Kittner (2007) developed a comprehensive analysis of more specific factors necessary for a terrorist safe haven for Islamist groups. She defines safe havens as geographical spaces where an operational and organizational base can be established. This base is used for financial activities that involve illicit actions, such as smuggling or drug trafficking. The Revolutionary Armed Forces of Colombia (FARC), with a haven in the mountains and jungles of Colombia and Venezuela, uses the cocaine trade to finance their ideological terrorism. The Taliban uses the relative security of southern Afghanistan and the tribal areas (FATA) of Pakistan to oversee their trafficking in opium. These areas are used to extract taxes from the local populace and to apply leverage on local families to tax immigrant and diaspora communities across the globe.

While the Internet can provide some indoctrination and training of recruits, it is not a complete substitute for combat and weapons training, focused communal indoctrination, and live training in operational security and intelligence tradecraft.

Geographical Factors

Favorable physical and human geography assist terrorist groups to maintain their safe havens. One category of geographic factors involves the site-specific physical aspects of an area. The roughness or complexity of the terrain is an important factor. In very complex terrain, groups can avoid detection, concealing operational and training facilities from both ground and remote sensing surveillance.

The land cover, especially dense natural or cultivated vegetation, is another factor making detection and surveillance difficult. Natural physical barriers such as rivers and mountains and lack of geographic proximity to established road networks are obstacles to centralized governmental control. Coastlines on edges of the safe haven provide easy, concealed access for groups to undertake operations, smuggling of weapons and supplies, and a route of escape if threatened. While remoteness of a haven can be an asset for safety, generalizations vary by geographic setting. Proximity of the haven with suitable safe landscapes and/or international borders to a target can be an asset. Berrebi and Lakdawalla (2006), in their study in Israel, state that terrorists seem to use a cost-benefit analysis for target selection. They indicate that terrorists are more likely to hit targets more accessible from their own home bases and international borders.

The second category of geographic factors involves the geographic context or situation in which the safe haven is located. The factors include the geography of the ethnic and cultural groups in the area. The linkages to clan and tribe are often a primary part of the network fabric of the group. Members of the group, sympathetic followers, and the supportive community at large actively support the group or are willing tacitly to support the group by not informing governmental authorities. Knowledge of these cultural patterns of tribal control, ethnic groups, and land utilization is essential to creating appropriate strategies to separate terrorists from community support.

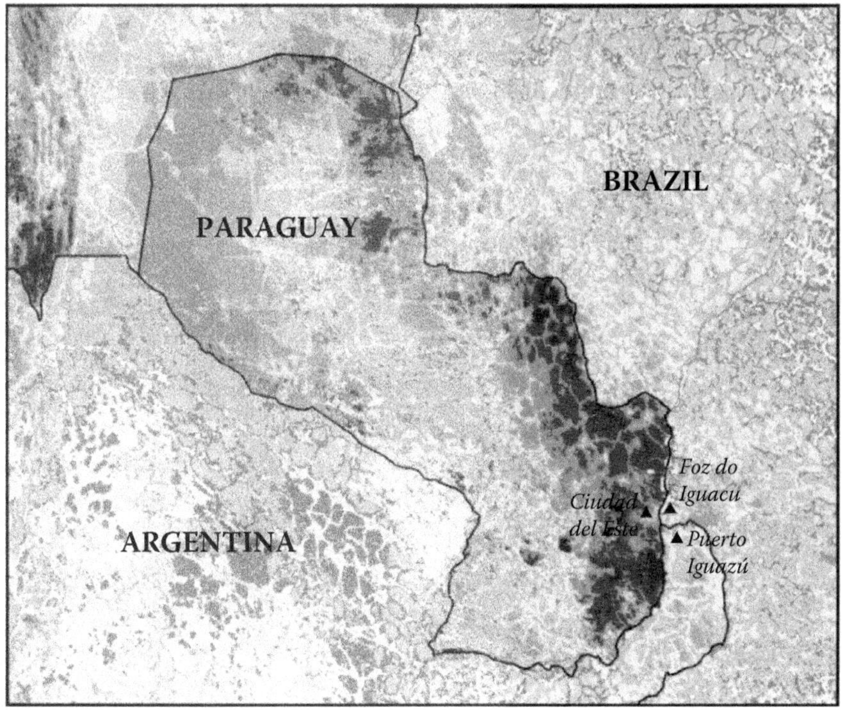

Darker tones indicate more suitable areas

FIGURE 3.5
Suitability as a terrorist haven: using GIS composite analysis.

Figure 3.5 shows a map of the frontier areas of Paraguay, Argentina, and Brazil, an area named the triborder area of South America. This map was part of a US government study using a geographical information systems approach to screen the globe for areas more suitable for the establishment of terrorist—in particular, Islamist—havens. The factors used were a physical geographical factor (terrain complexity, land cover, temperature), a geodemographical factor (population density, proximity to settlements, access to communications), a territorial situation factor (area size, contiguity and proximity to national borders and coasts), and a governance factor (legitimacy of government, institutions, and governmental capacity).

Location-specific data were collected on these factors for the entire globe. Areas were scaled from least suitable to most suitable for terrorist haven based on how well the areas meet the individual factor criteria. These results are mapped with white to black tones indicating the most suitable areas based on the composite of all factors. The black/dark are areas scoring 80% or more on the combined criteria. The moderate gray indicate areas are in the 65%–80% range; the lighter tones scored less, indicating the least suitable areas for a haven.

No single factor can be taken in isolation. The combination of geographical factors of landscape (terrain and vegetation complexity), proximity and porosity of borders, jurisdictional ambiguity, and inaccessibility—along with weak governance and absence of strong institutions, such as the legal system—provides the context for the establishment of a haven for terrorists.

In addition, the triborder area is the location of three linked cities: Puerto Iguacu, Argentina; Foz de Iguazu, Brazil; and Ciudad del Este, Paraguay. These cities and the surrounding areas have been the destinations for an estimated 60,000 Muslims relocating from the Middle East in the latter twentieth century. The area has a long history of illicit activities that provide both the economic support for terrorist groups and the channels to move weapons, money, and people between the adjacent nations. This area is viewed as a leading potential area of training of Spanish speaking Islamist militants for infiltration into North America.

Urban Havens

Due to modern communications in recent years, transportation and financial transfer technologies—urban rather than traditional rural areas—have become physical havens for terrorist groups. The urban area provided concealment along with close proximity to support and targets.

This concentration of a specific ethnic or cultural group within an urban area allows neighborhoods to function as physical havens, even within a city. Boyer (2008) termed cities that are composed of neighborhoods partitioned into ethnic and tribal groups and allegiances "tribal cities." Mogadishu, Grozny, and Baghdad are examples of tribal cities. Often terrorists hide within the high population density, urban ethnic concentrations, and complex built terrain of large urban areas.

Bale (2007) examines the case of "Londonistan," where numerous radical Islamists were able to have a safe haven in the center of the "infidel" Great Britain. Many operatives, organizers, and recruiting clerics maintained lives in London in spite of being wanted for crimes in other nations. Britain's openness for granting asylum for political refugees limited its cooperation to these other nations. Furthermore, the large numbers of recent migrants to London from Muslim nations created a community of support for global terrorist support operations. Recent migrants (foreign-born people) represented 34% of the 2.6 million people in London in 2006. Approximately 200,000 of these foreign-born individuals are Muslims, most from south and southwest Asia (Reid and Miller 2011). These migrants, even though living in Britain, are often resentful of colonial and postcolonial actions of the British. Many have been poorly assimilated within British society. Thus, they are open to economic support of Islamist groups and are willing recruits to the global jihad. The result is an isolated safe haven within the modern urban complex.

The religiously oriented neighborhood geography of Baghdad, Iraq, provides another example of an urban haven. Many of the neighborhoods are predominantly Shia, or Sunni with a few Christian enclaves. Under the Saddam Hussein regime, several neighborhoods were mixed with constant tension for dominance. With the removal of Saddam, the Shia neighborhoods, such as Sadr City and adjacent Shaab and Ur, are maintained as physical havens by Shia militia and terrorists. With "cleansing" of non-Shias starting in 2005, these areas provided haven for the Mahdi army and Kata'ib Hezbollah. Similarly, Sunni neighborhoods have been homogenized and act as havens for Sunni militia groups and al-Qaeda in Iraq.

Other Attributes of Havens

Safe havens are often located on the border between nation states. Porous borders allow terrorist groups to move with relative ease from one nation to another. Governmental control of these groups is hindered by the international border, which limits one nation's military, law enforcement, and political control at the border.

In some cases, the support community for a safe haven is not contiguous with the activity area of the terrorist group. Globalization effects to enhance the movement of products and people and weak border control allow geographic separation. The best havens for terrorists have a combination of these geographic factors.

Tamil Tigers of Sri Lanka

In the case of Sri Lanka, the Liberation Tigers of Tamil Eelam (Tamil Tigers) were able to maintain a presence and terrorist activity in northern Sri Lanka for decades, even though their haven was at most one-third of

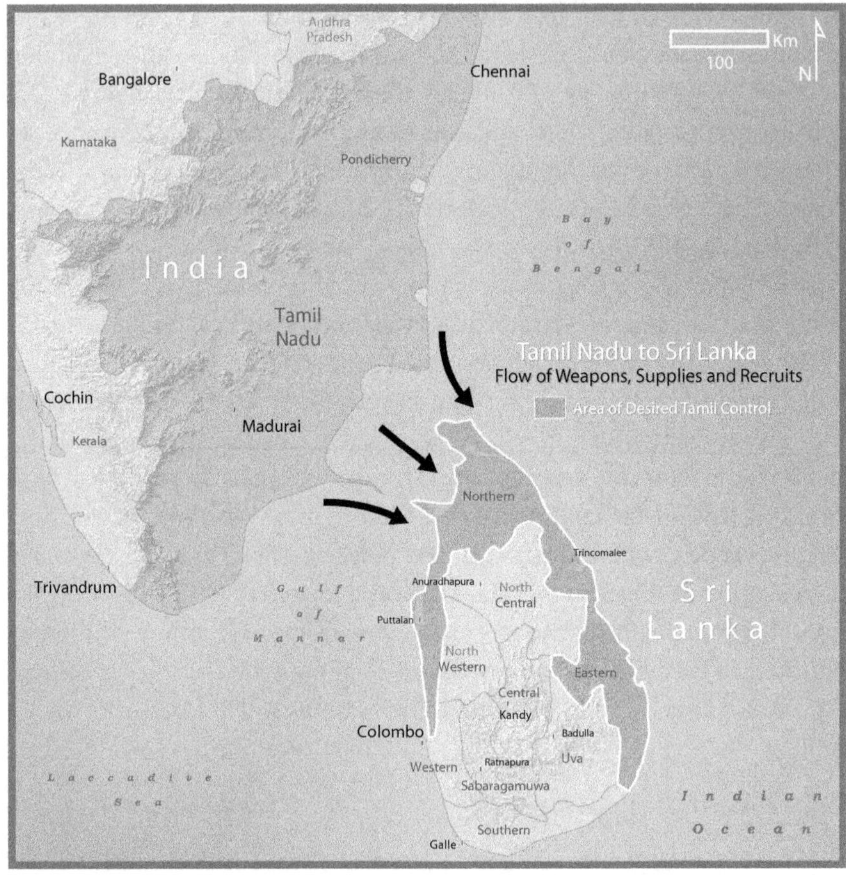

FIGURE 3.6
Tamil Nadu to Sri Lanka: flow of weapons, supplies, and recruits.

the relatively small 66,000 square kilometers (25,000 square miles) island of Sri Lanka. Sri Lanka is equal in size to the US state of West Virginia.

Sri Lanka has large swaths of remote jungle and rugged terrain. It has a loosely guarded coastal border of 1700 kilometers (1056 miles), which allowed use of the ocean for movement of people, weapons, and other supplies (Figure 3.6). The Tamil Tigers had their own navy (Sea Tigers), sinking over two dozen Sri Lankan government and private ships. This coastal access and boat fleet allowed the Tamil Tigers easy access to support communities and logistical support from the Indian state of Tamil Nadu, populated largely by ethnic Tamils. This extraterritorial haven and supply center in India provided everything from weapons to clothing, allowing the Tamil Tigers to become one of the deadliest, most resilient terrorist groups in the world. These geographic features allowed the Tigers to maintain their activities longer and in greater magnitude than would be thought possible given the small number of actual fighters and the size of their operational homeland base.

MEASURES TO DIMINISH GEOGRAPHIC SAFE HAVENS

Earlier sections examined the range of issues supporting the formation of havens. Diminishing the opportunity and availability of these havens for terrorist groups requires specific policies, programs, and tactics tailored to the group's motivations and goals and the physical and human geography of the haven. The lines of policy and tactics of counterinsurgency and counterterrorism are not clearly defined. Much of the current counterterrorism doctrine for safe havens is adapted from the more traditional counterinsurgency practices used in diminishing insurgent states. However, a few general ideas and actions have come from the many cases of terrorists creating havens and the limited number of successful campaigns to diminish these havens.

Havens are portrayed by the military and the media as rogue areas of hostility and lawlessness. They are not viewed as the complex places where ordinary people live according to the norms that are consistent with their societies. The terrorists only comprise a very small percentage of the population of the area. In these areas, such as the FATA in Pakistan, Chechnya, or the corridor of the Naxalites in India, most of the people are not hostile, lawless, or terrorists. The deliberate non-attention to that knowledge and understanding of these areas is designed to justify military action as reasonable and unavoidable.

In most cases, counterterrorism actions have relied on a military solution for the elimination of terrorist havens. In spite of a very poor record of success, the kinetic solution is the most used. History, as well as current conflicts, show that the use of military force as the sole measure has not worked in the past and will not work in the future.

The kinetic actions are deemed "surgical"—aimed at only the leadership or key logistical components of the terrorist haven.* The truth is that these strikes do not render an area a non-haven. Drone strikes by

* "Kinetic" action is a military term for killing terrorists and destroying their infrastructure.

US forces in violation of Pakistani sovereignty have killed numerous terrorist leaders, but the area remains a haven. Taken to its ultimate military conclusion, only occupation and control by massive numbers of troops will be an effective military solution. However, as the United States found in Vietnam, the Russians found in Chechnya, and both countries found in Afghanistan, attempts at complete control and occupation may not work as planned. In the end, the long-term occupation and control of foreign land, as both a means and an end to a terrorist haven, should be recognized as a dead-end strategy.

The additional downside consequences of the use of military force to eliminate terrorists are the loss of innocent civilian lives and property in these assaults. The special operations and drone strikes miss their targets in some cases and cannot be sufficiently selective in who is killed in these actions. These civilian losses, often of women and children, foster resentment and resistance to the counterterrorism efforts. In these days of generational terrorism, every terrorist cannot be killed faster than other terrorists are recruited or born and bred as such.

Thus, if one accepts that the current approach is not working and that diminishing the role of havens is to be a focus of counterterrorism strategy, then what can be done to be more successful in diminishing the role of these havens? The intent must be to influence the population of the haven, without necessarily controlling the territory:

1. One of the most important rules of counterterrorism and counterinsurgency is to know the enemy and its support community. Initially, the areas that are used as havens by terrorists must be recognized as complex areas for which a complex approach is needed. The complex human geography of these areas' cultures, economic activities, and tribal and family relations must be delineated and used as a basis for policy and tactics. Geographic, cultural, and temporal patterns of both the terrorists and the population must be studied as a foundation for actions. The focus must be on all source actionable research and intelligence integration.

   An example of this complexity is Somalia. Somalia has been characterized as the next al-Qaeda haven. Certainly, the country has multiple conflicts instigated by the al-Shabaab jihadists and the pirates of Somalia, which have captured the world's attention. However, on closer examination, Somalia is less of a candidate for an al-Qaeda haven and launching site for global jihad than has been portrayed.

The country has few of the landscapes (remote mountains and/or jungle) needed for a haven for foreign fighters. The pirates are criminals seeking money, not global jihad. The Somalis are extremely tribe and clan oriented; thus, many see the al-Qaeda foreign fighters and their ideology as negative, outside influences that can disrupt the existing cultural order.

Whether Westerners or al-Qaeda, outsiders have a difficult time infiltrating and influencing the Somali clans. While most Westerners recognize the Shia and Sunni split in Islam, the finer distinctions of Islamic beliefs are lost on them. Somalia has historically been influenced by Sufi thought; thus, it is an area with more moderate religious views. Al-Qaeda has not had the requisite physical landscape, means, or receptivity necessary to commandeer portions of Somalia as a haven to the extent initially forecast. In Chechnya, repeated brutal Russian actions to wipe out the nationalist-motivated insurgent terrorists drove them to align with al-Qaeda for financial and technical support. Ironically, outsider actions, such as the US-backed Ethiopian invasion and the Kenyan border incursions of Somalia, may foster al-Qaeda's presence in Somalia.

Cragin (2011) has suggested that the havens cannot be eliminated, so they should be isolated. The world of terrorism is a globalized world. As was mentioned earlier, terrorists increasingly rely on virtual havens within the Internet for recruiting and financing. Access to the Internet and modern communications for these haven areas should be restricted, along with interdiction of couriers by host nations. She calls for a focused effort to employ wider resources of host nations and for the non-military law enforcement agencies to put pressure on the people and activities that finance the maintenance of the safe haven for the terrorist group.

2. There should be limited and very focused use of military assets. These would include special operations and drone strikes deemed useful in a limited manner. Since collateral damage and killing of civilians are the primary reasons for tension and conflict with the local people, these military actions must be limited and specifically targeted. It must be acknowledged by those involved that these strikes are not effective in rendering havens unusable by terrorists, but only in limiting the terrorists' command and control structure and demonstrating their vulnerability. These actions should only be

directed toward terrorist regulars and, in limited cases, active but irregular members of the terrorist group.

3. The community of support for the terrorist group, both within and external to the haven areas, must be the focus of counterterrorism efforts. The terrorist group is composed of a very committed core leadership supported directly by fanatical regulars who perform the primary recruiting, training, logistical support, and attack functions. A larger group, who perform irregular support functions, such as informants, couriers, and concealing regulars, are the active supporters. The largest group supporting the group is those individuals who sympathize with at least some of the goals of the group and may be aligned by ethnicity or tribe, but may not fully support the terrorist tactics used. Beyond this, the area usually contains the largest segment of the population, who are neutral and only striving to survive in as secure a fashion as possible. This group may contain opposition to the terrorist group, but their opposition will only be expressed once the security situation allows them to do so with relative safety. Specifically, the small group of active supporters exerts significant influence on the majority of the population, who are neutral or opposed to the group. Influencing this group of active supporters and the neutral majority should be considered as key to undermining the control imposed by active terrorist regulars and irregulars in the area.

The terrorist insurgents have a distinct advantage in that they live and move freely among the people. One of al-Qaeda's strategies has been to intermarry with local clans in Chechnya and Pakistan. This fosters linkages that make separation from the population more difficult. To separate the terrorist insurgents from the population, counterinsurgents have to focus operations and efforts in four key areas: security, governance, services, and legitimacy. Furthermore, Galula (2006) states that providing the population with basic needs and addressing their grievances will assist in separating and isolating the insurgents from the population.

Vertical and horizontal coordination of counterterrorism efforts is essential. National and international entities must work with local political and tribal leaders and local law enforcement. Also, coordination must be maintained across the various political and social jurisdictions of the haven. The Indian governmental approach in the 1990s was to consider the Naxalite Maoist groups solely as a law enforcement issue to be dealt with by the individual states. This resulted in a lack of coordination of efforts both in time and across the corridor. This approach led to protracted, low-intensity conflicts between multiple popular movements and the states, along with their paramilitary allies. The results were that the Naxalites were not diminished and the community of support in the area strengthened due to abuses from the government and paramilitary units. In recent times, central Indian governmental coordination and focus has been more effective than past decentralized control efforts.

As Munoz (2011) suggests, greater inclusion of local governmental bodies, shuras, and jirgas with national and US decision makers in Afghanistan would have been a better approach. These traditional Afghan consensus leadership groups could have fostered the use of local defense forces for security and governance of many rural areas of Afghanistan. This approach assists in establishing civil order and civilian security at the local level, which is a prerequisite for altering community support for the terrorist groups and allowing other programs to be implemented. In addition, community projects that help the leader's clan or tribe are effective in helping win over community support. Recruitment of local leaders to assist in countering terrorist groups is a necessary but delicate task. Obvious collaboration with the central government could lead to an assassination of a leader by the terrorists. However, covert assistance to the leader or family, such as money, livestock, or medical supplies, is possible. One anecdotal story is that local Afghan tribal leaders, who are mostly older men, are provided erectile dysfunction medication, which is both rewarding to these leaders and covert.

4. Initial research has suggested little direct connection between poverty or education and participation in terrorism (Krueger and Maleckova 2003). However, the lack of economic opportunities and marginalization within a society provide the foundation for terrorist groups and the narrative for them to recruit local support. Thus, any long-term attempt to diminish a haven for terrorists must include culturally sensitive, local economic development, and infrastructure and institution building programs. Better roads and communications can benefit the local people and also assist in the control of the areas by governmental forces. Schools provide education of

the young and an alternative to indoctrination youth care facilities or religious madrassas run by the insurgent terrorist group. Having educational opportunities available for women is especially important as they are the primary caregivers to the next generation of potential terrorist recruits.

REFERENCES

Abbott, P. K. (2004) Terrorist threat in the tri-border area: Myth or reality? *Military Review* 84 (5): 51–55.

Bale, J. M. (2007) Hiding in plain sight in Londonistan. In *Denial of sanctuary: Understanding terrorist safe havens,* ed. Innes, M. A. Westport, CT: Praeger Security International, 131–151.

Bauder, H. (2011) Towards a critical geography of the border: Engaging with the dialectic of practice and meaning. *Annals of the Association of American Geographers* 101 (5): 1126–1139.

Berrebi, C. and Lakdawalla, D. (2006) *How does terrorism risk vary across space and time? An analysis based on the Israeli experience.* Santa Monica, CA: RAND Corporation.

Boyer, M. C .(2008) "Urban operations and network centric warfare," in *Indenfensible space: The architecture of the national insecurity state*, ed. M. Sorkin. New York: Routledge, 51–78.

CIA (2012) *World factbook: Afghanistan people and society.* Available from https://www.cia.gov/library/publications/the-world-factbook/geos/af.html

Cragin, K. (2011) The strategic dilemma of terrorist havens calls for their isolation, not elimination. In *The long shadow of 9/11,* ed. Jenkins, B. and Godges, J. Santa Monica, CA: Rand Corporation.

Culcasi, K. (2010) Locating Kurdistan, contextualizing the region's ambiguous boundaries. In *Borderlines and borderlands,* ed. Diener, A. and Hagen, J. New York: Rowman and Littlefield.

Ergil, D. (2007) PKK Kurdistan Workers Party. In *Terror, insurgency and the state,* ed. Heiberg, M., O'Leary, B., and Tirman, J., 323–356. University of Pennsylvania Press.

Galula, D. (2006) *Counterinsurgency warfare: Theory and practice.* Westport, CT: Praeger Security International, 52.

Gray, D. and LaTour, K. (2010) Terrorist black holes: Global regions shrouded in lawlessness. *Global Security Studies* I:3.

Innes, M. (2007) *Denial of sanctuary: Understanding terrorist safe havens.* Westport, CT: Greenwood Publishing Group.

Izady, M. (1992) *The Kurds: A concise handbook.* London: Taylor & Francis.

Jackson, R. H. (1990) *Quasi-states: Sovereignty, international relations and the Third World.* Cambridge Series on International Relations. Cambridge: University of Cambridge Press.

Kaplan, R. (2009) The revenge of geography. *Foreign Policy* May/June.

Kittner, C. C. B. (2007) The role of safe havens in Islamist terrorism. *Terrorism and Political Violence* 19 (3): 307–329.

Korteweg, R. and Ehrhardt, D. (2005) *Terrorist black holes: A study into terrorist sanctuaries and governmental weakness.* The Hague: Clingendael Centre for Strategic Studies.

Krueger, A. B. and Maleckova, J. (2003) Education, poverty and terrorism: Is there a causal connection? *Journal of Economic Perspectives* 17 (4): 119–144.

Lohman, A. (2000) Insurgencies and counter-insurgencies: A geographical perspective. In *The scope of military geography. The MOOTW context,* ed. Palka, E. and Galgan, F. New York: McGraw–Hill.

McColl, R. (1969) The insurgent state: Territorial bases for revolution. *Annals of the Association of American Geographers* 59:613–631.

Munoz, A. (2011) A long-overdue adaptation to the Afghan environment. In *The long shadow of 9/11,* ed. Jenkins, B. M. and Godges, J. P. Santa Monica, CA: RAND Corporation.

National Consortium for the Study of Terrorism and Responses to Terrorism [START] (2012) Terrorist organization profiles. Available from http://www.start.umd.edu/startdata_collections/tops/

Pillar, P. (2009) Who's afraid of a terrorist haven? *The Washington Post,* September 16, 2009.

Reid, A. and Miller, C. (2011) Regional characteristics of foreign-born people living in the United Kingdom. Regional Trends 43. Office for National Statistics.

Shane, S. (2009) Insurgents share a name, but pursue different goals. *New York Times* (NY edition), October 23, 2009, p. A12.

Simons, A. and Tucker, D. (2007) The misleading problem of failed states; a sociogeography of terrorism in the post 9/11 era. *Third World Quarterly* 28 (2): 387–401.

Sutton, M. (2009) The rising importance of women in terrorism and the need to reform counterterrorism strategy. School of Advanced Military Studies. US Army Command and General Staff College, Fort Leavenworth, KS.

Toft, M. (2003) *The geography of ethnic violence.* Princeton, NJ: Princeton University Press.

US State Dept. (2009) Terrorist safe havens, Chapter 3, www. State.gov/documents/organization/65466

Vaidya, S. (2012) The rising Naxalite rage. blog, naxaliterage.com

Wallensteen, P. and Sollenberg, M. (1997) Armed conflicts, conflict termination and peace agreements. *Journal of Peace Research* 34 (3): 339–358.

4

Sociocultural Understanding, Geospatial Data/Technologies, and Opportunities for Countering Terrorism

INTRODUCTION

Late in February 2012, in Afghanistan, US soldiers stood near the pile of burning Qurans in a landfill at Bagram Air Base, unknowing of the violence the act would cause in the near future. Seen by Afghan workers who transmitted the message outside the base, the incident was responsible for the deaths of over 30 Afghans, 5 US soldiers, and many other violent responses (Falk 2012). Other incidents that undermined the social and political relationships between the United States and the Afghan people include the murder of 16 innocent people including women and children (Shah and Bowley 2012). US soldiers taking pictures while posing with dead bodies of insurgents (Zucchino and King 2012), and US Marines urinating on dead Taliban fighters (Bowley and Rosenberg 2012). However, the Quran burning case is directly related to the lack of understanding of Afghani culture by US forces. Knowledge of events such as these is diffused through social media. Some information is volunteered, with or without the intention of the information ever reaching larger social circles. Events like these are used as points of propaganda by leaders of terrorist organizations to mobilize terrorists and potential terrorists, such as Ayman al-Zawahiri, who took command of al-Qaeda following the death of Osama bin Laden in 2011 (*USA Today* 2012).

The soldiers responsible for burning the Quran were responding in the way they thought was acceptable to local culture. The copies of the Quran burned were deemed desecrated, which is culturally correct, as they had been written in by prisoners. The act of burning the desecrated Qurans was also culturally correct. However, the burning is supposed to follow specific ritualistic acts. When the Quran is burned in a manner that is perceived to be demeaning, anger ensues by many of those who culturally/ethnically have an emotional connection to the symbolic meaning of the material item and witness the event directly or indirectly (Kalinski 2012). It is possible that the resulting outbreak from this event could have been avoided with a better understanding of local cultures, including knowledge of symbolic rituals.

Knowledge of the Quran burning traveled quickly throughout the world by information technologies—specifically, social media. Soon after the burning, US efforts, based on human geography, and using geospatial technologies alleviated the anger in the most affected regions. An automated search, or *crawl* as it is referred to in computational circles, was used to gather information on sentiments of the event, also referred to as *sentiment mining.* Locational properties of the sentiments were also gathered so that they could be mapped based on location, ethnic/tribal group, and socioeconomic characteristics. The identification of sentiments over geographic areas can be referred to as an indication of the *human terrain/landscape.*

Using these technologies, it was found that the most unstable regions, based on reactions to the burning, were the border regions between Pakistan and Afghanistan, even though the protests of the burning began in Bahrain. Five thousand new Qurans were directed to tribal and religious leaders within the identified regions with letters of condolence reflecting the misunderstanding that led to the burning. In some cases, formal presentation ceremonies were performed. The Qurans and apologies were welcomed by the local leaders and a fatwa* of peace and forgiveness was issued. The social media were then monitored to determine postactivity sentiment and found positive reaction to the US offerings in the same regions that were first identified as less stable.

* A fatwa is an Islamic law-based ruling given by a person in a leadership role in the Muslim religion. It is intended to be given by Islamic scholars, but recent fatwas have been given by Islamist terrorists whose legitimacy in initiating the fatwas is questioned by many.

THE IMPORTANCE OF SOCIOCULTURAL UNDERSTANDING (HUMAN GEOGRAPHY) ON GLOBAL SCALE TO LOCAL SCALE

The preceding case study provides an example of the importance of understanding geographic variation of sociocultural groups and beliefs and diplomatic efforts in wartime. In general, not understanding sociocultural rules and customs and their patterns across the landscape can lead to conflict. The United States lacks detailed knowledge on the sociocultural characteristics in regions of conflict. The "War on Terrorism" that began in the President George W. Bush era (2001–2009) was waged, for the most part, with insufficient knowledge of regional societies and cultures in Iraq and Afghanistan. The focus was on winning the war, but not managing and winning the peace.

Present US involvements are different from the state-centric conflicts of the past. The Cold War is over and, though the threat of state-to-state conflict is not gone, today's wars are being fought asymmetrically, by non-state groups rising up against the states in a war for power. As these asymmetric wars continue to be waged, more attention must be given to understanding and influencing the *hearts and minds* of the people. The United States is learning firsthand the importance of understanding region and culture and the damage from ignoring geography for extended periods of time. A 2004 report by the Department of Defense stated:

> The information campaign—or as some would have it, "the war of ideas," or the struggle for "hearts and minds"—is important to every war effort, and with respect to the separation of non-violent Muslims and violent jihadists American efforts have not only failed...they may also have achieved the opposite of what they intended (Defense Science Board Task Force 2004, pp. 39–40).

US efforts in some instances have created animosity between residents of countries in conflict and military forces, who are seen as occupiers and instilling a forced democracy through violence. One of the many lessons learned in US and coalition efforts overseas is that knowledge of sociocultural aspects of resident populations is vital in a battle for hearts and minds. To win irregular wars, knowledge of enemy and self is no longer enough (Hanzhang 2000). The *ambient population* must also be considered, as they are affected by actions of all sides and drive or deter the conflict. Today's war against non-state terrorist organizations is more complex than state-to-state wars of the past. Vital post-9/11 conflict-based operational gaps have been outlined by the US Army (2011a) as:

1. Understanding of the target area culture and its impact on operational decisions was insufficient. There was insufficient or ineffective transfer of knowledge to follow-on units via the relief in place/transition of authority (RIP/TOA) process.
2. There was limited joint service of interagency capability (organization, methods, and tools) to conduct research, visualize, understand, and explain the human terrain (i.e., population in which the unit operates).
3. Brigade combat teams (BCTs), regimental combat teams (RCTs), and division-level HQs engaged in counterinsurgency operations in Operation Iraqi Freedom and Operation Enduring Freedom lacked the operationally relevant human terrain knowledge base and social science staff experts necessary to optimize their military decision-making process.
4. Commanders were limited by the lack of joint, service, and interagency integrated capability (people, organization, methods, tools) to gather/consolidate, analyze, visualize, understand, database, and share sociocultural information effectively. The battalions, companies, platoons, and squads experienced firsthand the knowledge and capability gap.

These operational gaps are focused on the lack of sociocultural knowledge. The realization of the lack of sociocultural knowledge and the benefits of gaining this information, as well as using geospatial technologies, has brought geographic perspectives and efforts to the forefront of operations.

GEOSPATIAL INTELLIGENCE: THE INTEGRATION OF HUMAN GEOGRAPHY AND GEOSPATIAL TECHNOLOGIES

Geospatial intelligence, also known as GEOINT, "is an intelligence discipline and tradecraft that has evolved from the integration of imagery, imagery intelligence (IMINT), and geospatial information" (National

Geospatial-Intelligence Agency 2006). Imagery refers to reflected energy collected from air- and spaceborne platforms and visualized. The images are spatially and temporally specific and typically show land cover/land use characteristics. Because of the amount of coverage by satellite systems, images are available for any region in the world. Information derived from analysis of the imagery is referred to as imagery intelligence. The images through analysis become more than just pixels representing ground cover. Geospatial information as a category covers a wide range of information. The uniting factor is that the information has geographic characteristics of location. This can be population distribution, political boundary, ethnic region, or any other data with locational attributes.

Geospatial technologies and geographic information are used in geospatial intelligence efforts for strategic operations focused on the components of the geography thematic hierarchy—spaces, places, people, topologies, and activities, as discussed in Chapter 1. Geospatial intelligence has become commonplace in counterterrorism operations, specifically in the analysis of geospatial data from maps, geosensor systems, remote sensing, geographic positioning systems (GPS) integrated in geographic information systems (GIS) for decision support to locate, monitor, and assess terrorist groups and counterterrorism strategies and tactics. This integrated analysis of geospatial data leads to geospatial information, which leads to valuable intelligence for counterterrorist operations.

In the world of intelligence, GEOINT is the only INT that operates from a completely spatial perspective.* As such, it has its foundations in geography and for the task of counterterrorism, human geography specifically. Technological and data components of geospatial intelligence become much more valuable when informed with human geography knowledge. An image of settlements on the border between Pakistan and Afghanistan will only look like settlements to someone with no knowledge of the region. However, to a human geographer with prior knowledge of the region, the settlements can become temporary shelters for internally displaced people forced out of their homes by cultural conflict or environmental hazards. The people within the shelters, possibly nomads, are most likely unaffected by government rule in the autonomous region of the border. The trained eye may be able to derive demographic and cultural information from the image that adds further geospatial information. Gaining detailed

* Other INTs include human intelligence (HUMINT), signals intelligence (SIGINT), and measurement and signature intelligence (MASINT) (National Geospatial-Intelligence Agency 2006).

intelligence throughout the world is possible with geospatial technologies and human geography knowledge.

The remainder of this chapter will review aspects of geospatial intelligence, beginning with applied human geography efforts by the US Army, then on to the larger area of technology and conflict, and finally to more specific geographic data and geospatial technologies. Technologies, methods, and tools will be defined and examples of their usefulness for counterterrorism will be given.

The US Army Human Terrain System

Much of human terrain focus was initiated by the US Army in 2006 as the human terrain system (HTS). It began as a proof of concept effort for the Joint Improvised Explosive Device Defeat Organization (JIEDDO). The term *human terrain* describes the sociocultural variations of people over geographic space, a concept analogous to terrain analysis in physical geography and other earth sciences, which looks at variation in landforms over geographic space. The HTS has since deployed social scientists into conflict zones of Afghanistan and Iraq. Researchers of various social science backgrounds, including anthropology, geography, sociology, political science, and psychology, have been deployed. HTS activities include direct contact with local populations in the form of interviews, surveys, and other types of interaction (King, Bienvenu, and Stone 2011). The main goals of the HTS are to "[r]ecruit, train, deploy, and support an embedded, operationally focused sociocultural capability; conduct operationally relevant, sociocultural research and analysis; [and] develop and maintain a sociocultural knowledge base," with the purpose to "[s]upport operational decision-making, enhance operational effectiveness, and preserve and share sociocultural institutional knowledge" (US Army 2011a).

The HTS has evolved with greater emphasis on the practice of applied human geography for operational support of the war fighter. The system is structured into requirements of expert capabilities of understanding sociocultural characteristics and management of information in all stages from gathering to advanced analysis. This information is integrated into maps and graphics used in the training of military and government personnel on sociocultural and information management (Bartholf 2011). Figures 4.1 and 4.2 show examples of human terrain team members interviewing locals in Afghanistan about IEDs and prices of wheat. The *human terrain* of a

FIGURE 4.1
Interview about IEDs with a man who lost his leg on an IED in Afghanistan. (US Army, 2011b.)

FIGURE 4.2
Interview with locals on wheat prices in Afghanistan. (US Army, 2011c.)

region is not only focused on conflict based information, but also describes all aspects of sociocultural characteristics and patterns.

The HTS has been met with opposition from academic and scientific circles and has suffered its share of setbacks. One of the main arguments from the American Anthropological Association (AAA) is that HTS activities break the AAA code of ethics; active HTS teams have the potential to do harm to their subjects. Specifically, the AAA highlighted five concerns (American Anthropological Association 2007):

- The nature of the HTS deters those workers in the field from identifying themselves as researchers, which prohibits the full disclosure of their research intentions.
- Responsibilities to the US military may result in researchers directly or indirectly harming their study subjects.
- Because of the nature of war and operating in war zones, the ability of subjects to give "voluntary informed consent" is compromised.
- Information provided to the US military can be used for targeting of individuals.
- HTS operations can cause risk for the researchers and their subjects.

This statement and other efforts from the anthropology community have been a particularly damaging strike to the HTS reputation, as it was led by anthropologists. As a follow-up to the fifth concern, several researchers have died in the field as a result of conflict-based activities since the inception of the HTS program.

The HTS has also met harsh criticism from members of other military branches. Major concerns voiced by Major Ben Connable (2009), US Marine Corps, are that the HTS ignores standing doctrine, whereby, the military is mandated to maintain cultural capabilities, that cultural capabilities are much improved and the US military has proven to use "cultural terrain" to its benefit (p. 57), and that the activities can work negatively against the relationship between the military and social scientists. While Connable voices his negative opinions of the army-based HTS, he does emphasize shortcomings and the need for cultural capabilities in cultural competency in the military. Connable's stance is that cultural capability programs should remain in-house and that the military's cultural intelligence programs have greatly improved to the point where direct assistance from the academic community is not necessary.

Regardless of the ways in which cultural capabilities are being applied against terrorism, the realization that the US military lacks these capabilities is an important one. Focusing on local people and their culture within conflict areas is imperative to countering terrorism in the battle for hearts and minds of the asymmetric conflicts of the twenty-first century. Civilian residents play a much larger role in the conflict than they would have in state-to-state based conflict. They are the ones most affected by the conflict, they are potential recruits, and they can help alleviate sectarian or other types of local conflict. Reliable and effective information can be attained from the *ambient population* and used to better understand the situation and mitigate foreseeable problems. It is important to consider the sentiment of the people and their responses to various stimuli.

Human Terrain Shift to Human Geography

As described previously, today's wars and counterterrorism efforts have highlighted the lack of sociocultural knowledge in the United States, within the US military and diplomatic corps, coalition forces, and of private contractors working for the coalition. Human terrain was originally a limited qualitative practice of field researchers gathering information from and about local populations. Recently, using the broader concept, human geography, theories, methods, and techniques from the long history of qualitative and quantitative research have become available for use in military and diplomatic efforts. Recent changes to a human geography perspective have expanded to include quantitative spatial analysis, geostatistics, and geospatial technologies: mapping, GIS, GPS, and remote sensing with satellite and aerial vehicles. This combination forms the basis for integrated geospatial intelligence.

Technology and War

Technology has always been an important factor in how wars are fought and won. In the past, much of the technological advancement influencing war activities has been driven by firepower, but other technologies have played key roles. Transportation technologies led to the geographic decentralization of battles. For example, helicopters and airplanes allowed for troops to be deployed quickly to other countries. Aircraft and satellites led to high-resolution surveillance of the battlefield. Use of GPS and drones allows the military to accurately attack distant

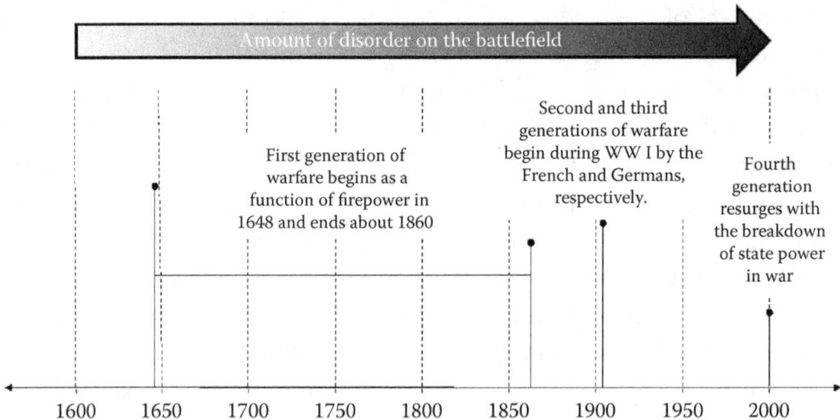

FIGURE 4.3
Time line: the four generations of war. (Adapted from Lind, W. S., 2004.)

places from the United States. Communications technologies have also changed warfare—from the days of Morse code to two-way radios to cellular phones. Each technological step of communications technology has changed mobility in warfare by allowing fighters more freedom and hence, has allowed more complexity on the battlefield. Terrorists are utilizing these and other technologies in all logistic activities.

Lind (2004) provides an overview of the relationship between weapons technology and warfare over time. At each generational step, there has been a greater tendency toward disorder on the battlefield that is facilitated by technology, ideas, or both (Figure 4.3). Warfare has moved from linear to non-linear forms where decentralization (social and geographic) in the present day provides a benefit for those who are fighting against state powers.

Warfare is shaped by aspects of technology and ideas. The first generation is characterized by linearity; the second, by firepower technologies that facilitated the move away from linear battles and forced non-linear movement through the use of barriers; and the third, by ideas that led to maneuver warfare.

The fourth generation of warfare is characterized by technologies in firepower, but also by technologies for spreading ideas and capturing information, including geospatial information. It is marked by shift of state control in war to the people. Because of this, more emphasis must be directed toward the people, the cultures, and the information. Political boundaries are becoming less important than often non-delineated cultural boundaries, which are at times fuzzy.

There can be an overlap for each of these generations. For example, countries can use second and third generation tactics, though the use of first generation tactics can be seen as "obsolete" or "suicidal" (Lind 2004, p. 12), though suicide as a tactic can be an asset in war.

Terrorists have found more value in the information war than with complex firepower, which is not a surprise since, traditionally, terrorists have had to use low-cost, low-tech weapons or weapons they can acquire through the enemy's losses. The difference is that today's technological advancements give almost everybody the ability to acquire and produce extreme amounts of information that in many ways facilitate the training, mission planning, and dissemination of propaganda. They use information age technologies, such as social networking and information diffusion tools Facebook and Twitter, are today seen by many as being more powerful in uprisings and fourth generational warfare than traditional weapons.

All the elements of the theorized fourth generation already exist and have been practiced throughout history. For example, Mao Tse Tung in China focused on political power before military power (Hammes 1994). The fourth generation war can be seen as a return to the world before state dominance, in the context of war, where the prominent strategy for warfare is guerrilla. Lind's conceptualization of these four generations illustrates the link between technology, ideas, and warfare. Today, technology is facilitating the move toward non-linearity, complexity, and decentralization of conflict strategy in the form of non-state terrorism.

TECHNOLOGIES OF GEOSPATIAL INTELLIGENCE AND THEIR USE IN TERRORISM AND COUNTERTERRORISM

Geospatial intelligence was described previously as having three main components: imagery, imagery intelligence, and geospatial information. This description leaves out important details of technologies working in the background. The path to a useable and useful image and, finally, the extraction of information from that image is a long one. However, the ease of accessibility to advanced technologies through free online services, such as Google Earth and NASA Worldwind, has made complicated geospatial processes less so.

Geospatial technologies are those used to collect, process, and analyze geographic data (i.e., data that have locational qualities). These technologies include GIS, GPS, and remote sensing. Geospatial technologies comprise one of the leading areas of research in the present day (Sui 2008). It is difficult to envision a world without these technologies used by many every day. They are integrated with our communications devices and modes of transportation, and that are accessible from any computer connected to the World Wide Web (WWW). They are used in terrorism and counterterrorism activities and are anticipated to continue to change the ways we live, as well as the ways in which wars are waged and countered.

Geographic Data as Geospatial Information

Geographic data are data that have locational references with associated attributes. These references are typically in the form of latitude/longitude coordinates, but can be linear or areal locational systems, such as kilometers on a roadway or presence in a specific tribal area or language area. Geographic data are widely available in many different forms and formats. In the twenty-first century, the increase of computational power and storage has facilitated the increased availability of geospatial data. Coordinates are embedded into digital photographs, remotely sensed images are georectified,* and mobile phone companies collect locational data of every customer. Online searches are now customized to factor in user locations, so a potential customer in Los Angeles will get different results in an online search than a user in Washington, DC, searching for the same item. For research purposes, many US agencies, such as the US Geological Survey, the National Oceanic and Atmospheric Agency, and the US Department of Agriculture, host geographic data clearinghouses online.

The acquisition of information, geospatial or otherwise, influences people's actions in many situations, including conflict and terrorism. People act on perceptions of reality and each new bit of information can change those perceptions; hence, activities of conflict will change with more information as terrorists and counterterrorists are in search of the optimal result. For example, geospatial information available online provides terrorists with the ability to better understand their operations and more accurately direct their attacks, though poor and/or outdated information

* Georectification refers to the processing of image data so that they appear to be at their correct geographic location.

may impact operations in a negative way. Either way, more information leads to a better perceived understanding of operations.

An example of the usefulness of geospatial data for counterterrorism is illustrated by the identification of Osama bin Laden's location in a 2001 al-Qaeda video. Scientists were able to derive the location from the sedimentary rock wall used as a backdrop for the videos. Bin Laden's location was first pinpointed to two provinces in eastern Afghanistan: Paktia and Paktika. Further research on geological aspects of the border region between Afghanistan and Pakistan, as well as the added cultural geography knowledge on the region, placed the likely location of the filming of the video in the Zhawar Kili cave region in the Khost Province (Beck 2003). Counterterrorism actions taken based on these findings are unknown. However, the potential of geospatial data and geographic knowledge from various sources for integrated analysis is clear.

Geographic Information Systems

Geographic information systems (GIS) were defined in the first chapter as an integrated collection of hardware, software, and data with a focus on geospatial data storage, processing, analysis, and visualization. Maps are the primary means of conveying geographic information from a GIS. Maps are conceptualized as models of a selected reality of the landscape. As statistics provide a value representative of numerical distribution, maps provide symbolic representations of physical and cultural features, distributions, and patterns across the landscape. When maps are combined with attribute information and numerical algorithms, spatial statistics, models, and projections of spatial patterns can be generated within the GIS.

The use of GIS has proven to be a great tool in research and operations for counterterrorism on all levels and in all aspects of the emergency management cycle: mitigation, preparedness, response, and recovery. GIS is designed as a tool for visualization and analysis. Aspects of the use of GIS for terrorism/counterterrorism include, but are not limited to, cartography, identifying patterns of terrorist activity with spatial statistics, and modeling populations at risk.

Much of a GIS sits on the back end of online applications, so not all users are highly trained technicians. Many users do not even recognize they are using a GIS. This is the case with applications including Google Earth, Google Maps, NASA Worldwind, OpenStreetMap, and others. GIS

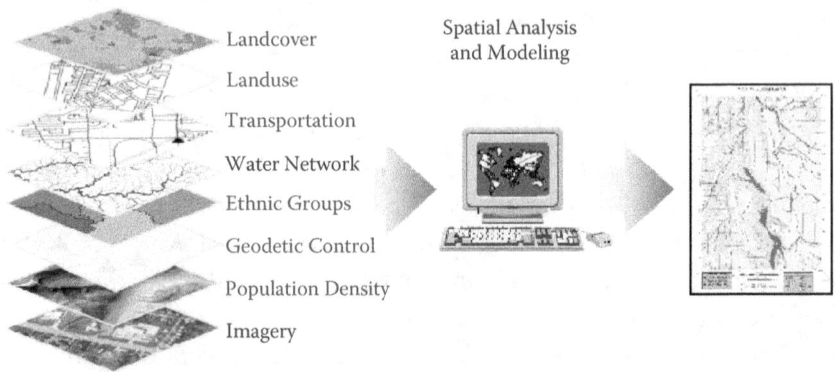

FIGURE 4.4
Data integration within a GIS.

makes the sharing of spatial information possible. Terrorists are using GIS to plan attacks if they use any online navigation or locational service.

The primary value of GIS over a simple map is that the GIS uses an information systems approach. It integrates different types of georeferenced feature data in the form of points, lines, and polygons and pixel data. These spatial data are combined with normally non-spatial tabular attribute data including cultural, demographic, and economic data (Figure 4.4). By using GIS, patterns of the physical and human environments can be detected and better understood.

One of the major benefits of GIS is the ability to do advanced spatial analyses, the focus of which is to find geographic patterns of people, places, things, or phenomena. For terrorism studies, one may be concerned with spatial patterns of terrorist attacks, recruitment, and vulnerable populations.

GIS can be used in all aspects of the fundamental issues of terrorism as defined by Cutter, Richardson, and Wilbanks (2003, p. 3): reducing threats, detecting threats, reducing vulnerabilities, and improving responses. Three examples of analysis are discussed here: a spatiotemporal analysis of terrorist/insurgent attacks in Iraq, an analysis of global terrorist social and geographic closeness (proximity) tendencies, and a viewshed analysis to locate areas of potential threat by sniper fire. One of the main points to consider with these analyses is that the incorporation of dynamics, whether spatiotemporal, sociospatial, etc., is key to understanding real-world cause and effect relationships. Humans do not operate motionless, void of space and time; thus, to obtain realistic results, researchers must conduct analyses that best reflect reality.

Analyzing the Connections between Social and Geographic Space Activities

Social and geographic space activities are interrelated. Humans tend to interact most with those that are near, and prefer to be near those they interact with most. GIS can assist in understanding these social and geographic space interactions. Activity locations in geographic space and connectivity in social space can be analyzed and visualized in a GIS. For example, Figure 4.5 shows a rendering of the Islamist terrorist social network to geographic space. Al-Qaeda as an organization sits at the center of this network, while leaders Osama bin Laden and Ayman al-Zawahiri are assumed to be in the border regions of Pakistan and Afghanistan. The locations of terrorists and extent of their connections are shown.

Identifying geographic and social connection patterns is imperative in today's struggle with global terrorism. Information campaigns and social networks are much more available and influential in instances of fourth generation warfare and netwar.* Today's terrorists are global people. They travel and maintain connections all over the world. Information technologies allow organizational leaders to maintain the sufficient leadership necessary for coordinated attacks. The world is a smaller place today, with decreasing costs and increasing efficiency of communications and transportation. This must be incorporated into how researchers view and analyze terrorism and the types of GIS analyses performed.

In a study of geographic locations of and social connections between terrorists on a global scale, Medina and Hepner (2011) substantiated the concept of the sociospatial network for terrorist network research and designed a new metric of analysis. This was done by incorporating graph theoretic and social network analysis methods within a GIS. They found that operational connections between terrorists are more likely to be at relatively shorter distances and that there is a relationship between social distance and geographic distance. Adding more social connections to further degrees† in a terrorist social network will result in longer average geographic distance connections. Thus, terrorist social networks operate

* Netwar is conceptualized as conflict waged by organizations structured in networks and attuned to the information age. These organizations are often decentralized such that little authoratative hierarchy exists (Arquilla and Ronfeldt (2001)).

† First degree social connections are adjacent members of one's social network. Second degree connections are friends of friends, third degree connections are connections with two intermediaries, and so on.

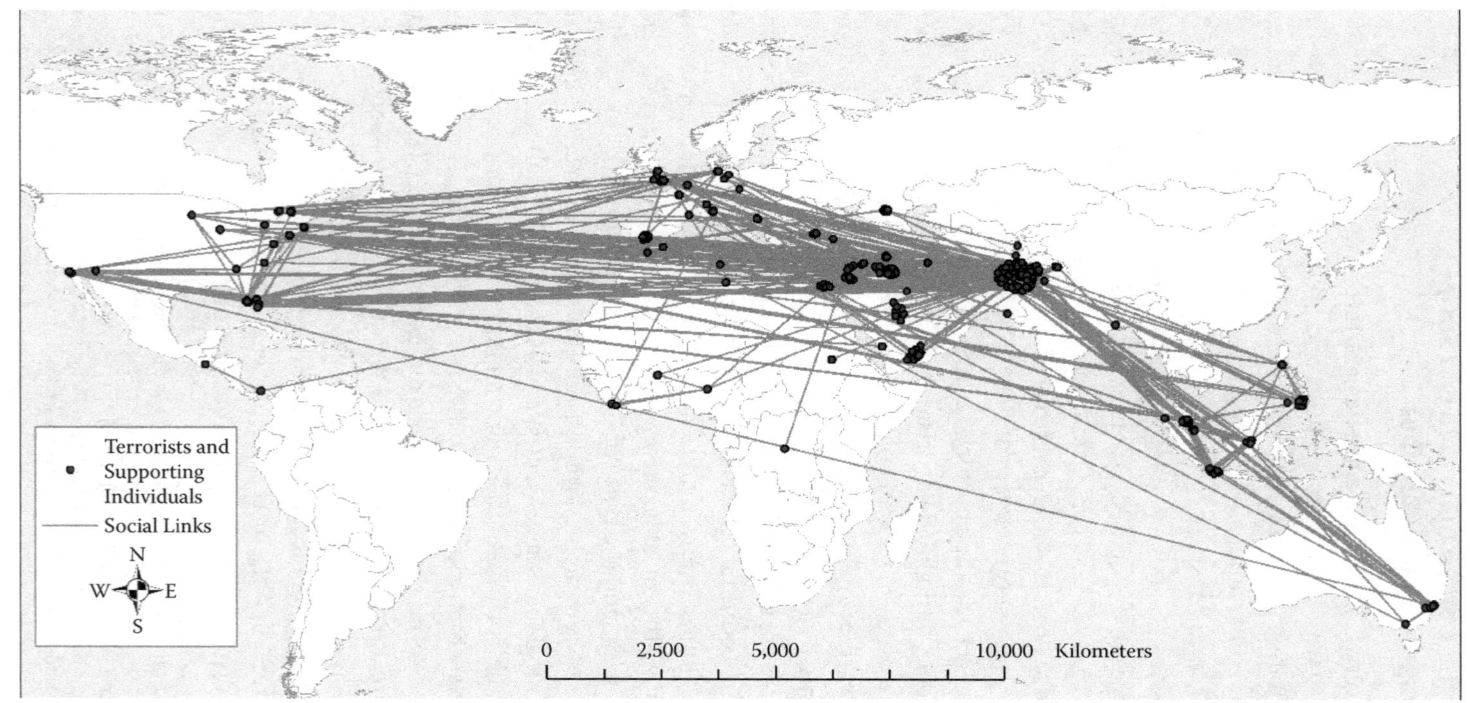

FIGURE 4.5
Islamist terrorist network rendered to geographic space. (From Medina, R. M. and Hepner, G. F., 2011, *Transactions in GIS* 15 (5): 577–597. With permission.)

similarly to general social networks in that they prefer to interact with those that are near or prefer to be near those with whom they interact.

This is not surprising when the history of the Islamist network is considered. Many connections are between longtime friends and were forged in jihadist struggles around the world. One of the most popular and partially responsible for today's Islamist network is the Russo-Afghan War in the 1970s and 1980s. Many connections in this network are family or clan based. Given these characteristics, the Islamist network can be seen as a subset of an already existing social network with similar characteristics.

Figure 4.6 shows the tendency for social network clustering of terrorists to be more likely within geographic clusters of terrorists. This analysis supports previously stated characteristics of geographic and social space dependencies. Members of terrorist networks need places to operate. If terrorists are clustered in a training camp or jihad arena, they are more likely to form social connections. If they are already connected, it is likely that at one point in time, if not now, they met at a specific place. This has implications for diaspora communities. Radical ideas are more likely to be shared with others who have similar sentiments about aspirational homelands, being alienated, and being marginalized.

The implications of this research do not lessen the importance of social connectivity through random interactions. The terrorist attacks on September 11, 2001, may have never happened if it was not for a chance meeting on a train, as described in Chapter 2. Chance and serendipity play a large role in Islamist network activities, as they do with social networks in general. Chance interactions can be connections for life, especially if those involved are of the same mind-set or cultural background, which are often geographically based traits. These interactions are important and are more likely to create lasting social connections if social distances are shorter between those involved.

Furthermore, social distances are more likely to be shorter if geographic distances are shorter. It is clear to see that coincidence in space and time, whether intentional or random, is vital for terrorist network operations. These meetings strengthen relationships, especially in warlike situations, and they increase the effectiveness of interactions, such as with training camps. Some may suggest a flaw in this argument. For example, cyberterrorists seem not to need geographic space interaction. Their social networks may all be contained in virtual space. However, their operations and targets also exist in virtual space. It is easier to operate in one

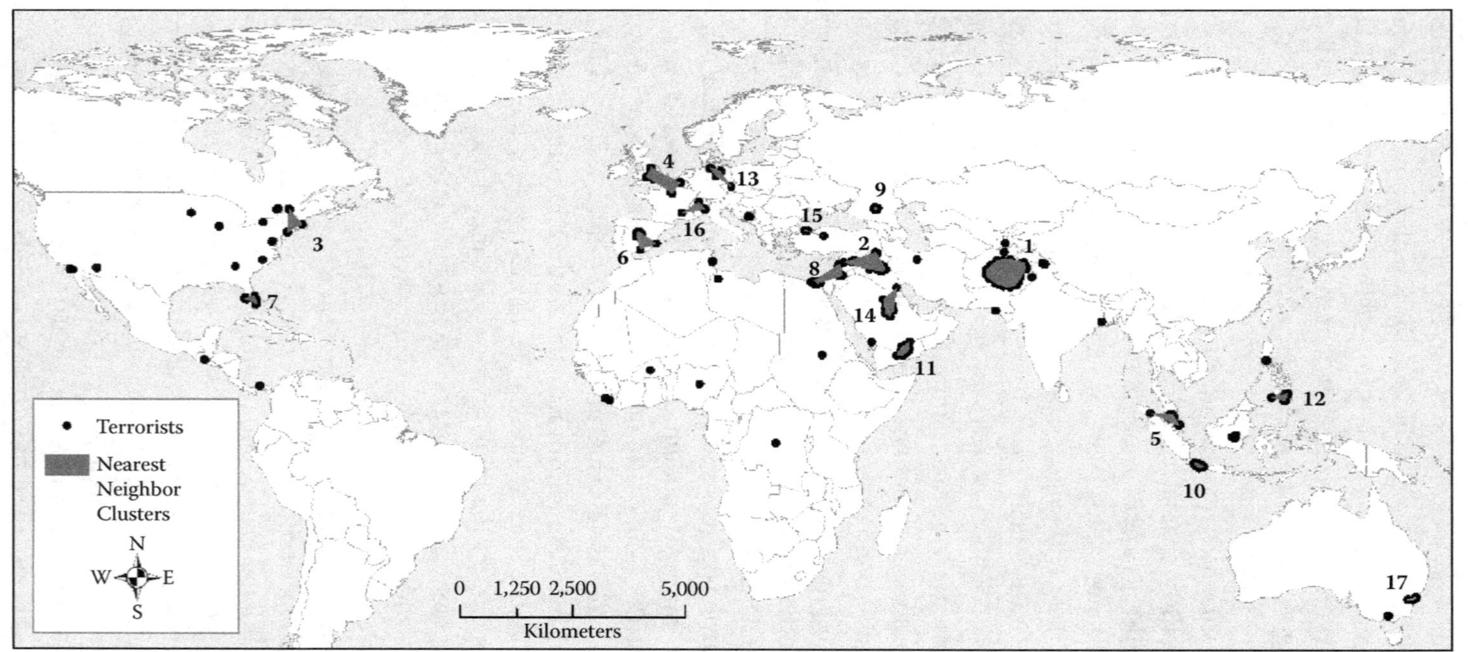

FIGURE 4.6
Sociospatial clusters of terrorists. (From Medina, R. M. and Hepner, G. F., 2011, *Transactions in GIS* 15 (5): 577–597. With permission.)

space. Terrorists operating in geographic spaces benefit much more from geographic space interactions.

One of the problems presented by this research is the lack of sociospatial dynamics. The entities represented are static on a global scale. Some of this is the result of poor or missing data on terrorists and their activities, but more so, this is the result of insufficient GIS tools and methods. Snapshots can be considered for different time intervals, but are inefficient for long time periods, and geovisualization would benefit from an intrinsically continuous model. Some tools and methods are available for spatiotemporal analysis and visualization, but when incorporating social network connections and other factors, the possibilities from industry standard software are minimal.

While sociospatial research is a promising area for GIS, technologies and methods are limited. Representing spatiotemporal dynamics and time geographies within a GIS is on the forefront of academic and industry research, as is complexity science and network analysis. However, there remains a gap between the two areas. Tools and methods to analyze and visualize dynamic social networks must be designed and/or customized for present-day research. Eventually this exciting new field of complex sociogeographic systems will have a collection of readily available tools and methods for important sociospatial analysis.

GIS-Based Spatial Analysis and Visualization of Terrorist Attacks

By analyzing spatial patterns of terrorist incidents,* it is possible to find clusters and hot spots of events and terrorist activity. Adding in temporal aspects of terrorist behavior to identify patterns over space and time provides results that offer much more information. Identifying a cluster of attacks in a region without respect to time does not take into consideration that smaller clusters of activity may be occurring in different districts throughout a larger area and that there may be spatiotemporal patterns of attacks that occur as a result of various stimuli. For example, terrorist attacks have typically been clustered in Baghdad since the US and allied troop invasion in 2003. Without consideration of time, an analyst would not be able to identify changes in behavior during trigger activities, such

* Terrorist attacks in the data set used for this study are termed "incidents" by the National Counterterrorism Center. Incidents are where "subnational or clandestine groups of individuals deliberately or recklessly attacked civilians or noncombatants" (2011, n.p.).

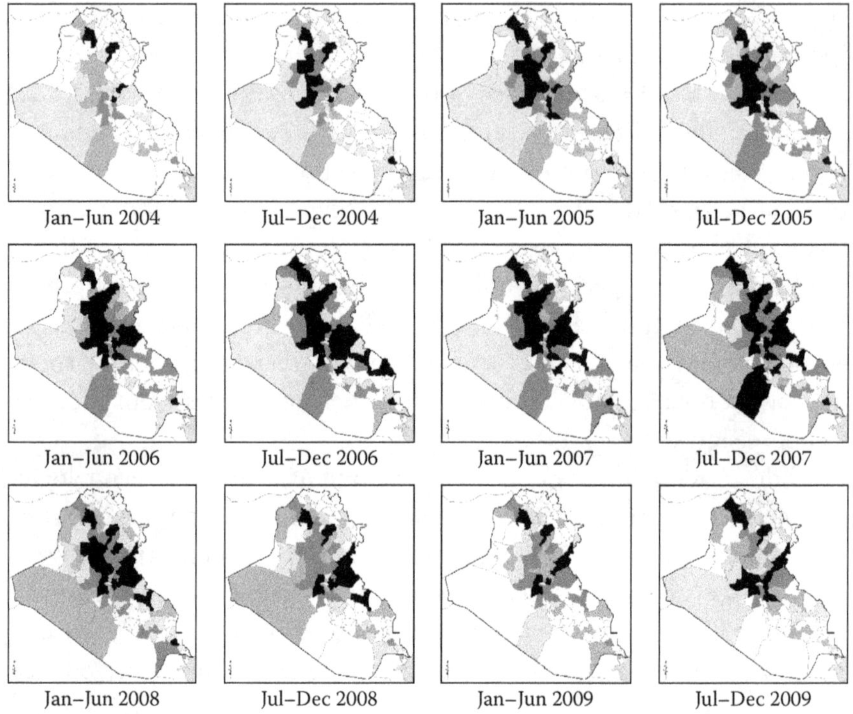

FIGURE 4.7
Space–time pattern of terrorist/insurgent attacks in Iraq districts, 2004–2009. (From Medina, R. M. et al., 2011, *Studies in Conflict and Terrorism* 34:862–882. With permission.)

as elections, counterterrorist/insurgent offensives, and leader deaths, that drive terrorist attacks. Spatiotemporal analyses provide a bigger picture of behavior and offer additional information. With added sociocultural information, an analyst is capable of determining in part why increased terrorist attacks are occurring, which can provide a better opportunity to thwart terrorism before it begins.

In a GIS based analysis of terrorist attacks in Iraq, Medina, Siebeneck, and Hepner (2011) were able to identify spatiotemporal patterns of attacks and several of the possible drivers for terrorism. Figure 4.7 shows the spatiotemporal pattern of terrorist/insurgent attacks in Iraq from 2004 to 2009, where darker shades represent greater numbers of attacks. The benefits of using GIS to map, analyze, and visualize the pattern of attacks over space and time are clear. One can see the growth and decline of attacks over the 6-year period and the districts that need more or less attention.

Attack intensity is the number of casualties divided by the number of attacks to give casualties per attack by district. Casualties in this

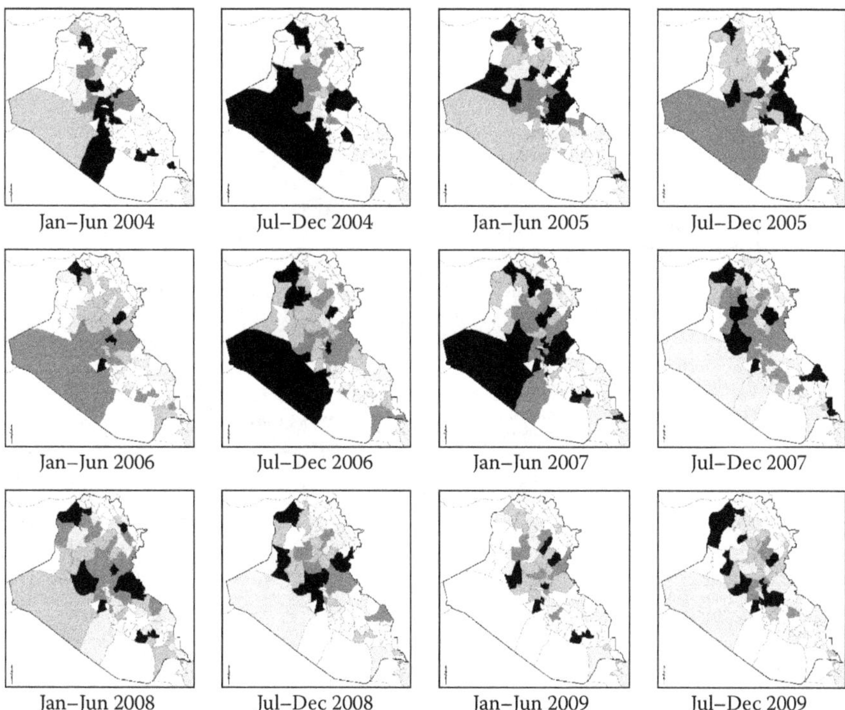

FIGURE 4.8
Space–time pattern of terrorist/insurgent attack intensities in Iraq districts, 2004–2009. (From Medina, R. M. et al., 2011, *Studies in Conflict and Terrorism* 34:862–882. With permission.)

research include deaths, injuries, and kidnappings (Siebeneck et al. 2009). Figure 4.8 maps the attack intensities to show the pattern differences between the incidence of an attack and the intensities of those attacks, which are characterized by the number of casualties per attack. One can see that the map of attack intensities has a much less coherent pattern. Further sociocultural information, such as communications and transportation flows, and social network connectivity may assist in explaining the intensity patterns. The most important factor in producing damaging terrorist attacks may be spatiotemporal coincidence. The ability to be a more professional, deadly terrorist is taught and learned. It requires time and practice, and if available, benefits are gained through spatiotemporal coincidence of social network members in training camps and other centralized places.

Combining attack and intensity trends with sociocultural data can assist in explaining patterns of behavior. One can identify temporal variations in reaction to sociocultural triggers. Figure 4.9 is a line graph of potential

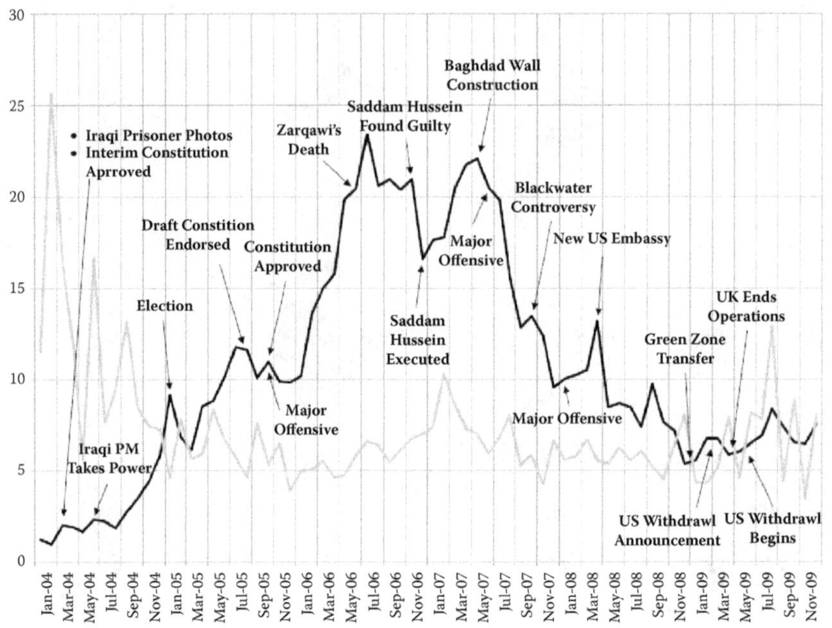

FIGURE 4.9
Time line of terrorist attacks and attack intensities with added sociocultural information. (From Medina, R. M. et al., 2011, *Studies in Conflict and Terrorism* 34:862–882. With permission.)

triggers for violent activity in Iraq with trends in attacks and intensities. A much more thorough investigation of spatial variation would analyze the attack trends for various districts to identify regions of greatest influence for each of the potential trigger events.

For more robust conclusions, this research would benefit from analysis of more events using spatiotemporal data mining* methods, where tens of thousands of attack events could be analyzed. Additionally, one could incorporate other factors of social and physical environment—demographics, climate, and infrastructure. Sociocultural systems are very complex, as are the challenges for designing models to analyze and visualize the geographic patterns of terrorism. This section serves as an introduction to the possibilities for GIS in terrorism research. Although only few examples are provided here, the potential of GIS for this research is much larger than can be summarized in this book.

* Data mining (also referred to as knowledge discovery) is the gathering of data through use of software and algorithms. It is used to find and analyze patterns in large databases or other data sets, online and off-line.

Viewshed Analysis: Line of Sight

The line of sight (LoS) concept is described as what can be seen from various standpoints given physical and built environment obstacles. It is modeled using a viewshed analysis, which is made possible and cost effective with today's geospatial technologies and available data. Viewshed analysis and LoS models are useful in many counterterrorism applications including finding potential locations of sniper placement and countersniper shelter, geosensor placement, and camera placement. It is also useful in determining likely placement locations for improvised explosive device (IED). IEDs have been an ongoing problem for counterterrorist/insurgent forces in Afghanistan, Iraq, and elsewhere. The trend that makes viewshed analysis an important tool for counter-IED activities is that those who place the IED typically wait and hide to detonate the explosive remotely or observe/record the attack for future use in planning. This makes it more likely that IEDs will be distributed within a LoS of a vantage point where terrorists/insurgents can remain hidden.

Analyzing the viewshed requires a vantage point and three-dimensional geographic data of the adjacent region at the extent of the desired results. The three-dimensional data must include physical terrain (for example, see Figure 4.15 later in the text) and built environment obstacles (see Figure 4.21 later in the text). Physical terrain data are available in the form of digital elevation models, while built environment data can be obtained by either manually inputting information for obstacle (buildings, walls, bridges, etc.) heights or acquiring remotely sensed data, such as light detection and ranging (Lidar) products. The data are then input into a GIS and a viewshed model is constructed using advanced algorithms. The output from a viewshed model approximates the LoS view from the selected vantage point (VanHorn and Mosurinjohn 2010).

The Naval Research Laboratory (NRL) has developed software for use in mission planning/training and combat simulation. The benefits of this software in the field are clear. Regions can be mapped for troops in combat situations and potential sniper/IED placement based on the best LoS can be identified in any region with geospatial data. Figure 4.10 is a screenshot from the NRL designed software, Navy Sniper/Counter-Sniper™: 3D Lines-of-Sight Mission Planning Software (Navy Research Laboratory n.d.).

The images in Figure 4.10 are based on visibility from the vantage point. Both images show the direct LoS from the vantage point marked by letter a. For troops in the field, these regions offer the least amount

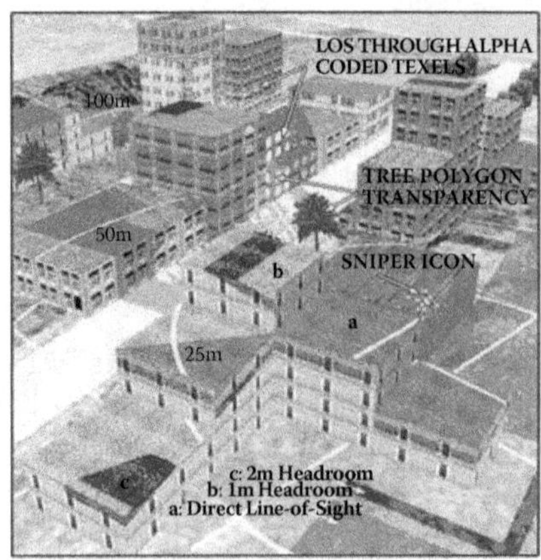

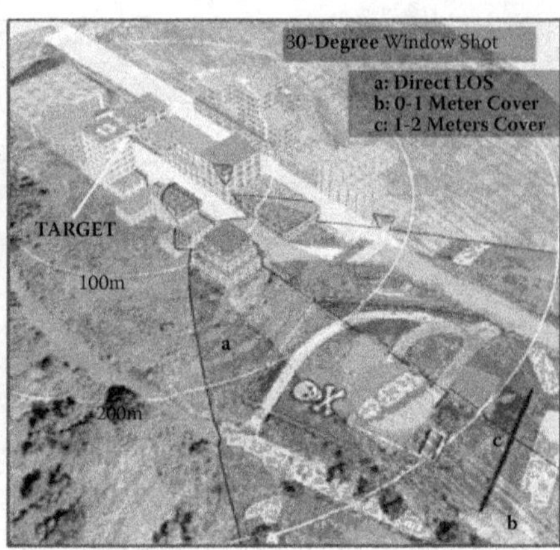

FIGURE 4.10
NRL designed software for viewshed analysis in preparation for combat situations. (Navy Research Laboratory, n.d.)

of coverage from snipers, while regions marked by b, c, and d offer some coverage defined in meters or amount of headroom.

Applications for viewshed analysis can be beneficial when used for mission planning and training. They give soldiers a visualization of regional coverage from sniper fire, which can lead to greater safety in combat situations. The greatest benefit from these types of tools, though, may be when they are utilized in the battlefield with potential for adaptive models that consider movement and number of snipers and countersnipers.

Consideration must also be given to the use of viewshed analysis, LoS models, and other geospatial technologies by terrorists. Undocumented reports of terrorists using GIS and viewshed analysis for mission planning do exist. They are as beneficial for terrorists for use to identify good locations for sniper placement as they are for countersniper forces to find shelter from snipers—if not more so. In the situation where the terrorists have more knowledge of the battlefield, this added information can make a big difference in the outcome of the conflict.

Global Positioning System

The Global Positioning System (GPS) is a system of satellites launched by the Department of Defense that provide locational and navigation information with the combined use of a handheld or transportation-based receiver. GPS was originally a military asset, but has since become a very successful commercial industry. GPS technologies provide us with

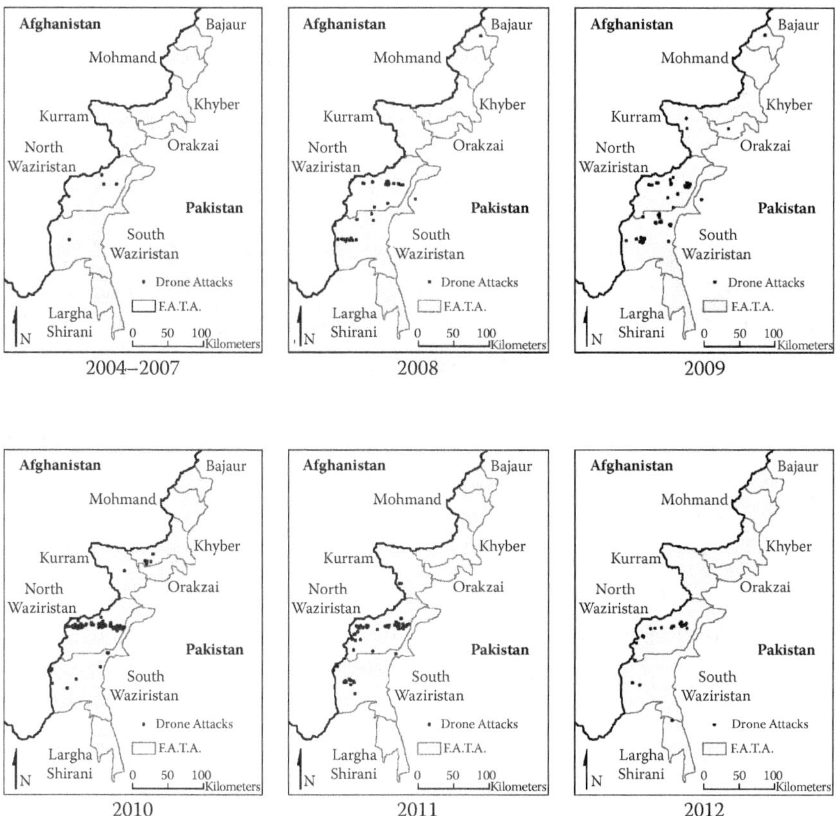

FIGURE 4.11
US drone attacks in Pakistan by year (2004–June 14, 2012). (Data from New America Foundation, 2012.)

absolute location of features and routes across the landscape. The use of drones by the United States to target high-level Islamist terrorists remotely would not be possible without GPS technologies, which are embedded in warheads of all types.

Figure 4.11 shows the pattern of US drone targets in Pakistan from 2004 through June 14, 2012. The majority of these targets have been within the FATA on the Pakistan/Afghanistan border. Many top leaders and other members of terrorist organizations including al-Qaeda, the Taliban, and the Haqqani Network have been killed by drone attacks, and while collateral damages exist, the increasing accuracy of today's geospatial technologies helps to minimize those damages.

GPS technologies will increasingly be embedded into other location-based technologies, such as mobile phones. The main concern is that these technologies are easier to come by and more affordable. Already terrorists use GPS receivers to detonate bombs at specific locations using GPS guidance and mobile phones.

Remote Sensing

Remote sensing is defined in Chapter 1 as the acquisition, processing, and interpreting of reflected electromagnetic radiation. It includes scanners on remote platforms, such as satellites, airplanes, unmanned aerial vehicles (UAVs) and ground-based *in situ* sensors; methods; and algorithms for the processing spectral signal data into information (Sabins 1996). Every chemical element and compound comprising natural and human-made materials have a unique spectral identification or signature based on the manner in which specific wavelengths of radiation are reflected by those materials. These wavelengths of radiation compose portions of the electromagnetic spectrum called spectral bands. Objects and features reflecting light in the visible portion of the spectrum can be seen with the human eye. Materials without radiation reflectance in the visible portion of the spectrum can be discerned using spectrometers and other sensors. Remote sensing is used for many different applications including navigation; identification of soils, vegetation, and urban areas; and detection of change in land cover/land use.

For terrorism and counterterrorism activities, remote sensing is a valuable tool to acquire information from a secure location at a distance, without risking lives on the ground. Remote sensing can be used for persistent surveillance, detection of change over time, identification of chemicals in the air, and a multitude of other related uses.

The most valuable application of remotely sensed imagery in terrorism and counterterrorism may simply be to visualize areas and features from a distance—to see terrain, land cover/land use types, human presence, complex urban areas, and transportation routes. Current commercially available imagery has 1 meter spatial resolution, which means that features on the ground larger than 1 meter in size can be seen from a satellite 644 kilometers (400 miles) up in space. Military systems, such as the KH series of satellites, purportedly have a spatial resolution of 10 centimeters (4–5 inches) or less. Smaller features can be delineated on aerial imagery from aircraft or UAVs, but have less areal coverage than a satellite. Remotely sensed images are used to generate realistic maps that provide more detail than possible without air- or spaceborne sensors. Also, since

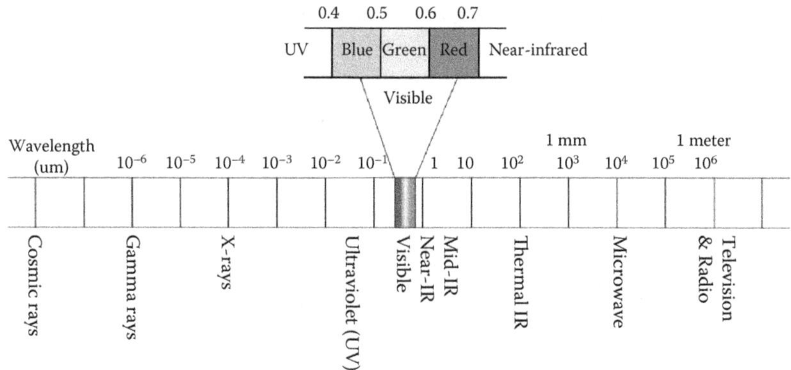

FIGURE 4.12
The electromagnetic spectrum. (Blodgett, C., n.d.)

the platforms can be flown over the same geographic locations over time, changes in the landscape can be detected.

As sensors improved, the number of wavelengths recorded has increased. Panchromatic sensors record only one value representative of the amount of reflected radiation. Multispectral sensors today record true color, infrared, and sometimes radar wavelengths of radiation; hyperspectral sensors generally record more wavelengths than multispectral sensors and they record them continuously (i.e., there are no gaps between the bands). The wavelengths collected by multispectral sensors are discrete. Both multispectral and hyperspectral sensors are capable of recording wavelengths that are not visible by the human eye.

Figure 4.12 shows the electromagnetic spectrum. The wavelengths visible by humans make up a small section of the spectrum labeled "visible" and appear to humans as blue, green, and red. Other wavelengths of reflected radiation, such as infrared (near/mid/thermal IR), are detectable by sensors and assist in identifying land cover and other reflective objects that humans cannot see. Each surface material has different reflectance characteristics.

Figure 4.13 illustrates the reflectance properties of various urban surfaces over a spectrum of wavelengths between 350 and 2,500 nanometers. The visible spectrum is approximately between 390 and 750 nanometers.

Depending on the combination of bands used to produce an image, natural and human-made surfaces such as vegetation, soils, gasses, buildings, and pavement can be much easier to detect on a visual representation (see Figure 4.13), where healthy vegetation is easily detectable in green (520–565 nanometers). Various arrangements of wavelength bands provide better visualizations for different types of surface materials.

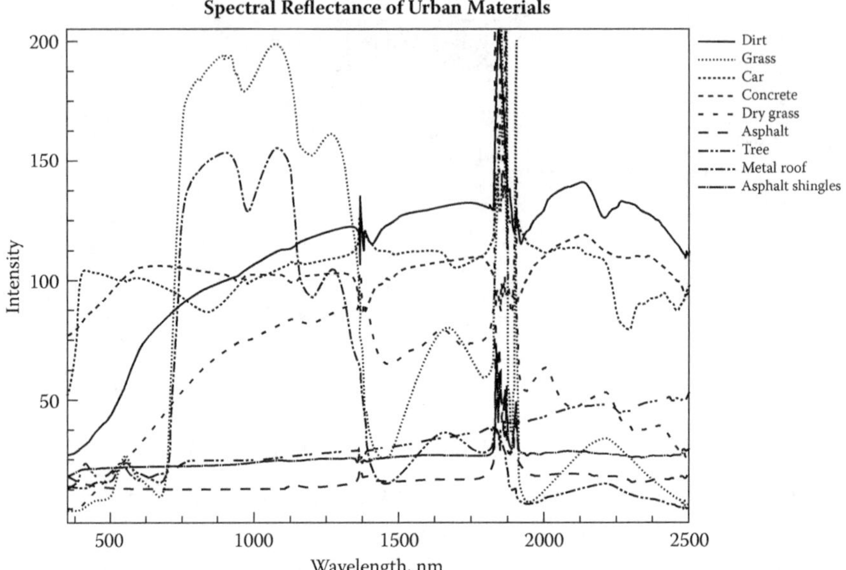

FIGURE 4.13
Spectral reflectance of urban materials.

The more bands of data collected, the more detail of surface cover is provided. All types of remotely sensed images are used for counterterrorism and security research—from panchromatic and natural color images of land use and land cover that show what is on the ground, to terrain and elevation images that show barriers, passageways, and regions of cover, to hyperspectral images that have the potential to detect agents of chemical and bioterrorism (see Figures 4.14–4.22).

Remotely sensed images are used in counterterrorism operations such as the US attack of the bin Laden compound in Abbottabad, Pakistan, in 2011 (Figures 4.16 and 4.17). If used over periods of time, sensors can be used to detect change on the ground, where triggers for conflict, such as environmental hazards, may be detected early. The ability to identify regions of hazardous climate change with knowledge of population vulnerabilities can assist in predicting future regions of conflict.

Change detection has many uses, especially when combined with other geospatial information. An example of change detection is given in Figures 4.16 and 4.17, where Osama bin Laden's compound is shown before (2004) and after (2011) construction. Other applications of change detection for terrorism security include locating regions of internally displaced

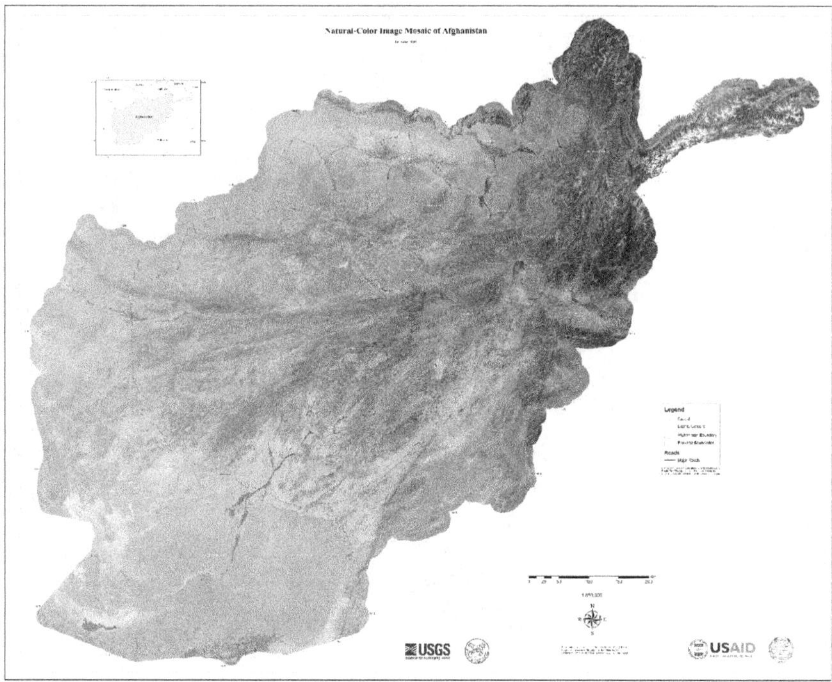

FIGURE 4.14
True color Landsat mosaic of Afghanistan. True color is a type of remotely sensed image. (US Geological Survey, 2011b.)

persons through temporary residence structures, locating construction of new weapons of mass destruction facilities, and identifying environmental changes that can result in regional conflicts.

Remotely sensed imagery is used for emergency management purposes: to detect hazards, vulnerable populations, escape routes, and safe zones. Following 9/11, remotely sensed images were used for many applications. Figures 4.19–4.21 show the 9/11 ground zero site from different scales and through a Lidar sensor. Using images like these, emergency responders are able to identify damages, potential dangers, distribution of debris, and passageways and barriers. Thermal band images were used by 9/11 responders, but onsite temperature sensors proved more useful (Huyck and Adams 2003).

One of the present-day concerns with remote sensing is the concept of *information from pixels,* or *imagery-to-information.* Remotely sensed images are used to provide a visual of the ground and are available for

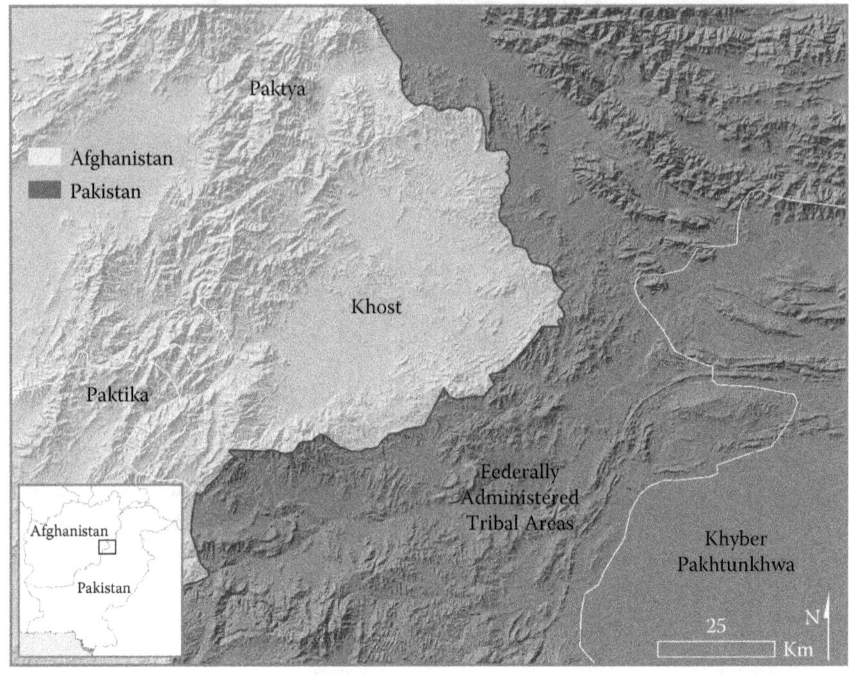

FIGURE 4.15
90 meter SRTM digital elevation model (DEM) terrain map of the Afghanistan/Pakistan border region. (Data from US Geological Survey, 2011a.)

most of the world and at many different times, though at various resolutions. These images are now included in many free services provided by software companies such as Google and Microsoft as a background for map and direction/routing applications.

As useful as the remotely sensed visuals are, there is a need to extract more information from the images in defense and security efforts. Scientists and researchers are focusing more on what information they can extract from the imagery data. This process benefits from the inclusion of other geospatial data, such as demographics, infrastructure, and economic data. For example, Figure 4.22 shows an image of a terrorist training camp in Afghanistan collected in the 1990s. It would be beneficial for counterterrorist operations to know how many attendees the camp had, where they were from, the types of training activities being used, and the intended targets, if any. This information may be available based on the resolution, amount of detail provided, number of recorded wavelengths (also called bands) of the sensor, and integration with knowledge of human geography.

FIGURE 4.16
Osama bin Laden's compound, Abbottabad, Pakistan, 2011. (US Department of Defense, 2011.)

Volunteered Geographic Information and Data Mining

The term volunteered geographic information (VGI) was first introduced by Goodchild in 2007. VGI is geographic information provided by users and can either be focused on a goal of producing a specific result, such as with mapping effort, or volunteered as locational information with no specific purpose in the mind of the volunteer, such as with geotagging* of digital photos. These two sources of volunteered information are termed here *intentionally* and *unintentionally* volunteered information, respectively.

Intentionally volunteered information is a straightforward concept. It describes the process of users choosing to share geographic information with the intention that others will utilize the volunteered information for a specific application. Unintentional volunteered information refers to user information that is collected by communications tools, software applications, digital photos, or other information technologies and used without the volunteer knowing of the specific applications the

* Geotagging refers to the added locational information, typically into digital media, though the concept of geotagging could be applied to nondigital media just as effectively.

FIGURE 4.17
Construction of Osama bin Laden's compound. (US Department of Defense, 2011.)

information is being used for. Even though users may not have any motivation to share their geographic information, it can be collected as a contractual agreement upon initiating use of the technology or as a function of the specific technology. These types of information can be leveraged by those collecting the information for many uses, including traffic data, individual route taking, and emergency updates.

Both terrorists and counterterrorists can use VGI in activities as simple as navigating to a targeted location or as complex as identifying a target based on user posts about the characteristics of specific locations. In many cases, terrorists and supporters have been open about their intentions and offer detailed geographic information in online forums and other websites. By tracking these posts over time, counterterrorist organizations can identify regions of potential conflict, threat, and, with added geographic and sociocultural data, vulnerabilities. Humans can be used as sensors. Presently, volunteered information on websites such as Twitter is mined for geolocated information and key terms. Geolocated Google searches are used to identify global influenza patterns.*

---

* For more information, see www.google.org/flutrends.

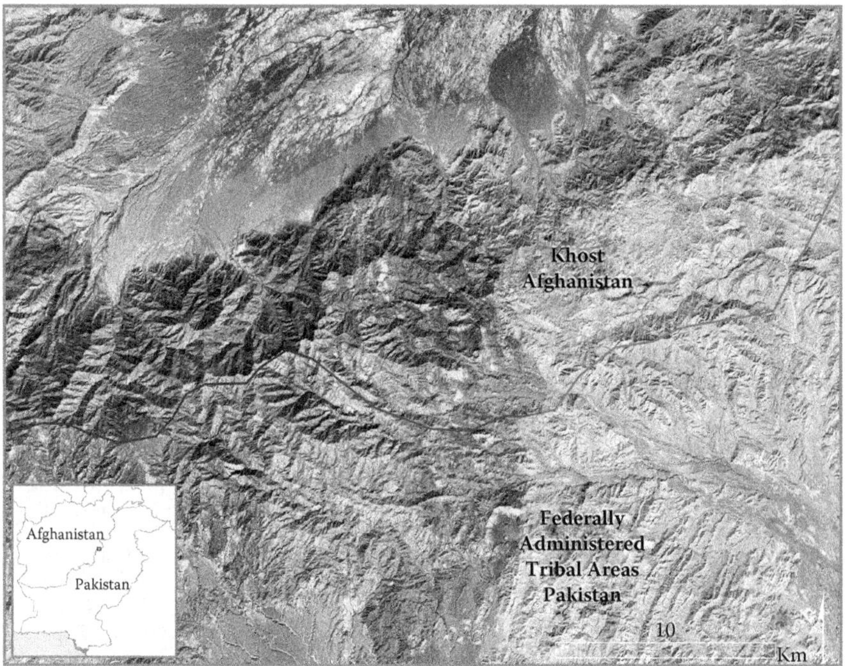

FIGURE 4.18
False color (bands 7, 4, 2) image of border area between Khost, Afghanistan, and the Federally Administered Tribal Areas, Pakistan. (Data from US Geological Survey, 2011c.)

Information can be extracted from digital media, especially when media are geotagged and time coded. Many times detailed spatiotemporal information is provided by the content itself. Photos and videos are now uploaded to the web at large scales and can be mined for pertinent counterterrorism and human/physical geography information. Mining of spatiotemporal data can also be used in emergency preparedness activities previous to and following terrorist attacks. Information collected on human movement patterns, which is possible through the harvesting of cell phone data, can provide knowledge of movement preferences and other environmental attributes.

The ubiquity of VGI allows for extraction of geographic information through data mining. Data mining by counterterrorist organizations can be used to identify spatiotemporal patterns in terrorist and other radical activities and sentiments. Results of data mining do not provide an indication of how or why phenomena are related, but only that they are related. In this way, it is possible to detect human behavior that precedes a terrorist attack. Why that behavior precedes the attack is not necessary

FIGURE 4.19
Landsat 7 image of ground zero, taken on September 12, 2001. (NASA/Goddard Space Flight Center Scientific Visualization Studio, 2002.)

information; however, to understand the motivations and activities behind terrorist attacks completely, understanding correlations between phenomena are key.

Mobile Phones and the Ubiquity of Spatial Information and Tools

Mobile phones and other information technologies are ubiquitous in the information age, even in areas where communications were previously limited by physical or economic constraints. Mobile phones are used by many in countries without infrastructure to support landline phone services. Mobile communications infrastructure is more affordable, so in a technology sense, landline communications were "leapfrogged" by new technologies in many parts of the world (Hahn and Passell 2012). For example, the number of households in Kenya with a phone increased from 3% in 1990 to 93% in 2011 (Demombynes and Thegeya 2012). In many socially and physically vulnerable places in the world, the cell phone is the primary form of communication other than face-to-face, and if signals

FIGURE 4.20
High-resolution aerial photo taken on September 23, 2001. (National Oceanic and Atmospheric Administration, 2001a.)

are not jammed or restricted, the users will have access to the Internet and other technologies.

No longer does one have to own an expensive GPS unit or be tethered to a desktop computer to access valuable locational/relative locational information. Mobile phones today provide access through wireless networks to the World Wide Web and contain GPS technologies with an increasing accuracy. Even with the GPS capabilities switched off, mobile phone locations can be tracked by phone tower triangulation, though with less accuracy. These phones can be considered geospatial tools.

Mobile phones provide terrorists with greater opportunities for operational efficiency and communications when carrying out an attack. Real-time navigation and relative geographies are available and can assist terrorists in adapting to situations and escaping authorities. Mobile

FIGURE 4.21
Lidar images of ground zero. (National Oceanic and Atmospheric Administration, 2001b.)

phones can be used as remote detonators and tracking tools to keep a close eye on operations and, when paired with GIS, GPS, and remote sensing, become much more powerful for operations.

Mobile phones can be used to receive and distribute social media to mobilize populations and organize movements. Social media are becoming a much more powerful tool, as seen with instances in the Arab Spring in Egypt, Tunisia, and other regions. In the right setting, social media networks using mobile phones can be used to mobilize people for violence, send early warnings, and maintain social connectedness. In these ways, social media postings can be seen as high tech smoke signals accessible to anyone with a mobile phone.

Geosensors and Geosensor Networks

Geosensors are instruments that detect physical properties and changes in these properties in specific geographic locations. They can be used to record radiation reflectance, as with remote sensing; to detect seismic activity; or to detect quantities of biological, chemical, or nuclear agents. When on the

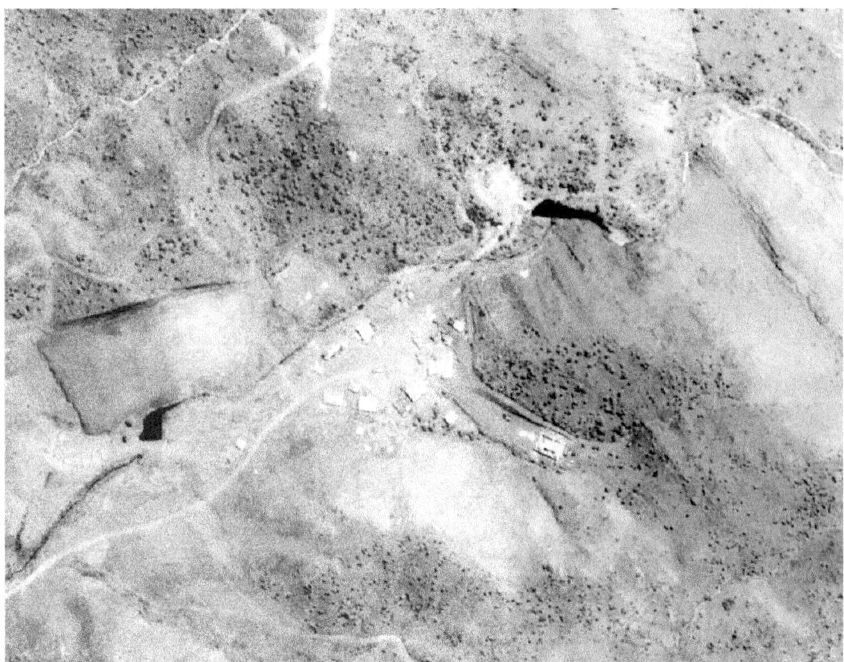

FIGURE 4.22
Zhawar Kili Al-Badr camp (west), Afghanistan. (US Department of Defense, 1998.)

ground, sensors are connected in networks and in communication with each other; the potential for complex information integration is increased. Today's networked sensors have increased capabilities for data processing, dynamic space-time pattern detection, and decision making.

Geosensor networks are used as counterterrorism tools for early detection of chemical, biological, radiological, or nuclear (CBRN) terrorist attacks. Combined with terrain, weather, land use/land cover, and sensor data, the release of a CBRN agent can be detected, tracked, and modeled. With early detection, the risk to vulnerable populations is greatly decreased, as evacuations can begin and those incoming can be deterred. Examples of geosensor networks for counterterrorism are the joint biological remote early warning system (JBREWS) for biological agent detection and tracking by Lawrence Livermore National Laboratory (LLNL) and the wide area tracking system (WATS) for the detection and tracking of nuclear material, also by LLNL.

In battlefield situations, sensors can be placed and operated through use of UAVs as illustrated in Figure 4.23. In this figure, the sensors are

FIGURE 4.23
Placement and operation of sensor networks by UAV. (Lawrence Livermore National Laboratory, 2001.)

dropped by UAVs in rugged terrain. The network is formed autonomously by the sensors and information is projected skyward back to the UAVs.

Future technologies may see sensor networks in major cities throughout the world. These networks along with mobile phones are used as dynamic sensors, so that geolocated sensors can detect movement and change anywhere in the world.

USE OF GEOSPATIAL DATA/INFORMATION AND TOOLS BY TERRORISTS

While geospatial data/information and tools provide great benefits for counterterrorist activities, they also provide terrorists with useful information when organizing attacks. The same benefits exist for both terrorist and counterterrorist sides: increased information and high-level geospatial detail. Terrorists use geospatial data for target selection and planning. Initial planning for attacks benefits from the visualization of places through geospatial data, but a more detailed account of the location and environment benefits more from "ground truthing," or visiting the potential attack site in person for a firsthand account. Terrorists have been known to visit sites before attacks for "dry runs" to get a better feel for the area and attack processes. However, in the initial target selection and mission planning stages, geospatial information can be invaluable.

Terrorists use cell phone GPS, laser range-finding GPS units, and Google Earth to get exact coordinates of target sites for attack. Enhanced information age threats from the use of geospatial technologies for terrorism are from a combined use of GIS, GPS, and remote sensing. Google Earth alone is a powerful tool for terrorism, but when it is combined with GPS, new possibilities arise. For example, precise locations for a target based on latitude and longitude coordinates can be found using Google Earth, and a location-based detonator with an integrated GPS can be set to trigger the explosives upon arrival at the target. This would ensure that suicide bombers hit their target with no hesitation by simplification of the bombing process. Bombs such as these could be placed on children, animals, modes of transportation, etc. In the future terrorists may be able to buy or build missiles with GPS-based guidance systems onboard where the target coordinates need only be entered. This would give terrorists longer range and greater payload capabilities.

There have been multiple cases of terrorists using freely available geospatial information. For example, Google Earth images were used to attack British military bases in Basra, Iraq, leading to one death and several injuries. The most vulnerable structures for attack within the bases, such as tents, were identified by insurgents. Google was cooperative with government concerns and removed the images from the Internet. However, the efforts were futile, as the images had already been archived and printed versions were being distributed for attacks against the British bases. Printouts were confiscated from Iraqi insurgents (Hearn 2007; Harding 2007). Other examples include the al-Aqsa Martyrs Brigade incorporating Google Earth images with other maps for rocket strike target selection into Israel from Gaza (Chassay and Johnson 2007) and Google Earth images being used extensively by Lashkar-e-Taiba for the 2008 Mumbai attacks in India (*Times of India* 2008).

One of the most interesting and probably unexpected examples of targeted attack facilitated by geospatial information is when four AH-64 Apache helicopters were destroyed by mortar attack in Iraq as a result of soldiers taking pictures of the new arrival of the fleet and posting them online. The digital photos were embedded with relatively accurate locational information (geotagged) used by insurgents to attack the precise location of the helicopters (Rodewig 2012).

Google Earth images and imagery from other geospatial data servers are used by terrorists because they are more recent than paper maps, provide more detail, include many attributes of the physical and human environment, have the precision necessary for different types of attacks, and are easily and freely accessible. Terrorists are benefiting from detailed topography and land use information, which includes buildings, roads, and other aspects of relative geography, as well as user-volunteered photographs linked to locations where even more detail is offered, such as building identifiers and other text and heights of walls and fences for potential escape routes.

Figure 4.24 shows the Google Maps account of the Mumbai attacks generated by users, with each attack site marked and information given for each attack. Digital photos of the area following the attacks are also included. One can imagine that the terrorists identified these locations previous to the attacks and used an image like this for planning and organization purposes.

Future online geospatial applications, such as Google Earth, will only become more detailed. The next step for Google, it seems, is the incorporation of within-building navigation capabilities in their proposed Google Maps Floor Plans. This detail, already described as offering information on shopping malls and airports, has obvious implications for terrorist attack planning.

CRITERIA FOR PUBLICLY AVAILABLE GEOSPATIAL INFORMATION

There is always a question as to what and how much geospatial data should be made public. Much available geospatial data can be used for terrorist attacks, but its usefulness may be minimal. While restricting access to some geospatial data may reduce the terrorist threat, the pros and cons must be weighed before removing these data from open sources. These same maps, images, and attribute data are useful for private sector business, civilian government, and citizens for economic development, disease monitoring, agricultural assistance, transportation, and emergency response in many nations where these data are the only available support for critical decisions. In many totalitarian nations, maps are one of the

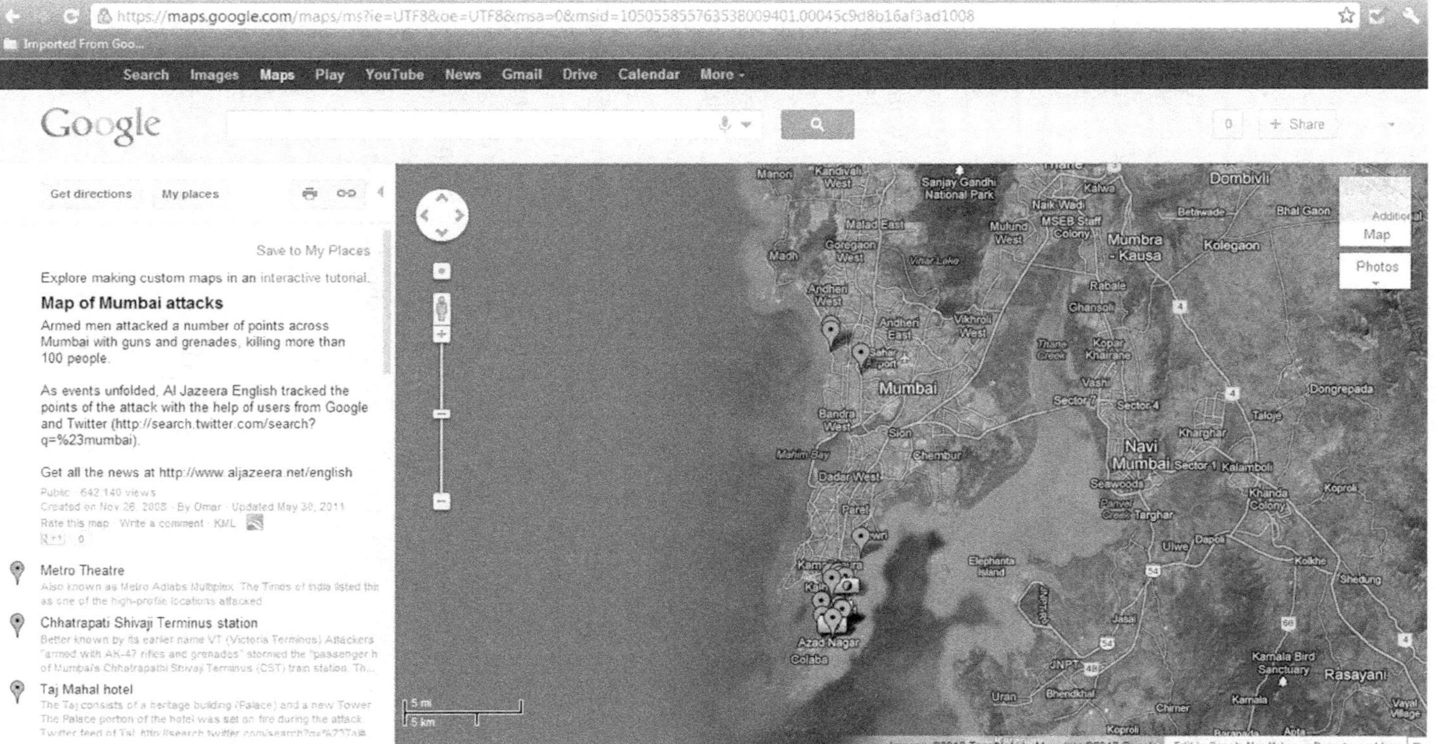

FIGURE 4.24

Google Maps: user-generated content for the 2008 Mumbai attacks in India. With permission.)

most controlled types of information. Access to information provides power to citizens and ensures transparency in democratic nations.

In a study for the US government, Baker et al. (2004) developed three general guidelines for decisions to restrict access to geospatial data and information. The guidelines address the *usefulness, uniqueness,* and *benefits and costs* of the geospatial data in question.

The specific data set must be evaluated for its usefulness to terrorists for mission reconnaissance, mission planning, organization, and targeting purposes. If the data are found not to be useful for violent activities, there is minimal need to remove them from the open source. Some geospatial data are very detailed and therefore can prove to be dangerous if utilized by terrorists. Aeronautical charts and many maps of critical infrastructure have been removed from the Internet. It is possible to modify content rather than remove it completely. Modifications are useful to remove critical information from maps and imagery, while still allowing public access. Examples include removal of critical facilities from satellite imagery before release on the Internet.

The second criterion for control of geospatial data/information involves the uniqueness of the data set. If a geospatial data set is important and unique (meaning that terrorists cannot get the same information elsewhere), it should be controlled. For example, a satellite image showing an airbase is not unique if that same airbase is shown on multiple public sources.

The final criterion considers the societal costs and benefits of restricting access to the geospatial data in question. Data sets that have value for terrorist activities may also be useful for public and/or private sector operations. The benefits of these data to the public enterprise should be evaluated against the actual risk of terrorist use. This does not imply that usefulness and uniqueness of data for legal use should limit the restriction of those data, but that the costs and benefits should be weighed prior to restriction (Baker et al. 2004).

FINAL THOUGHTS ON GEOSPATIAL INTELLIGENCE AND TERRORISM

The concept of geospatial intelligence is not new, though some geospatial technologies introduced here are. Maps have been used for centuries, but geospatial intelligence has become more technologically advanced over

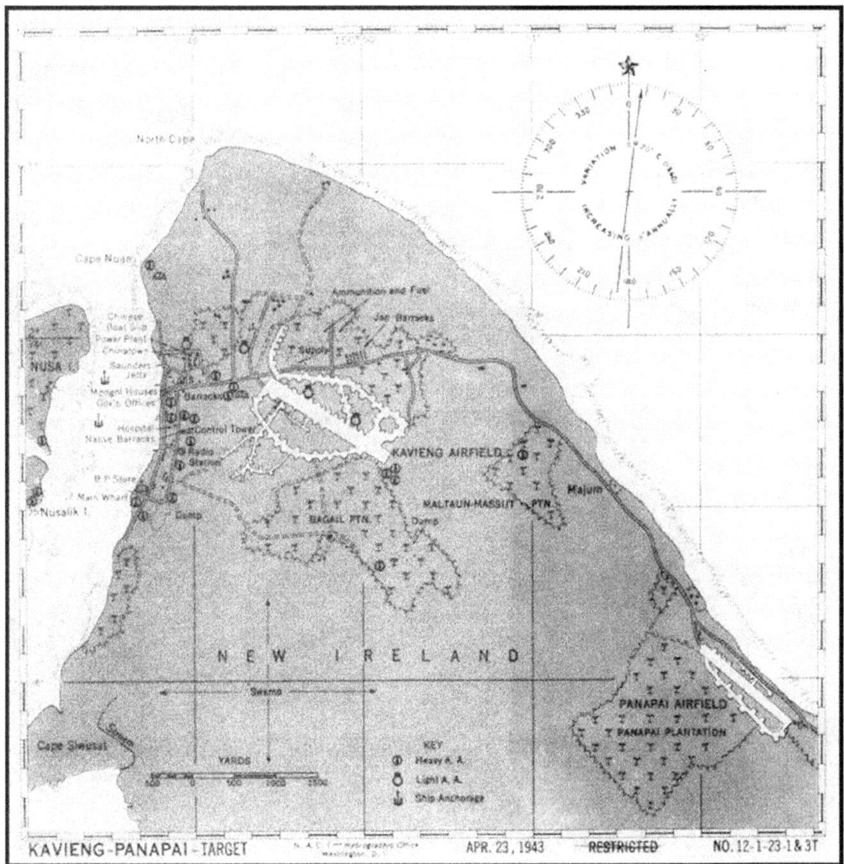

FIGURE 4.25
Target chart used in World War II depicting airfields and other structures in Japan. (US Navy, 1992.)

the years. The transition into fourth generation warfare does not change the need for geospatial intelligence; rather, it enhances it. Terrorist elements are more difficult to identify and find than nation-based troops. They can move within, between, and around political and social boundaries that would stop their nation counterparts. And the world today is changing much faster socially and physically than it has in the past.

Figure 4.25 shows a target chart that highlights Japanese airfields for pilot targets in World War II. Points of interest also include hospitals, government offices, and antiaircraft positions. Aerial photography has been used for operational support in many conflicts, as has geospatial information. Figure 4.26 shows an aerial photo of Auschwitz during World War II

FIGURE 4.26
Auschwitz-Birkenau complex, 12/27/1944. (National Archives, n.d.)

in 1944. The military understands the importance of spatial knowledge and human geography. When comparing these maps with the potential for analysis and visualization possible with today's GIS, GPS, and remote sensing technologies, it is clear that capabilities are greatly improved, but the key concepts of space, place, people, topologies, and activities remain. There is no substitute for geospatial knowledge in counterterrorism.

The present focus on geospatial intelligence and human geography is necessary for effective counterterrorism. International terrorism today is much more complex than the state-to-state conflicts of the past. Counterterrorist forces have more to do now than just win battles. They must also win over hearts and minds, or at least not lose them to terrorists and insurgents. This requires sociocultural understanding, which levels the field of communications between counterterrorist troops and elements of the ambient population. Sociocultural capabilities teamed with geospatial intelligence will continue to help counterterrorist forces connect with local people and save lives at home and in the field. All types of sociocultural information are important and new geospatial methods, tools, and techniques must be constructed for future counterterrorist activities.

Geospatial intelligence and technologies provide a great benefit for counterterrorism, but one must not forget that they provide terrorists with similar benefits of spatial knowledge for planning and strategy. The ease of access makes today's geospatial information and technologies a good starting point for terrorists. In the foreseeable future there will be a trade-off between security and progress due to the distribution of geographic information.

REFERENCES

American Anthropological Association (2012) American Anthropological Association Executive Board statement on the Human Terrain System Project. October 31, 2007. Available from http://www.aaanet.org/about/Policies/statements/Human-Terrain-System-Statement.cfm (last accessed June 14, 2012).

Arquilla, J. and Ronfeldt, D. (2001) Networks and netwars: The future of terror, crime, and militancy. Santa Monica: RAND Corporation.

Baker, J. C., Lachman, B. E., Frelinger, D. R., O'Connell, K. M., Hou, A. C., Tseng, M. S., Orletsky, D., and Yost, C. (2004) *Mapping the risks: Assessing the homeland security implications of publicly available geospatial information*. Santa Monica, CA: RAND Corporation.

Bartholf, M. C. (2011) The requirement for sociocultural understanding in full spectrum operations. *Military Intelligence Professional Bulletin* October–December: 4–10.

Beck, R. A. (2003) Remote sensing and GIS as counterterrorism tools in the Afghanistan War: A case study of the Zhawar Kili region. *Professional Geographer* 55 (2): 170–179.

Blodgett, C. (n.d.) What is hyperspectral imagery (HSI)? Missouri Resource Assessment Partnership (MoRAP), Missouri Department of Natural Resources. Powerpoint presentation online. Available from http://www.cerc.usgs.gov/morap/Assets/UploadedFiles/Projects/HSI/HSI.pdf (last accessed June 26, 2012).

Bowley, G. and Rosenberg, M. (2012) Video inflames a delicate moment for US in Afghanistan. *The New York Times*. January 12, 2012. Available from http://www.nytimes.com/2012/01/13/world/asia/video-said-to-show-marines-urinating-on-taliban-corpses.html?pagewanted=all

Chassay, C. and Johnson, B. (2007) Google Earth used to target Israel. *The Guardian,* World News Section. October 24. Available from http://www.guardian.co.uk/technology/2007/oct/25/google.israel (last accessed June 20, 2012).

Connable, B. (2009) All our eggs in a broken basket: How the human terrain system is undermining sustainable military cultural competence. *Military Review* March–April.

Cutter, S. L., Richardson, D. B., and Wilbanks, T. J. (2003) The changing landscape of fear. In *The geographical dimensions of terrorism,* ed. Cutter, S. L., Richardson, D. B., and Wilbanks, T. J. New York: Routledge.

Defense Science Board Task Force (2004) *Report of the Defense Science Board Task Force on Strategic Communication*. Office of the Under Secretary of Defense for Acquisition, Technology, and Logistics. Department of Defense. Washington, DC.

Demombynes, G. and Thegeya, A. (2012) Kenya's mobile revolution and the promise of mobile savings. Policy research working paper 5988, The World Bank, Africa Region, Poverty Reduction and Economic Management Unit.

Falk, R. (2012) Quran burning: Mistake, crime, and metaphor. *Al Jazeera*, Opinion Section. Available from http://www.aljazeera.com/indepth/opinion/2012/03/20123785644715832.html (last accessed May 24, 2012).

Guevara, E. (2007) *Guerrilla warfare*. Thousand Oaks, CA: BN Publishing.

Hahn, R. and Passell, P. (2012) How cell phones are boosting Kenya's economy. *US News*, Economic Intelligence Section, April 12. Available from http://www.usnews.com/opinion/blogs/economic-intelligence/2012/04/12/how-cell-phones-are-boosting-kenyas-economy (last accessed May 4, 2012).

Hammes, T. X. (1994) The evolution of war: The fourth generation. *Marine Corps Gazette* 78 (9): 35–44.

Hanzhang, T. (2000) *The modern Chinese interpretation: Sun Tzu's Art of War*. New York: Sterling Publishing Co.

Harding, T. (2007) Terrorists use Google maps to hit UK troops. *The Telegraph*, World Section, January 13. Available from http://www.telegraph.co.uk/news/worldnews/1539401/Terrorists-use-Google-maps-to-hit-UK-troops.html (last accessed July 10, 2012).

Hearn, K. (2007) Terrorist use of Google Earth raises security fears. *National Geographic News*. March 12. Available from http://news.nationalgeographic.com/news/2007/03/070312-google-censor.html (last accessed June 20, 2012).

Huyck, C. K. and Adams, B. J. (2003) Remote sensing in response to September 11th. *Proceedings of the 2003 ESRI User Conference*, July 7–11. San Diego, CA.

Kalinski, A. (2012) Quran burning riots: How geospatial tools helped calm the waters. *GPS World*, Geointelligence Section, May 9. Available from http://www.gpsworld.com/gis/geointelligence/qur-burning-riots-how-geospatial-tools-helped-calm-waters-12971 (last accessed May 25, 2012).

King, C. A., Bienvenu, R., and Stone, H. (2011) HTS training and regulatory compliance for conducting ethically based social science research. *Military Intelligence Professional Bulletin* October–December: 16–20.

Lawrence Livermore National Laboratory (2001) Sensing for danger: Correlated sensor networks can help fight against nuclear terrorism and other threats. *Science and Technology Review*, July/August.

Lind, W. S. (2004) Understanding fourth generation war. *Military Review* 84 (5): 12–16.

Lind, W. S., Nightengale, K., Schmitt, J. F., Sutton, J. W., and Wilson, G. I. (1989) The changing face of war: Into the fourth generation. *Marine Corps Gazette* 73 (10): 22–26.

Medina, R. M. and Hepner, G. F. (2011) Advancing the understanding of sociospatial dependencies in terrorist networks. *Transactions in GIS* 15 (5): 577–597.

Medina, R. M., Siebeneck, L. K., and Hepner, G. F. (2011) A geographic information systems (GIS) analysis of spatiotemporal patterns of terrorist incidents in Iraq 2004–2009. *Studies in Conflict and Terrorism* 34:862–882.

NASA/Goddard Space Flight Center Scientific Visualization Studio. (2002) Landsat 7 image of New York City taken on September 12th, 2001. Instrument: Landsat 7-ETM. Image completed on 8-30-2002.

National Archives. (n.d.) Auschwitz–Birkenau complex, *12/27/1944*. Records of the Defense Intelligence Agency, 1920–2006. Available from http://arcweb.archives.gov (last accessed July 10, 2012).

National Counterterrorism Center (2011) Worldwide Incidents Tracking System Methodology Criteria. Available from http://www.nctc.gov/witsbanner/wits_subpage_criteria.html (last accessed April 18, 2011).

National Geospatial-Intelligence Agency (2006) National System for Geospatial Intelligence: Geospatial Intelligence (GEOINT) Basic Doctrine. Office of Geospatial-Intelligence Management. September.

National Oceanic and Atmospheric Agency. (2001a) NOAA WTC high resolution aerial photo. Image taken by NOAA's Cessna Citation Het of September 23, 2001, from an altitude of 3,300 feet using a Leica/LH systems RC30 camera. Available from http://www.noaanews.noaa.gov/stories/s798b.htm (last accessed June 28, 2012).

——— (2001b) Lidar images of ground zero. Available from http://celebrating200years.noaa.gov/magazine/disaster_response/9_11.html (last accessed June 28, 2012).

Naval Research Laboratory (n.d.) Navy Sniper/Counter-Sniper™: 3D Lines of Sight Mission Planning Software. Available from http://www.fhwa.dot.gov/planning/census_issues/ctpp/

New America Foundation (2012) The year of the drone: An analysis of US drone strikes in Pakistan, 2004–2012. Available from http://counterterrorism.newamerica.net/drones (last accessed June 11, 2012).

Pattison, W. D. The four traditions of geography. *Journal of Geography* 63 (5): 211–216.

Rodewig, C. (2012) Geotagging poses security risks. US Army news article, March 7. Available from: http://www.army.mil/article/75165/Geotagging_poses_security_risks/ (last accessed May 4, 2012).

Sabins, F. F. (1996) *Remote sensing: Principles and interpretation,* 3rd ed. New York: W. H. Freeman and Company.

Shah, T. and Bowley, G. (2012) An Afghan comes home to a massacre. *New York Times*, World Section. Available from http://www.nytimes.com/2012/03/13/world/asia/us-army-sergeant-suspected-in-afghanistan-shooting.html?pagewanted=all (last accessed May 24, 2012).

Siebeneck, L. K., Medina, R. M., Yamada, I., and Hepner, G. F. (2009) Spatial and temporal analyses of terrorist incidents in Iraq, 2004–2006. *Studies in Conflict and Terrorism* 32 (7): 591–610.

Sui, D. Z. (2008) Geospatial technologies and homeland security: An overview. In *Geospatial technologies and homeland security: Research frontiers and future challenges,* ed. Sui, D. Z. Berlin: Springer.

The Times of India (2008) How Google Earth helped Mumbai attackers. December 19. Available from http://articles.timesofindia.indiatimes.com/2008-12-19/india/27909393_1_mumbai-police-lashkar-terrorists-terror-strike (last accessed June 20, 2012).

US Army (2011a) The human terrain system. Online. Available from http://humanterrainsystem.army.mil/ (last updated March 24, 2011) (last accessed May 4, 2012).

——— (2011b) Interview about IEDs with a man who lost his leg on an IED. Photo. Available from http://humanterrainsystem.army.mil/htsImageSliderAfghan.aspx (last accessed June 14, 2012).

——— (2011c) Interview with locals on wheat prices. Photo. Available from http://humanterrainsystem.army.mil/htsImageSliderAfghan.aspx (last accessed June 14, 2012).

USA Today (2012) Al-Qaeda leader: Avenge Quran burning in Afghanistan. News Section. Available from http://www.usatoday.com/news/world/story/2012-05-09/al-qaeda-quran-burning/54856714/1 (last accessed May 24, 2012).

US Department of Agriculture (2011) National agriculture imagery program (NAIP) images of Salt Lake County. Available from http://www.fsa.usda.gov/FSA/apfoapp?area=home&subject=maps&topic=arc (last accessed June 28, 2012).

US Department of Defense (1998) Zhawar Kili Al-Badr camp (west), Afghanistan. Released August 20. Available from http://osd.dtic.mil/photos/Aug1998/980820-O-0000X-001.html

——— (2011) DoD news briefing, Monday, May 2, 2011, 11:30 a.m. Available from http://www.defense.gov/news/briefingslide.aspx?briefingslideid=359 (last accessed June 16, 2012).

US Department of Transportation (2012) Census transportation planning products (CTPP). Available from http://www.fhwa.dot.gov/planning/census_issues/ctpp/ (last accessed June 28, 2012).

US Geological Survey (2011a) 90 meter SRTM digital elevation model data of Afghanistan. Available from http://afghanistan.cr.usgs.gov/geospatial-reference-datasets (last accessed June 17, 2012).

——— (2011b) True color Landsat mosaic of Afghanistan. Available from http://afghanistan.cr.usgs.gov/geospatial-reference-datasets (last accessed June 17, 2012).

——— (2011c) False color (bands 7, 4, 2), 14.25 meter Landsat ETM data of Afghanistan and Pakistan. Available from http://afghanistan.cr.usgs.gov/geospatial-reference-datasets (last accessed June 19, 2012).

——— (2007) Figure 9. Data integration is the linking of information in different forms through a GIS. Geographic information systems (webpage). Available from http://egsc.usgs.gov/isb/pubs/gis_poster/ (last accessed June 15, 2012).

US Navy (1992) Target charts. Reference information paper 79. National Archives and Records Administration. Washington, DC, p. 27. Available from http://www.history.navy.mil/library/guides/wwiirecords_cartographic_natlarch.htm (last accessed July 10, 2012).

VanHorn, J. E. and Mosurinjohn, N. A. (2010) Urban 3D GIS modeling of terrorism sniper hazards. *Social Science Computer Review* 28 (4): 482–496.

Zucchino, D. and King, L. (2012) Photos of US soldiers posing with Afghani corpses prompt condemnation. *Los Angeles Times*, US Section. Available from http://articles.latimes.com/2012/apr/18/nation/la-na-afghan-photos-20120419 (last accessed May 24, 2012).

5

Terrorism Risk and Vulnerability

TERRORISM AS A HAZARD

As has been indicated earlier, terrorism is not a new or unique threat to people, property, and societal order, and it is not a threat impacting only one region or group. In a relative context, twenty-first century international terrorism is a much smaller threat to global society and order than the Cold War nuclear threat of global annihilation of the latter part of the twentieth century. Even the largest, worst terrorist weapon of mass destruction attack would be relatively small compared to thousands of nuclear warheads being unleashed. In the future, terrorist actions on the cyber or financial infrastructure of the world may be the worst possibility, although still arguably less than nuclear destruction and contamination of most of the earth. Thus, terrorism in the twenty-first century is international in scope, but it is not an omnipotent global threat.

Terrorist targeting is a place-based or geographically focused activity related to the nature and goals of the terrorist group and the group's perception of impediments to their goals. They attack places, groups, and symbols that fit within their narrative of the wrongful situation necessitating the need for terrorist actions. Given this more constrained and less emotional view of the terrorism threat as not being unique and globally catastrophic, the vast and insightful research, policy, and programs that have been devoted to psychopathological violence, organizational criminal behavior, and analogs in countering other natural and technological hazards can be applied to the terrorist hazard (Piegorsch, Cutter, and Hardesty 2007; Egan 2009). This chapter will focus on the latter.

Terrorism does present some special challenges when viewed as a conventional hazard. Natural hazards are associated with known earth processes and a constrained number of locations, such as geological fault zones for earthquakes. Terrorism is not so deterministic, but focused analysis can constrain the activity and target locations for terrorist groups. Terrorism by non-state groups is a targeted violence, rather than impulsive violence (Schouten 2010). Terrorists exhibit patterns of behavior and action within their geographic activity space—those areas of preferred operation. Since terrorists establish activity patterns, these patterns can be used to anticipate their likely future actions, or at least the range of possible actions within a given time and space (Medina, Siebeneck, and Hepner 2011). However, the activities of terrorists are mostly covert, which makes information gathering and delineation and monitoring of the activity spaces extremely difficult.

Unlike an earthquake or even a technological hazard, such as a nuclear power plant, terrorists adapt to changing situations. Terrorists modify their activities in response to countermeasures taken against them. Terrorism presents a psychological threat and impact on people, often in excess of the actual physical and economic damage. As implied by Chinese military strategist Sun Tzu, "Kill one; frighten ten thousand"; the psychological impacts of terrorism are heightened and must be addressed. The susceptibility of social structures and populations is termed social vulnerability (Cutter et al. 2008).

Terrorists will likely attack using one of the unfortunately termed BNICE weapons. Also, another commonly used acronym for these weapons of mass destruction (WMD) is CBRN (chemical, biological, radiological, or nuclear). BNICE means biological, nuclear, incendiary, chemical, and explosive events, each of which has varying degrees of risk and impacts. Conceptual knowledge, human behavioral knowledge, and, of greatest focus in this chapter, the geographical dimensions of terrorism risk and hazards research can be applied to the terrorism hazard.

Hazard as an Evolving Interaction of Risk and Vulnerability

The study of hazards, risk, and vulnerability is a multidisciplinary field comprising numerous areas of expertise. Unfortunately, there is no single accepted definition or consistent usage for these several related concepts and terms across and within the intelligence community, the risk and decision research community, and lay citizens (Willis et al. 2005; National Research Council 2008). This brief overview of a complex and extensive field will attempt to define terminology and provide consistent use.

A hazard, whether natural or anthropogenic, is the integrated combination of risk and vulnerability. The concepts of hazard, risk, and vulnerability are crucial to dealing with terrorism, especially if one is viewing terrorism from a societal security perspective. Not all places or locations are equally at risk from a terrorist attack, nor are all places equally vulnerable. This hazards approach fosters a scientific view toward analyzing the actual risk of a specific type of terrorist attack and the ability of an area or people to withstand and recover from that attack.

Thus, resource allocation to reduce risk and vulnerability of places needs to consider the variable geographic differences in the social, built, and natural environments (Piegorsch et al. 2007). This more objective, scientific approach has been sorely lacking in the development of terrorism countermeasures and homeland security. The United States has spent over 635 billion dollars on homeland security since September 11, 2001 (National Priorities Project 2011). Much of this spending was done, especially in 2001–2006, without a scientifically based plan, priorities for resource allocation, or metrics of success.

Risk

Risk is defined in several ways depending on the situation. Star, Rudman, and Whipple (1976) state that risk is the probability per unit time of the occurrence of a unit cost burden. This can be modified to be more inclusive if an indication of the geographic unit at risk is included along with the per-unit time. The US Agency for International Development defines risk as a measure of the expected losses due to a hazard event of a particular magnitude occurring in a given area over a specific time period (Atwell 1999).

The probability of a hazardous event is estimated in different ways. For natural events, such as an earthquake, the probability is estimated based on the number, size, and geographic location of previous earthquakes. For terrorist events, the estimation of probability is based on the patterns of actions, including the number, type, target, and geographic location of previous attacks from either a specific terrorist group or a profile of actions of an individual terrorist or type of group. This information would be combined with current actionable intelligence on leadership tendencies, current issues, confidential informants, and potential targets of the group.

For example, al-Qaeda has long targeted US and Western European airline systems for using planes as weapons or the bombing of planes with explosive devices in shoes, underwear, and even body implants in passengers. Thus, based on the group's doctrine of action, goals, and history of airline-related targets and attempts, the probability of risk of an airline-related attack is higher than for other possible targets.

The cost burden is the total costs of an event, such as a terrorist bombing, measured in terms of injuries, deaths, economic costs, including actual losses as well as costs to recover. The total costs should include the less tangible social and environmental costs, such as social disruption and contamination of land and water.

Risk is extremely difficult to estimate, especially for terrorist actions (Willis et al. 2005). A conditional risk estimate is made using a baseline of information on possible terrorist actions in specific locations. The probability of an event taking place would ideally be a specific probability value, but in terrorism events, that probability is often expressed as a range, such as 40%–60% or a high, moderate, or low categorical designation. The probability is combined with the range of possible magnitudes of destructive consequences of an event. These are integrated with the range of deaths, injuries, and other costs associated with the various ranges of magnitudes to provide an estimation of the risk.

Probabilities of risk are difficult to assess and estimate; therefore, experts often decompose the overall event probability into component probabilities (Ezell et al. 2010). These component estimates might include the target city, the weapon choice, and the date/timing of the terrorist action. These components are then ordered into event trees or decision trees to culminate in an overall estimate.

Vulnerability

Vulnerability is defined as the extent to which a community, structure, service, or geographic area is likely to be damaged or disrupted by the impact of a particular hazard (Atwell 1999). The level of vulnerability associated with a geographic place is composed of social, physical, and built-environment characteristics that make a place more susceptible to hazards and influence the ability to recover from an event. The level of vulnerability can change based on changes in any of these components (Borden et al. 2007). Mitchell (2003a, 2003b) addressed the issues of the failure to focus on vulnerability being a principal detriment to US security policy against terrorism:

$$\text{Vulnerability} = \{\text{Exposure Resistance Resilience}\}$$

Mitchell (2003b) explains vulnerability more concisely as the combination of exposure, resistance, and resilience. Thus, facilities, populations, social organizations, and environments that exhibit a high degree of exposure to terrorist actions—along with minimal safeguards against terrorist tactics (resistance) and a minimal capability to recover from a terrorist event (resilience)—are the most vulnerable.

Exposure is a major issue in the United States. In the United States, public buildings, symbolic targets; public events; and physical, financial, and communications infrastructure are plentiful and have relatively open access, thus giving them a high degree of exposure as terrorist targets. This is one of the fundamental security trade-offs in American society, pitting freedoms of movement, access, and privacy against terrorist countermeasures, which tend to limit all three of these freedoms.

Resistance is the ability of a terrorist target to prohibit, withstand, and/or minimize damage from an attack. This involves the design, construction, and operation of infrastructure and systems for redundancy and robustness. Increased use of security guards, deployment of sensors and cameras to detect intruders, use of barriers around facilities, and geographic dispersion of critical support systems can increase the resistance to a terrorist attack.

Resilience is the ability to diminish the spatial and temporal duration of damage of a terrorist attack. The measures that limit the deaths, destruction, geographic extent, and time duration of the impacts of a terrorist attack involve emergency response and the ability to recover from the impacts.

THE BNICE POSSIBILITIES—GEOGRAPHICAL IMPLICATIONS

Terrorists use BNICE weapons because most of the materials and agents to create them are available, inexpensive, and the delivery systems are relatively easy to create. A nuclear device would be the exception. The impacts of several of the BNICE agents can be spread over large areas with great psychological impacts on a populace. The geographical implications related to BNICE events include:

- Location of the event relative to the location of people and infrastructure
- Proximity of the event to people and infrastructure

- Geographic distribution and density of people, their age structure, income level, and other relevant demographic factors
- Location of critical facilities, such as schools and hospitals
- Land cover and land use activities of the surrounding impact area
- Ambient environmental conditions, such as wind direction and speed, temperature, relative humidity

The following is not meant as a comprehensive overview of the BNICE weapons. It only provides an explanation with a few of the primary geographically related implications:

Biological: the use of bacteria or viruses to infect humans and domestic animals, causing disease. The most likely biological agents are anthrax and plague bacteria, smallpox virus, and biological toxins, such as ricin and botulinum. Each of these agents that might be employed by terrorists has very complex chemical/biological, human exposure, and epidemiological implications for the actual event and the response and recovery. Impacts of the release would not be immediately evident, thus allowing time for the spread of the agent by human contacts or through the atmosphere. Factors of population density, the ambient temperature and moisture, and the land activity/use would influence the ability of the agent to survive and spread. Rapid response spatial epidemiology (Auchincloss et al. 2012; Legrand et al. 2009) is one of the measures necessary to reduce the impacts and aid the recovery.

Nuclear: the deployment of a nuclear bomb would have devastating concussive impacts on the target area, as well as long-term contamination of the target site and the surrounding area. The long-term impacts on the surrounding area would be determined by the rate and direction of spread of the nuclear contamination plume through the atmosphere (see the example in Figure 5.3) and by the water drainage system.

Incendiary: the ignition of a fuel storage tank farm, pipeline, or refinery would have large close-proximity impact, but would be limited in both time and area. The largest threat is the combination of the use of an incendiary device, such as a railroad tanker car of flammable chemicals, in close proximity to a critical infrastructure facility, such as an electrical generation or chemical plant.

Chemical: terrorists can cause the release of chemical toxins into the environment, usually in enclosed spaces such as subways or buildings. These agents are industrial chemicals, such as chlorine, or manufactured toxins, such as cyanide, sarin, and VX (Disaster Information Management Research Center 2012). These toxins can be harmful through both skin contact and inhalation; thus, proximity to the release and directionality of the chemical plume are critical to the impact. Environmental conditions affect the lethality of chemical weapons. Colder temperatures generally increase the duration of effectiveness of these chemicals, by slowing down their dispersion and chemical reactions with environmental chemical compounds.

Explosive: explosive devices have been used very often and effectively as terrorist weapons. The 2004 railroad bombings in Madrid, Spain, inspired by al-Qaeda using mining explosives killed about 200 people. The Oklahoma City bombing of the federal courthouse by US domestic terrorists used a mixture of fertilizer and fuel oil (termed ANFO) as a cheap, obtainable explosive.

An explosive device combined with non-fissionable radioactive laboratory test and waste materials is used to create the "dirty" bomb. Laboratory and medical testing and waste materials are more available than a nuclear bomb device. These radioactive materials, combined with a conventional explosive, would achieve widespread radioactive contamination and psychological impact. For these reasons, the dirty bomb is one of the more likely and destructive weapons (Rosoff and Winterfeld 2007).

Figure 5.1 provides a useful view of the relative probability of risk of specific types of terrorist events versus the impact of each event on human lives and societal systems. As shown, the use of a nuclear weapon by a terrorist group has a low probability, but a high impact if used on a population. Terrorists are able to access chemical, explosive, or biological materials for terrorism more easily, although the impacts on humans and property are relatively less than those from a nuclear explosion. It is for this reason that most terrorist attacks use the more readily available terrorist weapons: a fertilizer bomb in the Oklahoma City bombing, explosive airplanes (World Trade Center, 9/11), and release of sarin gas in the Tokyo subway by the Aum Shinrikyo cult.

It should be noted that the psychological impacts on a population vary with the type of terrorism event, likely even more than the physical and economic impacts. Fear and the duration of fear caused by a bacterial

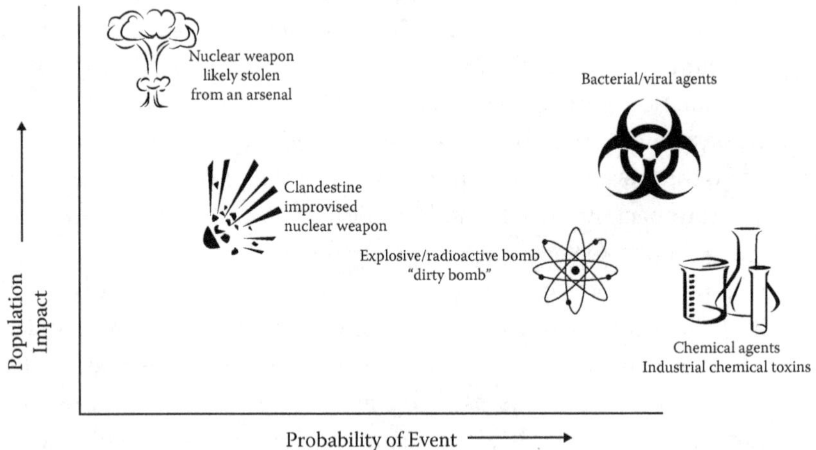

FIGURE 5.1
Probability of occurrence versus impact on population.

attack may be greater than by an explosive attack. In doing scientific assessment of the risk component of the terrorist hazard, this continuum must be evaluated to assign priorities and resources to minimize the risk of an occurrence.

ACTIONS TO DIMINISH RISK OF AND VULNERABILITY TO TERRORIST ATTACKS

To paraphrase Mitchell (2003b) in a simple manner: risk reduction is keeping threats away from people; vulnerability reduction is keeping people away from threats. In the terrorism context, countermeasures must operate on both sides of the risk–vulnerability equation. The view and actions should be on security, not defense. Security is a much more comprehensive approach to the protection of people, infrastructure, and society.

The emphasis for risk reduction is to deter terrorists from attacking and detecting them prior to the attack. The deterrence part of risk reduction for the United States and Western Europe has been on "kinetic" solutions, which is a military term or euphemism for killing terrorists and destroying their havens and infrastructure. The primary reason given for the invasion of Afghanistan by coalition forces in 2001, known as Enduring Freedom, was to deny al-Qaeda, the Taliban, and associated groups use of Afghanistan as a safe haven. Hundreds of billions of dollars have been spent in the last two decades on this effort in Afghanistan, the hunt for Osama bin Laden and other al-Qaeda leaders, and military actions against terrorists across the globe.

While the core of al-Qaeda has been weakened by these kinetic actions, terrorists groups, unlike natural hazards, adapt. Killing of leadership works most effectively with organizations that have a hierarchical structure. Al-Qaeda has changed its structure to a geographically dispersed network of franchises in Southeast Asia (Abu Sayyaf), Northern Africa (al Shabaab and al-Qaeda in the Islamic Maghreb), and al-Qaeda in the Arabian Peninsula. Additionally, with the advent of generational terrorism, where sons and daughters are indoctrinated and take up the cause of their parents, it is impossible to kill every terrorist or dismantle every network.

This deterrence component of risk reduction has fostered strategies including increased airline passenger screening, immigration/border controls, and foreign and domestic intelligence collection and integration. These actions attempt to deny access of terrorists from source nations to target nations and deter them from carrying out a terrorist action. Detection and deterrence require a much greater focus on intelligence analysis, rather than the conventional law enforcement mind-set. In countering terrorism, the actions must be on finding and stopping terrorist actions rather than apprehending the terrorists after the event.

One obvious aspect of this rethinking has been the reconfiguration of the US Federal Bureau of Investigation (FBI) (Feldstein 2008). Traditionally, the FBI has been used to find and arrest criminals after the fact. The authority hierarchy of the FBI has tended to favor those individuals successful in investigating and arresting criminals. The new role of the FBI counterterrorism effort requires individuals skilled in computer technology, statistical analysis, and intelligence interpretation. Analysts of networks, data, and patterns were necessary, but were not usually on the fast track for advancement and higher authority. This is and should be part of the change in culture of any organization countering terrorism in the twenty-first century. Arguably, the fact that the United States has not experienced another major attack since 9/11 supports the conclusion that these measures of risk reduction have worked to detect, neutralize, and deter terrorists away from the US homeland.

EFFECTIVE PLANNING AND RESPONSE TO MINIMIZE VULNERABILITY

On the vulnerability side, the coordinated strategy of focused efforts, the proper allocation of resources, and an integrated plan to reduce vulnerability are less apparent in governmental policy and understanding of the citizenry. Vulnerabilities are infinite. Not every city, infrastructure component, or population can be protected. Decisions about what cities, facilities, and populations are most at risk and most vulnerable must be made and constantly reevaluated.

With a few critical exceptions, preparation and response to a terrorist event are similar to actions necessary to diminish vulnerability for any hazard. The primary constituents of effective response to a hazard event are *awareness, prevention, preparedness, response,* and *recovery.*

Cities are identified as prime targets for obvious reasons: numerous economic and physical infrastructure targets, high density of population, guaranteed media notification and coverage, and the ability of terrorists to hide in plain sight, especially if there is a diaspora or supportive community in the city. For this reason, cities are a prime focus for vulnerability analyses. These analyses are being done at various geographical scales. From governmental buildings or critical infrastructure facilities, such as energy or financial systems, to entire cities and to national and international scale, measures are being implemented to decrease vulnerability. A terrorist attack in the financial center of New York City would have impacts throughout the United States and the world.

Prevention of an attack centers on actions to diminish risk, which were already discussed. Prevention also involves the difficulty of the terrorist attacking a target successfully weighed against the real and/or symbolic value of that target to the terrorist goals. New York City, which has been a target for terrorists on several occasions, has its own foreign intelligence unit in several foreign countries whose goal is to prevent future attacks. Difficult or hardened targets, in general, have less vulnerability. Security personnel prevent a facility from being a target by using obvious demonstrations of security with barriers, guards, and cameras.

Preparedness involves having the resources available to diminish the geographic and temporal duration and/or mitigate the impacts of a terrorist attack. Training of employees and citizens on evacuation and/or shelter-in-place plans is a means of preparation. Less obvious means to prepare for an attack deploy sensor networks linked to geographic information systems for identification and monitoring of radiation, chemical, and biological releases across the city.

Response actions include the prepositioning of emergency supplies, such as antibiotics and medical supplies, gas masks, and decontamination units, in locations that are in the higher risk areas of cities and having the accessibility necessary to make these supplies rapidly available after an attack.

The availability of event impact and response information along with trained personnel in accessible locations to deal with the physical and social aftermath of the attack is a most critical response support.

Recovery is the ability of the facility or city to regain function after the attack. The time for a city to recover vital services, restore security and order, and alleviate the psychological impacts of the event is the primary metric of successful programs to reduce vulnerability.

Much of the information that is required to minimize all types of vulnerability is variable and comes from disparate sources. The communications pipeline and street networks, the areas of higher population density, hospital capabilities, first responder personnel, and equipment are all critical types of information to prepare, respond, and recover. These sets of information likely only have one attribute in common—that they all exist in a physical location, which can be defined by geographic coordinates (Koch 2010). This is termed georeferencing or geocoding of data. Thus, all of this information can be analyzed for proximity, connectivity, and accessibility to each other, can be mapped, and can be combined and dynamically modeled in a geographic information system to aid in response to and recovery from a terrorist event.

Infrastructure Vulnerability

The physical or infrastructure vulnerability has been a critical focus for preemptive management of terrorist events in the United States. In 2002, the National Geospatial-Intelligence Agency (NGA) and the US Geological Survey (USGS) undertook an effort to locate and map critical infrastructure, such as transportation networks, electrical grids, pipelines, and chemical storage facilities. This program, the Homeland Security Infrastructure Project (HSIP), combined these map layers with public health and demographic data, symbolic landmarks, and elevation data. The USGS has worked with state and local governments to acquire data, information, maps, and imagery for 133 major urban areas in the United States (Alness 2012). As of 2011, HSIP had compiled over 450 layers of information for GIS use. The project goal is to provide a nationwide, vertical (local to national government and private sector), secure web-enabled information portal (Palanterra) to portray a common operational picture for assessing infrastructure vulnerability and managing response to terrorist attacks.

Social Vulnerability

Physical and social vulnerabilities include geographical constituents and implications. Arguably, social vulnerability has the most connection with geographic concepts, methodologies, and techniques. The concept of social vulnerability, being a function of the geographic place that is under threat, has provided a valuable approach to assessing vulnerability of urban places beyond the more engineering-focused infrastructure vulnerability assessment. One cannot consider vulnerability of a city only in terms of destroyed buildings or downtime for the banking system, but the terrorist event must consider the consequences to the human population and their supporting social systems (Cutter, Boruff, and Shirley 2003).

The variables used in assessing social vulnerability include the various infrastructure systems and critical facilities (hospitals, schools), but also include population density, ethnicity and race, socioeconomic status, and employment—all georeferenced. Piegorsch et al. (2007) found that social vulnerability for terrorism incidents in a US urban area can be characterized as a function of ethnicity, wealth, age, race, and gender. The five most vulnerable cities overall were New Orleans and Baton Rouge, Louisiana; Charleston, South Carolina; New York; and Richmond, Virginia—likely due to their location on coastlines, the high vulnerability of their built environment, and their race and socioeconomic class factors.

The recognition that the geographic variation in social vulnerability modifies the total vulnerability picture within an urban area and between areas across a nation is important. Furthermore, doing hazard-specific event risk assessment yields important results tailored to the specific hazard threat (Willis et al. 2005). However, the social vulnerability approach provides a picture of an urban area's vulnerability without emphasis on correct anticipation of the type of terrorist event. This provides a justification for a robust and rational allocation of resources to diminish vulnerability within a city or across a nation (Borden et al. 2007), which strengthens the city regardless of whether a terrorist or natural event occurs.

Mapping Vulnerabilities Using Dynamic Populations

Urban areas have the highest density of civilians, infrastructure, and symbolic targets. These conditions make urban areas more at risk for terrorist attacks as evidenced by terrorist attacks in London, Madrid, New York, and Mumbai. The main considerations when conceptualizing the vulnerability of urban areas and people are the dynamics of this population. Urbanites tend to be more mobile and have specific diurnal patterns (e.g., traveling to work, picking up children, shopping). In most cases, population estimates used for emergency planning do not consider diurnal population dynamics. Planning uses census numbers, which typically count people in their residences at night at various scales (e.g., block group, census tract, and county). While it is important to know where people live, this information is not as useful for emergency responders because attacks are often on business or governmental facilities in the central areas of cities.

Population dynamics influence the terrorist attack planning and the vulnerability of an urban area to attack. For example, an attack on a downtown area at 2 a.m. on a Saturday will not result in as much loss of life as it would at 2 p.m. on a Wednesday. The estimate of location and timing is essential for emergency responders to determine which people are at greatest risk and plan material and human resources to meet these estimates. GIS is used to map these population dynamics in proximity to places of symbolic target value, vital infrastructure, land use/land cover, terrain, and locations of hospitals and schools. This type of geospatial analysis aids in planning and preparation for future attacks, as well as providing the information foundation for more timely and effective response after the attack.

Figure 5.2 provides a graphical rendition of population dynamic estimates in Salt Lake City, Utah, at midnight and at noon on a typical weekday.* The central business and governmental areas are just north of the intersection of major roadways, I-15 and I-80. Note that the high peak indicates the very high population density in the central business district of Salt Lake City at noon, relative to more prominent areas in white in the outlying areas at midnight.

In a study by Kobayashi, Medina, and Cova (2011), diurnal population estimates were compared to static residential estimates for Salt Lake

* It should be noted that the diurnal population data used for this study were generated as a combined effort between the US Census and the US Department of Transportation. For more information, see the Census Transportation Planning Products (CTPP) (US Department of Transportation 2012).

Midnight

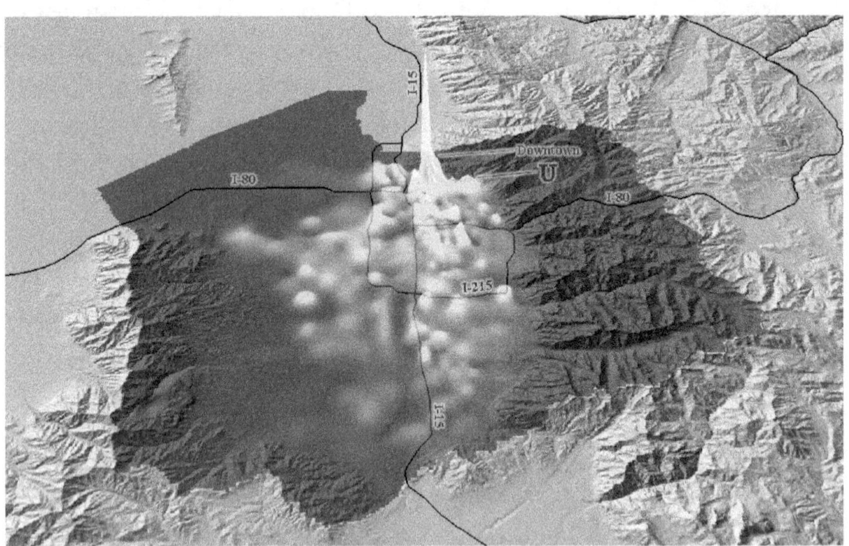

Noon

FIGURE 5.2
Population dynamics in an urban area—a case study in Salt Lake County. (From Kobayashi, T. et al., 2011, *Professional Geographer* 63 (1): 113–130. With permission.)

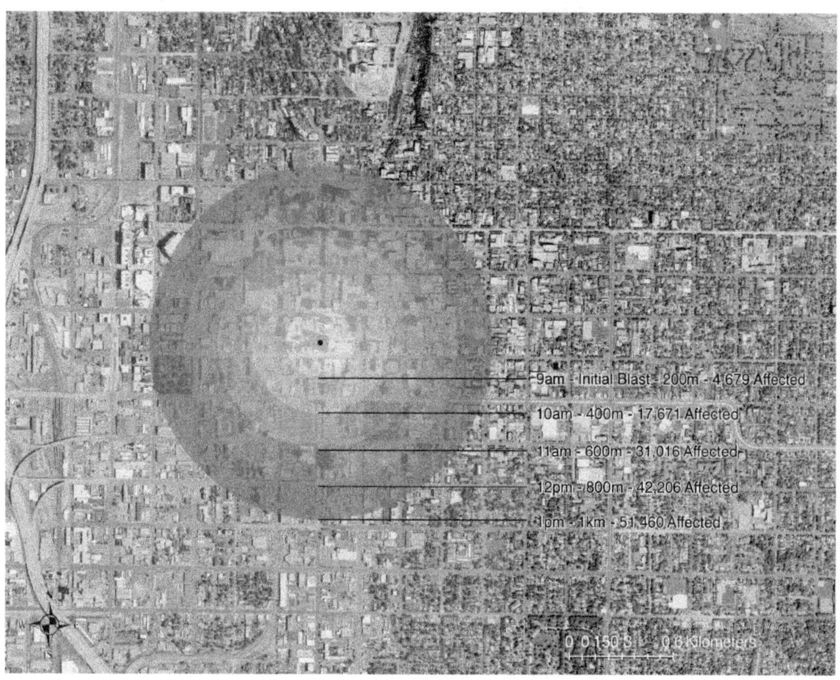

FIGURE 5.3
Vulnerable population over time in the event of a hypothetical dirty bomb. The remotely sensed background image is used for visualization purposes. (From Kobayashi, T. et al., 2011, *Professional Geographer* 63 (1): 113–130. With permission.)

TABLE 5.1
Dirty Bomb Radius and Affected Population

Time	Radius (Meters)	Affected Population Based on Interpolation	Affected Population Based on Block Data
9:00:00 a.m.	200 (initial blast)	4,679	167
10:00 a.m.	400	17,671	461
11:00 a.m.	600	31,016	972
12:00 p.m.	800	42,206	2,601
1:00 p.m.	1,000	51,460	4,820

Note: From Kobayashi, T. et al., 2011, *Professional Geographer* 63 (1): 113–130. With permission.

County, Utah, in the event of a dirty bomb attack. The scenario has an explosion and diffusion of radiation in a circular pattern in 1-hour increments (Figure 5.3). The assumed dirty bomb blast occurs at 9 a.m. when many people are commuting to or are at work, school, or shopping.

The variation in the impact on people is shown in Table 5.1. This table compares estimates of people affected in the attack area using interpolated dynamic population estimates derived from employment and route to work data. These dynamic estimates are compared to estimates using census block residential (nighttime) data. The estimates of those affected using the dynamic population data are much higher than with the nighttime population data. At the end of the 5 hours and 1 kilometer of radiation exposure, 4,820 people are affected based on the nighttime population data, while 51,460 people are affected using the dynamic population estimate.

The radiation from the dirty bomb is assumed to travel outward at 200 meters per hour at a constant rate and shape, without consideration to land use, terrain, and meteorological factors, and people are assumed to go about their daily employment-based routine. The study does not consider levels of injury or death—only that people are affected. However, even with the level of model simplification, the implications of the results are clear.

This geospatial-based research indicates the utility of more refined spatial and temporal data, spatial analysis of these data for dynamic estimates, and the use of GIS for analysis and conveyance of results to support emergency planning, response, and recovery.

REDUCTION OF THE TERRORIST HAZARD AND HOMELAND SECURITY

Recent terrorist events and the recovery from these events have led to some important insights and changes in dealing with the terrorist hazard. The cost and unending duration of the effort to capture and kill terrorists, thus reducing the risk, have fostered more emphasis on decreasing our vulnerability to terrorist attacks. Shortly after the World Trade Center terrorist attack of 2001, Seifert (2002) emphasized the need to establish comprehensive continuity and recovery plans. Most experts agree that a comprehensive risk assessment (Jenkins 2007) and comprehensive vulnerability assessments integrating non-economic costs and benefits and tailored to specific geographic settings are essential to sound planning and allocation of resources.

Viewing the terrorist threat as one of many hazards fosters a cooperative and more efficient approach to dealing with other hazards. Thus, the steps necessary for confronting any hazard lend themselves to addressing the terrorist hazard. The need for geographic decentralization and redundancy of critical facilities is essential, as it reduces vulnerability regardless of the hazard.

The perspective of dual use of investments in reducing vulnerability to the terrorist hazard is being recognized. Facilities, systems, and people developed against terrorism can be utilized for response and recovery from the impacts of any hazard. For example, creating medical centers with specialized capabilities in highly vulnerable areas can be used whether the disaster is terrorist or natural.

In the end, terrorism is not going to be totally eliminated. It has proven to be an effective means of conveying a group's agenda. Thus, all nations need to adopt a security view that recognizes and works to address both the risk and vulnerability sides of terrorism security. However, the development of a more informed and aware society should not devolve into an obsession with and fear of terrorist attack. To allow this to happen threatens individual freedoms and liberties beyond any realistic view of the actual threat of terrorism to an individual or nation.

REFERENCES

Alness, S. (2012) Readiness, response and recovery. Homeland Security Infrastructure Program (HSIP) Update. www.nsgic.org

Atwell, L. (1999) Report on Natural Hazard Mapping and Vulnerability Assessment Workshop, St. Georges, Grenada, March 2–5, 1999, OAS-USAID.

Auchincloss, A., Gebreab, S., Mair, C., and Diez Roux, A. (2012) A review of spatial methods in epidemiology, 2000–2010. *Annual Review of Public Health* 33:107–122.

Borden, K. et al. (2007) Vulnerability of US cities to environmental hazards. *Journal of Homeland Security and Emergency Management* 4 (2): 1–21.

Cutter, S. L., Barnes, L., Berry, M., Burton, C., Evans, E., Tate, E., and Webb, J. (2008) A place-based model for understanding human resilience to natural disasters. *Global Environmental Change* 18:598–606.

Cutter, S., Boruff, B., and Shirley, W. (2003) Social vulnerability to environmental hazards. *Social Science Quarterly* 84:242–261.

Disaster Information Management Research Center (2012) Chemical warfare agents. National Institute of Health (2012) http://sis.nlm.nih.gov/enviro/chemicalwarfare.html

Egan, K. (2009) *The terrorscape: Geography of urban terror risk.* El Paso, TX: LFB Scholarly Publishing.

Ezell, B. C., Bennet, S. P., Winterfeldt, D. V., Sokolowski, J., and Collins, A. 2010. Probabilistic risk analysis and terrorism risk. *Risk Analysis* 30 (4): 575–589.

Feldstein, M. (2008) Designing institutions to deal with terrorism in the United States. *American Economic Review* 98(2): 122–126.

Jenkins, B. M. (2007) Basic principles for homeland security. Testimony presented before the House Appropriations Committee, Subcommittee on Homeland Security on January 30, 2007.

Kobayashi, T., Medina, R. M., and Cova, T. J. (2011) Visualizing diurnal population change in urban areas for emergency management. *Professional Geographer* 63 (1): 113–130.

Koch, D. (2010) A geospatial integrated problem solving environment for homeland security applications. *IEEE Proceedings on Technologies for Homeland Security,* 211–215.

Legrand, J. et al. (2009) Estimating the location and spatial extent of a covert anthrax release. *PLoS Computational Biology* 5 (1): e1000356.

Medina, R. L. Siebeneck, L. K., and Hepner, G. (2011) Geographic information systems (GIS) analysis of spatiotemporal patterns of terrorist incidents in Iraq 2004–2009. *Studies in Conflict & Terrorism* 34:862–882.

Mitchell, J. K. (2003a) Urban vulnerability to terrorism as hazard. In *The geographical dimensions of terrorism,* ed. Cutter, S., Richardson, D., and Wilbanks, T. J., 17–25. New York: Routledge.

——— (2003b) The fox and the hedgehog: Myopia about homeland security in US policies on terrorism. In *Terrorism and disaster: New threats, new ideas (research in social problems and public policy),* vol. 11, ed. Clarke, L., 53–72. Bingley, UK: Emerald Group Publishing Limited.

National Priorities Project (2011) http://nationalpriorities.org/analysis/2011/us-security-spending-since-9/11

National Research Council (2008) Department of Homeland Security bioterrorism risk assessment: A call for change, appendix A. Washington, DC: The National Academies Press.

Piegorsch, W., Cutter, S., and Hardesty, F. (2007) Benchmark analysis for quantifying urban vulnerability to terrorist incidents. *Risk Analysis* 27 (6): 1411–1425.

Rosoff, H. and Winterfeld, D. (2007) A risk and economic analysis of dirty bomb attacks on the ports of Los Angeles and Long Beach. *Risk Analysis* 27 (3): 533–546.

Schouten, R. (2010) Terrorism and the behavioral sciences. *Harvard Review of Psychiatry* Nov./Dec.: 369–378.

Seifert, J. (2002) Homeland security—Reducing the vulnerability of public and private information infrastructures to terrorism: An overview, report for Congress, Congressional Research Service.

Starr, C., Rudman, R., and Whipple, C. (1976) Philosophical basis for risk analysis. *Annual Review of Energy* 1:629–662.

US Department of Transportation (2012) Census Transportation Planning Package (CTPP). Available from: http://www.fhwa.dot.gov/planning/census_issues/ctpp/

Willis, H. H., Morral, A. R., Kelly, T. K., and Medby, J. J. (2005) *Estimating terrorism risk.* Santa Monica, CA: RAND Corporation.

6

Influences on the Future Geography of Terrorism

GLOBAL INFLUENCES ON THE LOCATION OF CONFLICT

The preceding chapters have focused on the influence of physical and human geography in delineation of the location, strategies, and operational tactics of various non-state terrorist groups across the world. Symmetric and non-symmetric warriors are being influenced by geography and, conversely, affect the geography of places to a larger degree than has been recognized in the insurgency and terrorism research literature. While the future is impossible to predict, one can provide informed speculation about the geographic locations and character of terrorism in the future.

There are several global processes that will continue to influence the occurrence, location, and character of terrorism in the twenty-first century. These drivers create the conditions that lead to social and economic instability in a region, to conflict, and, in a number of cases, to terrorism. The most dominant of these drivers are globalization and global environmental change.

While the correspondence between areas left behind in the globalization process and terrorism is clearer, solid evidence of the linkages between environmental change and increased conflict, especially terrorism, is lacking (Scheffran et al. 2012). A systematic, causal relationship between climate change and terrorism has not been defined empirically. The absence of an empirical linkage may reflect the actual absence of such a relationship, or it may be the consequence of theoretical and methodological limitations of existing research in this new and complicated arena. However, historical evidence supports the linkage between changing environments and conflict, as does current research using scenario and modeling methodologies (Buntgen et al. 2011; Zhang 2008; Devitt and Tol 2011; Raleigh and Kniveton 2012).

Areas adversely impacted by globalization and/or climate change likely will have increased social and political upheaval in the future. Simons and Tucker (2007) conclude that all nation-states (rich or poor) fail some portions of their populations. Poorer nations will be less able to respond to and mitigate these changes, resulting in more potential for upheaval. Terrorists come from the alienated groups or communities within populations. The areas that continue to have their populations disenfranchised and alienated, without redress, will be opportune sources of terrorist recruits, areas of terrorist actions, and havens for international terrorists. While researchers are still debating the issues, policy makers are developing plans for addressing the impacts of globalization and climate change. The consensus among many is that weakened governments, with an already thin margin for survival, will face conditions of increased internal conflicts, extremism, and movements toward radical ideologies (Mazo 2009; CNA 2007; Moran 2011).

This look into the future requires that one accept that the globalization and environmental change drivers provide the precursors for conflict and terrorism in some areas of the globe, while fostering success in other economies and societies. In other words, these global changes will manifest in regional and local winners and losers as the effects of globalization continue and environmental change becomes more pronounced. The processes of globalization and global environmental change can work in a mutually reinforcing manner. Those areas that are undergoing environmental change, which will disrupt their water supplies, agriculture, and coastal areas, will have time to mitigate and recover from these impacts, if they have the economic and human resources to do so. If the resources and societal infrastructure are absent, then mitigation will not take place and instability and conflict will be more likely.

The patterns of differential impacts of globalization will be key in the capability of the areas impacted by environmental change to withstand and recover without major instability. Those areas in the globalization gap not benefiting from continuing globalization have been and will continue to be the areas where terrorism, as both a means and an end, takes place.

Thus, if one pictures a map overlay of the geographic distribution of negative impacts of both drivers; those areas experiencing geographically coincident negative impacts of both globalization and environmental change are the most likely conflict and terrorism areas of the latter part of the twenty-first century. The following is a look into the geography of areas impacted by globalization and climate change. One cannot predict with certainty that they will be sources of terrorists and target areas for terrorism. However, this approach should provide a reduced set of likely future areas in which, combined with the necessary other factors discussed earlier in this book, terrorism will continue or arise in the future.

GLOBAL ENVIRONMENTAL CHANGE

Environmental change resulting from global warming is a reality (IPCC 2007). The primary questions involve which regions of the earth's surface will experience these impacts and the nature of the impacts on the humans and ecosystems in these regions. Global environmental change is a process that will have both beneficial and negative impacts on various regions and nations. The warming of the climate will affect the temperature and precipitation amounts and their geographic distribution across the areas of the globe. The frequency and geographic distribution of droughts, floods, and severe weather and the timing of seasonality will change. In turn, productivity of the oceans, the natural landscape, and land use by humans will be affected.

Global temperature has risen over the last 150 years. The earth's average surface temperature has increased about 0.8°C (1.4°F) with most of the warming in the latter twentieth century since 1975 (NASA 2012a). A 1° change is significant because it takes a vast amount of heat to warm all the oceans, atmosphere, and land by that much. In the past, a 1°–2° drop in the earth's average temperature was all it took to plunge the world into the Little Ice Age. A 5° drop was enough to bury a large part of North America under a towering mass of ice 20,000 years ago.

These temperature changes vary by land and water and by region based on latitude. In the past decade (2000–2009), land temperature changes were 50% greater in the United States than ocean temperature changes, two to three times greater in Eurasia; and three to four times greater in the Arctic and the Antarctic Peninsula. These higher relative levels of warming are resulting in the melting of the Antarctic ice sheet, the Arctic sea ice pack, and the Greenland ice sheet.

Still unknown are the geographic variability and implications of these changes across the globe. In any scenario, climate change will act as a threat multiplier for instability in some of the areas of the world that are already very unstable (CNA 2007). Scheffran et al. (2012) examined potential conflict issues in light of the most recent forecasts on the regional variations in environments related to global climate change.

Changes in Water Supply

Changes of climate and the environment create changes in the human and natural environmental base and the ecosystem services available from this environmental base. These changes include regional variations in precipitation amounts and seasons. These water supply changes impact agricultural production, human water supplies, natural vegetation, and disease and pest patterns across the landscape. It is estimated that 40% of the world's population (approximately three to four billion people) will reside in nations undergoing water shortages by 2025 (World Resources Institute 2000). These impacts stress the political and social structure of regions, especially in those regions with already diminished water supplies and drought.

The map focused on China (Figure 6.1) shows the source region of several of the major river systems of south and east Asia in the Himalayan Mountains and Tibetan Plateau. These systems include the Indus River in Pakistan; the Ganges and Brahmaputra systems primarily in India, Myanmar (Burma), and Bangladesh; and the Mekong system flowing through China, Laos, Thailand, and Viet Nam. The Yangtze and the Yellow Rivers are primary systems within China with their sources in the Tibetan Plateau. These systems are especially vulnerable to disruption by climate change as they are dependent on the Himalayan snowpack, which is highly dependent on south Asian monsoon precipitation. Changes in the amounts of water, the geographic distribution of the precipitation, the timing of the monsoon, and the temperature of the river source regions regulating snow pack melt will greatly impact the future availability of water in these nations. The multinational management of these river systems will be a challenge to the downstream nations, which tend to be the more at-risk nations in the regions.

Directly related to the monsoon and Himalayan Mountain changes are food issues in south Asia. Recent research done by the India Meteorological Department (Kashyapi et al. 2012) contains a projection that indicates a rise in rainfall during the summer monsoon or *kharif* season. Kharif crops include rice, maize, oilseeds, soybeans, and coarse grains. An increase in precipitation in one period or area often results in a lessening in another area. Production of rice and maize has declined in parts of Asia due to increasing water stress as a result of a rise in temperature, increasing

FIGURE 6.1
Himalayan Mountains and Tibetan Plateau are the source areas for several major rivers of south and east Asia. (CIA maps and publications.)

frequency of El Niño, and decline in number of rainy days. Net cereal production in south Asian countries is projected to decline by 4% to 10% by the end of the twenty-first century. This region includes India, Pakistan, and Bangladesh—nations currently experiencing the impacts of globalization and terrorism.

In addition to south Asia, the Andean region of South America (Peru, Bolivia, Ecuador, and Columbia) faces major impacts on water availability, agricultural production, and electrical power generation. The Andean glaciers are melting with the same impacts as the Himalayan glaciers. The fragile ecosystem of this region is at great risk (IPCC 2007). Also, the disruption may force migration from these areas to increasingly overcrowded and overburdened cities and to North America.

The region most vulnerable to impacts of environmental change on water supply is Africa. Over 250 million people are projected to suffer from water and food insecurity (IPCC 2007) in the next few years. Much of Africa has chronic drought conditions, with several desert areas such as the Sahara, Namib, and Kalahari Deserts. Not only are precipitation amounts low in many areas, but also, due to the low latitudinal position of much of the continent, evaporation and evapotranspiration are higher than mid-latitude areas with the same amount of precipitation. The result is that less water is available to humans, crops, and natural systems.

Along with the physical geography, Africa has several factors present that contribute to making it more vulnerable to induced environmental changes of global warming. Many of the nations are extremely poor, with limited infrastructure and services to deal with change. The lack of political representation, poor governance, and a history of political violence make these nations more vulnerable than most (Busby, Smith, and White 2011).

Figure 6.2 indicates the most vulnerable areas of Africa. This map portrays a composite measure of vulnerability. This measure includes a factor representing climate hazard exposure combined with population density, a household and community resilience factor, and a governance and violence factor. One can see that most of the Sahel area bordering the Sahara Desert on the south has moderate to high vulnerability (darker shades) with a few areas in central Africa having the highest vulnerability.

These areas in the nations of the Congo River basin, South Sudan, and Somalia exhibit higher vulnerability, likely due to the resilience and governance factors. Thus, environmental disruptions will have a more pronounced impact on these dark areas resulting in conflict and, possibly,

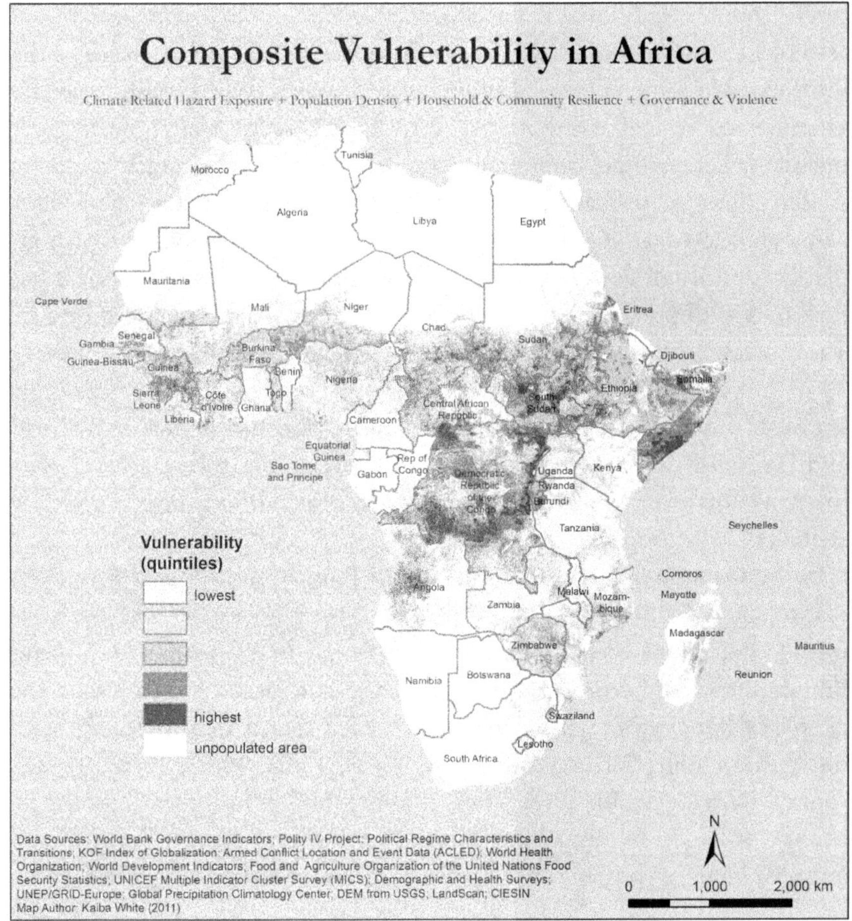

FIGURE 6.2
African areas of most vulnerability to environmental change. (From Busby, J. W. et al., 2011. With permission.)

terrorism. As events in 2012 have shown, even the models of democratic stability in Africa, such as Mali, are very fragile to ethnic (Tuareg) unrest for an autonomous area, disputes over water and land, and Islamist terrorism.

Coastal and Estuarine Inundation

Global warming is causing global sea levels to rise at approximately 3.2 millimeters per year (NASA 2012b). Geological records indicate the earth has experienced as much as a 20-meter rise in a 500-year time frame, when previous ice sheets have melted. Should both the Antarctic and Greenland ice sheets melt entirely, a sea level rise of approximately 80 meters would result from the additional water in ocean basins and the thermal expansion resulting from heating of that water (Usery 2007). A global rise of a not unreasonable 5 meters would inundate approximately five million square kilometers of land affecting almost 700 million people, most in the developing world. For example, only about 1% of Africa's land is located in low-lying coastal zones, but this land supports 12% of its urban population (UN 2007).

Bangladesh had a 2012 population of over 140 million people with a population density of 964 people per square kilometer (USAID 2012). It has the greatest population density of any major, non-island nation on earth. The projected 2050 population is 200 million. Bangladesh is known to have 30 or more distinct terrorist groups. These groups are overwhelmingly Islamist; the most well known are Jamatul Mujahedin Bangladesh (JMB) and Harkat-ul-Jihad-al-Islami Bangladesh (HuJI-B). India claims that as many as 100 groups operate in Bangladesh, including over 100 training centers (Cochrane 2009).

In the Ganges delta—a large portion of Bangladesh supporting a population of 144 million in 2000—inundation by a 2-meter sea level rise would affect areas where 9.4 million people live (CARE 2008). A 5-meter inundation would cover almost 50% of the land area of the nation. The people of Bangladesh will be forced into even higher density living, with likely mass migrations to unfriendly Hindu India, which currently surrounds Bangladesh on three sides. It seems highly unlikely that climate change will not reinforce the conflict in Bangladesh and its use as a terrorist haven in pursuit of the pan-Islamic arc surrounding India.

Indirect Consequences of Environmental Change

In addition to water supply changes and coastal inundation as major direct changes brought on by global warming, other less direct natural changes will likely take place. Natural vegetation change and geographic redistribution of insect pests will take place as they respond to the changing vegetation patterns (Jarvis 2008). Given the temperature and moisture changes, there will be a geographic redistribution of human and domestic livestock diseases. Since many diseases, such as hanta virus, malaria, and West Nile virus, depend on rodent and insect hosts, as the hosts relocate, so too will the diseases that they transmit to humans.

The physical impacts of environmental change induce indirect consequences where existing conflicts are heightened by these changes. Barnett

(2007) elaborates on several of these indirect and multiplier effects of environmental change on societal and socioeconomic conditions. Many people in the areas negatively impacted by global change have vulnerable livelihoods. They are poor people employed as farmers, fishers, or other harvesters dependent on primary resources. Climate change may directly increase poverty by undermining access to natural resources. Impacts on livelihoods will be more significant for those with high resource dependency and in socially and environmentally marginalized areas. Many of the world's poorest people are subsistence farmers who will experience crop failure or, at minimum, the need to alter agricultural cropping and cultural practices in a short time—not an easy task.

Climate change may indirectly increase poverty through its effect on resource sector markets and logistics, and the ability of governments to provide social safety nets. These environmental changes are likely to increase the costs of providing public infrastructure and services and may decrease government revenue. Disasters may result in more disruption and costs. At the very least, the adaptation to climate change will affect the ability of governments at all levels to create a receptive setting and opportunities for citizens.

Migration

The largest single impact of climate change may be on human migration (IPCC 1990). People whose livelihoods are undermined by climate and environmental change may be forced to migrate. The disruption and resulting instability will create "push" factors for large-scale migrations, increasing the risk of conflict in both origin and, more often, destination communities.

The complexity of the situation, shortages of data, and the lack of proven methodologies result in the absence of consistent, reliable estimates of climate-change-induced migration. It is difficult to isolate environmentally induced migration from other migration drivers and to calibrate estimates based on institutional effects on the migration numbers. In 2008, 20 million persons were displaced by extreme weather events, compared to 4.6 million internally displaced by conflict and violence over the same period (Laczko and Aghazarm 2009). Gradual changes in the environment tend to have an even greater impact on the movement of people than extreme events do. For instance, over the last 30 years, twice as many people have been affected by droughts as by storms (1.6 billion compared with approximately 718 million).

Future estimates are for 200 million people to become environmental migrants by 2050 (Myers 2005; Brown 2007). However, forecasts vary from 25 million to 1 billion environmental migrants by 2050, moving either within their countries or across borders, on a permanent or temporary basis.

THE ENVIRONMENTAL CHANGE–CONFLICT NEXUS

It is evident that gradual and sudden environmental changes are already resulting in alteration of water availability, destruction of existing subsistence livelihood activities, and substantial population movements. These changes and impacts are likely to continue and increase in the future. The locations of potential conflict areas are at the nexus of both the increased risk of impacts of global environmental changes and increased vulnerability due to location, poverty, and insufficient institutional resources to cope with the changes. These areas are the most prone to conflict and, potentially, terrorism in the future.

The regions that fit this nexus more fully and have existing terrorist groups present are Sahelian and central Africa, central Asia, the Middle East, south Asia, and Andean South America. These conditions act to multiply the threat when there are terrorist groups already active in these areas, ready to exploit the instability. The presence of the Shining Path and the Revolutionary Armed Forces of Columbia (FARC) in Peru and Colombia, the Islamist groups such as al-Qaeda in the Islamic Maghreb and Boko Haram in Nigeria, and the multigroup visions of a pan-Islamic arc to encircle India composed of Afghanistan, Pakistan, Kashmir, western China, Nepal, and Bangladesh will exploit climate-induced instability and conflict in these regions.

GLOBALIZATION AND TERRORISM

Globalization is the integration of social, political, and economic properties and processes on a global scale. Nations, regions, cities, and people have become more interconnected and interdependent. Presently, much of the globalization is driven by the West and, in many cases, led by the United States. This is in part due to US economic standing and its serving as a base for media outlets fostering cultural diffusion. Globalization is often seen negatively by the non-Western world and referred to as Westernization, secularization, and democratization (Cronin 2002/2003).

Globalization has geographic implications. Although the term alludes to the merging of all world units into a unified entity, the truth is that the degree and impacts of globalization are geographically variable. In processes of what some call premodern globalization (i.e., colonization in Africa, Asia, and the Middle East), animosity was generated from colonial imposition of political boundaries and mixing of ethnicities that are still in place today. On an economic platform, inclusion in the benefits of globalization requires that a region has properties of complementarity (i.e., that region must have something to offer in the global market). This can be cheap labor, natural resources, technology, capital, or a receptive market. On a cultural platform, globalized communications and media assist in the diffusion of ideas, technology, and people.

There are two major negative impacts of globalization processes that fundamentally drive conflict on all geographic scales. First, citizens of many regions, other than the power elite, are in adapt-or-die situations, where adaptation means acceptance of a globalized economy and cultural redefinition. The second impact of globalization is the redistribution of wealth, which creates or worsens poverty in many regions throughout the world. As globalization processes take place, conditions of poor and disenfranchised populations in marginalized regions are worsened.

STATE WEAKNESS AND VULNERABILITY TO TERRORISM

State weakness can be a hindrance to connecting with the globalizing world. There is not a firm connection between failed or weak states and the creation of terrorists (Simons and Tucker 2007). However, linkages between terrorism, poverty, weak governments, and social inequalities do exist. Environments of governmental weakness, corruption, and instability should be considered as potential facilitators of conflict and terrorist activity.

Figure 6.3 shows state weakness of 141 developing countries based on economic, political, security, and social welfare factors, as determined by Rice and Patrick of the Brookings Institute (2008). States are coded based on their weakness on a standard deviation scale. This figure is similar

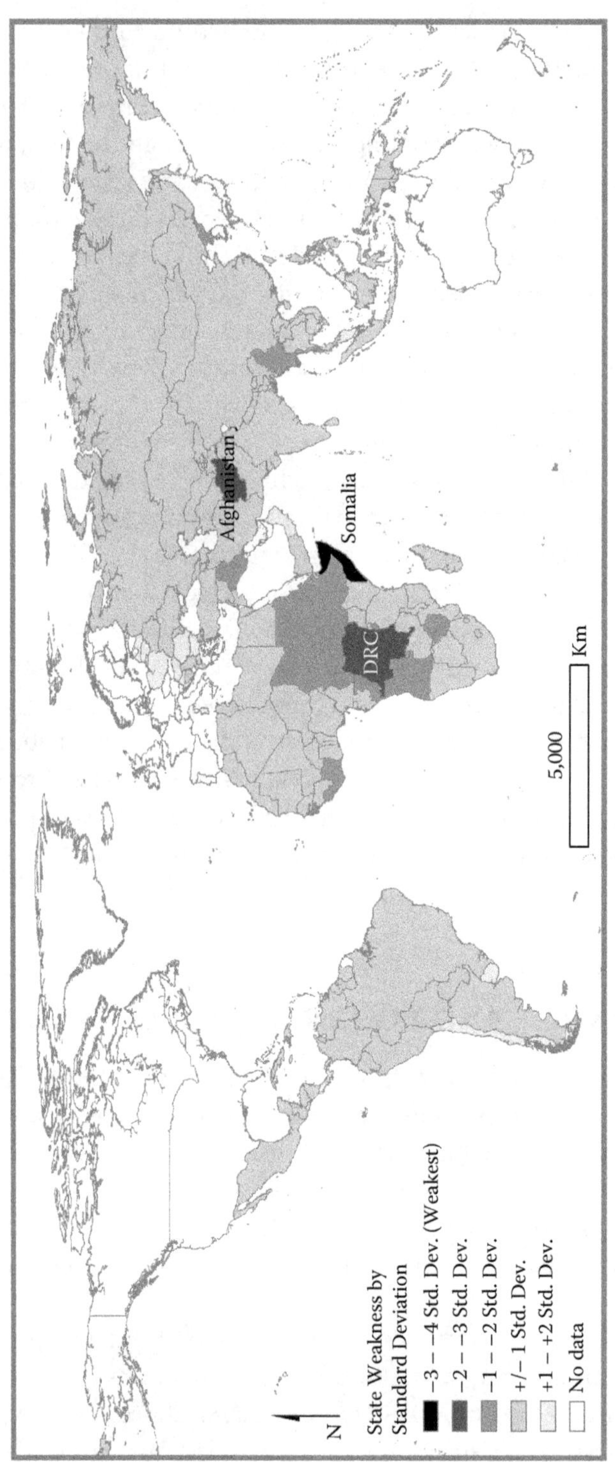

FIGURE 6.3
State weakness of developing countries by standard deviation. (Data source: Rice, S. E. and Patrick, S., 2008.)

to Figure 1.5 in Chapter 1 in that it uses the same data, but by mapping standard deviations it identifies only the weakest states at less than two standard deviations from the mean. Extreme state weaknesses (less than two standard deviations) are located mostly in sub-Saharan Africa. In general, much of the continent of Africa, and parts of the Middle East, Southeast Asia, and East Asia are relatively weaker. The three weakest states are the Democratic Republic of the Congo (DRC), Afghanistan, and Somalia. Other weak states include Iraq and Myanmar.

In regions of political, economic, and security weakness, portions of the population can become disenfranchised. This increases the vulnerability of these people to the terrorist narrative and radicalization. Some of the weak countries identified here have experienced terrorism in one way or another. For example, Sudan, Somalia, Iraq, and Afghanistan have served as residences for al-Qaeda and other terrorist organizations. On the other hand, countries such as Yemen and Pakistan, which are known residences for terrorist networks, are not shown here as weak. Statistical analyses of state failure and terrorism would likely result in no significant correlations. State weakness alone is not responsible for the creation of terrorists, though these conditions can increase the likelihood of terrorist activity. As quoted from Simons and Tucker (2007), "From disenfranchised populations can come foot soldiers, from alienated populations can come terrorists" (p. 400). As terrorist ideologies and actions spread to different regions in the world, the potential for recruitment from weak states, where disenfranchised and alienated populations exist, is greater.

BECOMING CONNECTED TO THE GLOBALIZING WORLD

Prospering in today's globalized environment is an issue of economic and social connectedness. To be connected requires the ability to (1) absorb the content flows necessary for integration with the global economy, and (2) adapt internal rule sets with rule sets of the globalizing world, which include "democracy, rule of law, and free markets" (Barnett 2004, p. 127). Countries that are already or are becoming disconnected are at a great disadvantage. Ultimately, this is a struggle between the haves and the have-nots.

Factors of adaptation play a large role in connectedness. Since globalization is driven by Western influences, it has been much easier for Western countries to adapt, than countries that are culturally more distant. Fear of losing cultural identities will result in nationalist ideals that can result in violence. Adaptation today requires much more progressive thinking and freedoms that are not always afforded by many regions in the world. These countries and regions that can adapt to all the drastic changes brought about by globalization will remain connected.

Given the role of connectedness, globalization can drive terrorism directly and indirectly. It can facilitate terrorism, drive people to terrorism through direct government or corporate activities, or create environments where the likelihood of terrorism is increased. For example, globalization is responsible for the disenfranchisement of many Muslims in southwest Asia and the Middle East. The colonial powers of the nineteenth century created the geopolitical framework based on controlling the oil and people within these regions. As beneficial impacts of modern globalization took hold in other parts of the world, the engagement of these regions was stifled by Western control and a lack of personal and economic freedoms due to domestic regimes. Along with marginalization of the masses in these regions, globalized communications and media provided the means for the spread of "decadent" Western lifestyles to very traditional cultures.

Terrorist groups used these same advances to spread radical ideas and people to places throughout the region. This includes the spread of al-Qaeda personnel and al-Qaeda-based ideologies out of Pakistan and into Palestine, Iraq, Yemen, and Somalia. Indirectly, processes of globalization can create regions of poverty, alienation, and degradation. Direct, causal connections between poverty and terrorism do not exist. Many terrorists are not poor. However, in many cases, discrimination and inequality leading to poverty also exist as potential factors leading to violent activities.

MARGINALIZED REGIONS AND THE POTENTIAL FOR TERROR

There are many more disconnected and marginalized countries in the world than connected ones. The disconnected regions include much of Africa, South America, and a large portion of Asia. It is also noted, as described by Barnett (2004), that the great majority of US military operations from 1990 to 2003 took place in the non-integrated gap of disconnected countries. While military operations do not necessarily equate to terrorist activity, many of these operations were linked to terrorist groups or actions.

Effects of globalization will likely drive terrorism based on the four most prominent factors contributing to terrorism flourishing, as stated in a report by the National War College (2002, p. 54):

- Economic and social inequities in certain societies are marked by both abject poverty and conspicuous affluence
- Poor governance, along with economic stagnation or decline, that alienates many segments of a nation's population
- Illiteracy and lack of education that leads to widespread ignorance about the modern world and resentment toward encroaching Western values
- US foreign policies, particularly regarding the Middle East, that have caused widespread resentment toward the United States

Within these four factors are key concepts that can be used to understand terrorism on a higher level, though the actual causes of terrorism are still debated. Terrorism exists in or is related to regions where there is a noticeable gap between the rich and the poor, problems with governance and economies, alienation, ignorance, and policy disagreement. Each of the factors are influenced by globalization. Distributions of wealth and regime/corporate control expand the gap between the rich and the poor. Poor governance, illiteracy, and lack of opportunity due to government corruption and ineptitude, as well as the inability to function in an increasingly sophisticated economic marketplace, cause alienation and feelings of hopelessness among the people. These conditions further lessen the willingness for future aid and investment in these nations, creating further decline. These outcomes create a receptive audience to be the foot-soldiers of terrorist movements.

The following sections will discuss specific examples of possible globalization-based influences on terrorism within regions of weak states disconnected from the globalizing world.

Sub-Saharan Africa

The majority of sub-Saharan Africa is not an acknowledged focus of international terrorists. Exceptions include Nigeria and Sudan where terrorist networks are already established. However, many of sub-Saharan Africa's nations are stricken with unemployment, poverty, disease, and poor governance, while having oil and mineral resources in abundance. All of

Africa, except South Africa, is in the non-integrated gap. Regions of ethnic and sectarian conflict are less likely to become connected. These insecure environments pose economic risks for investors who may act as brokers to global markets.

The influx of terrorist network elements can radicalize and recruit from within destination countries (Stewart 2008). In the case of many sub-Saharan African countries, the existence of radical Islamist ideologies and people has only increased since 9/11. Much has diffused from source areas in the Middle East. Perhaps more ominous for those nations of Africa not on the transition zone of Islamic spread is the creation of ideological and nationalistic terrorist groups.

The events of the twenty-first century have shown that terrorism is an effective means to precipitate change. The non-Islamist, homegrown terrorist groups in sub-Saharan Africa may plan an increasing role as conditions deteriorate. Integrating this region with the globalized world could diminish much of the terrorist threat from the African continent. As shown by a study in Peru, the Shining Path insurgency was not successful in mobilizing locals in regions of farmers in the Mantaro Valley that were dependent on the capitalist economy. The Shining Path diminished in prominence and had to move on to other Andean regions for support (Kent 1993). Economically integrating the at-risk populations for radicalization will decrease the pool of candidates for terrorist activities.

Central and South America

All of Central America, except Mexico, and all of South America, except Argentina, Brazil, Chile, and Uruguay, is in the non-integrated gap. Regions of South America, such as Peru, Columbia, Venezuela, and the triborder area discussed previously, have had issues with terrorist organization activities (Sullivan 2012).

In these regions, there is the potential, possibly with the highest likelihood in the world, for terrorist networks using the assets of a globalized world to merge with transnational criminal networks for mutual benefit. Central and South America are home to many criminal organizations engaged in drug production and trade. Regions that are destabilized or ungoverned, such as the triborder area, can serve as havens for terrorists who can collaborate for profit from criminal activities. Groups such as the Shining Path in Peru and the FARC in Columbia were initially ideological groups motivated by providing more egalitarian society for indigenous and peasant groups. At present, these groups have embraced the illicit economy using their ideological goals as part of their narrative to justify dealing in drugs, weapons, and other criminal activities.

Better governance is a key to stemming this trend. Lessening the drug trade activity would stabilize the region by decreasing terrorist motivations for operating in the area. Entrance and sustained interaction of these nations into the global market could relieve poverty as the region is rich with resources and abundant lower cost labor.

The Middle East and North Africa

The Middle East and North Africa have had difficulty connecting with Western-based globalization processes. A report by the National Intelligence Council (2008) states that "[a]s long as turmoil and societal disruptions, generated by resource scarcities, poor governance, ethnic rivalries, or environmental degradation, increase in the Middle East, conditions will remain conducive to the spread of radicalism and insurgencies" (p. 68). If this is the case, terrorism-based violence will likely continue and possibly increase with the potential for climate-induced environmental hazards in the future. The hope is that Middle Eastern governments will lead their people into the globalized world or that the people will have the ability to enter it themselves. Present situations with resources, ethnic rivalries, and environmental conditions are hindering the Middle East's move to globalization. The situations are not likely to reverse in the near future, so the marginalization of the Middle East may increase, leaving it as a region vulnerable to the presence of terrorists.

The Middle East and North Africa are low on the human development index, experiencing ethnic and sectarian conflict. Much of the wealth in the region is located in the oil-rich countries, where approximately only 9% of the region's population is located (Salehi-Isfahani 2010). While the numbers of disenfranchised people in the region are increasing, the support for al-Qaeda as a solution appears to be decreasing in the Muslim populace. A Pew Research study (2012) identified the waning popularity of al-Qaeda in the Middle East. In a survey of Muslims in five countries: Egypt, Jordan, Pakistan, Turkey, and Lebanon, al-Qaeda was found to have the most favorability at 21% of the sample in Egypt. Confidence in Osama bin Laden in 2011 was most in the Palestinian territories at 34%. Other countries of interest for confidence in bin Laden were Indonesia at 26%, Egypt at 22%, and Pakistan at 21% (Pew Research Center 2012). The decrease in popularity of al-Qaeda is linked to the fact that most of their victims come from the Muslim population. There may also be a greater motivation among the masses to integrate with global systems, which can be better accomplished without violent means.

Southeast Asia

While much of Asia has had success in integrating into the globalized economy, portions of Southeast Asia, especially the peripheral areas outside the urban areas, have not. This is true in the border areas of the Philippines and Thailand. For example, the Bangsamoro people in the southern Philippines have struggled for decades with the central government over control over and access to educational and economic opportunities. This has led to the formation of terrorist groups including the Moro Islamic Liberation Front (MILF), the Moro National Liberation Front (MNLF), and the splinter group Abu Sayyaf. These areas are a great distance from the economically active cities, especially the primary city of Manila. The southern islands have been ignored by development policies initiated by government based in the north. Also, the central government has traditionally been Christian and allied with the United States. Thus, the people in the southern island, predominately Muslim and less supportive of US interests, have been marginalized. These areas in the south are havens for nationalist and religious terrorists, with an increased following of jihadists since the 1990s.

Terrorist networks in Southeast Asia benefit from four main factors (Abuza 2011):

1. Operations and support bases are located at the weakest regions of weak states, which are often the border regions where cultural overlap and minority persecution exist.
2. Weakness of states allows room for planning, training, and other terrorist activities.
3. Grievances include great economic inequalities.
4. States are unwilling or unable to cooperate with neighbors.

There are many interstate disputes in the region including one over the border between Thailand and Cambodia, one over territorial resources between Malaysia and Indonesia, and issues between Myanmar and neighboring countries over involuntary migrant flows out of the country.

Based on these four factors, the present situation may worsen if the region does not exit from the non-integrated gap.

Eastern Europe

The Eastern European region in the non-integrated gap is typically referred to as the Balkans and includes Bosnia and Herzegovina, Albania, Serbia, Romania, Bulgaria, Croatia, Moldova, Kosovo, Yugoslavia, and Macedonia. The Balkans have had a long history of poverty, ethnic conflict, and insecurity. The region is presently a minor threat for terrorism on the global stage and is home to many foreign fighter terrorists. It is also a source of terrorist fundraising (Rom 2010). As with areas in Central and South America, parts of Eastern Europe are heavily involved with crime syndicates, drug trafficking, and other illegal activities. Large amounts of heroin from Asia find their way to Europe en route through the Balkans. As with Afghanistan, globalization may push this region into a dependence on the drug trade. This would lead to a weaker state and a greater potential for an influx of terrorist organizations who may find reciprocating relationships with criminal networks. Terrorist organizations require funding for their ideological pursuits.

Entering the global market could lessen the need for dependencies on illegal trade; however, challenges of ethnic conflict and corruption in the Balkans can turn away investors. High unemployment rates make terrorism look favorable over a life of poverty for young adults, especially if combined with criminal networks. More opportunity must be generated so that those at risk of being recruited by terrorist organizations are minimized. Inclusion of this region, as well as others, into the globalized world will require a multinational effort.

GLOBALIZATION AND SPATIAL REDISTRIBUTIONS OF PEOPLE AND IDEAS

Globalization is facilitating the movement of people. Within the refugee diasporas, terrorists are redistributing for conflict haven. Some terrorists migrate to initiate the fight at their destination, while others migrate to be hidden and safe from authorities in their nations of origin. Increases in global mobility will increase the likelihood of geographically redistributed conflict on local (e.g., rural to urban), regional, and international scales (Committee on Strategic Directions for the Geographical Sciences in the Next Decade 2010).

Diasporas are common in the world today. Violence from diaspora communities typically occurs as a factor of alienation, where societal integration is hindered. Hence, the alienation following terrorist attacks in a nation can foster additional radical behavior. Countries with diaspora communities that are cause for future concern include the UK, Canada, the Netherlands, and the United States. Though other countries of concern for terrorism exist, only these few will be mentioned here as an example of the threat.

In the UK, the influence of radical Islam linked to the Middle East and South Asia has become more effective and widespread. The mobilization of many radical Muslims is fueled by foreign political processes, rather than local, UK-based issues. Those in Muslim diasporas are finding more acceptance and are bolstered from entities of the worldwide Umma (Muslim community), while being denounced and marginalized by the non-Muslim populations in the UK. The UK is presently being used as a haven for members of several Islamist terrorist organizations. Following the London bombings in 2005, at least three other attacks have been thwarted. Because of the effects of alienation of the migrants and the tendency toward radicalization in the UK, this country is one to be watched for terrorist attacks, as well as planning, training, and funding terrorism for attacks in other regions.

Because of Canada's open immigration policies, it has a large and diverse foreign population that has become an outpost for many terrorist organizations. These organizations are finding support from the local diaspora communities. Canada is home to members of al-Qaeda, Hezbollah, Hamas and, most of all, the LTTE (Liberation Tigers of Tamil Eelam). Another concern for Canada is the rate of converts to Islam (approximately 3,000 per year)—many to radical sects. The relative location of Canada as a neighbor increases the likelihood of terrorists entering the conterminous United States by way of the 6,400 kilometer, mostly unguarded border between them.

The Netherlands, like Canada, is home to many radicals and terrorist organizations. Of biggest concern is the Moroccan diaspora, which is one of the largest diasporas in the world. Many of the young of Moroccan descent are radicalizing as a result of the perceived lack of opportunity in Dutch society. They find hope for the future in radical Islam.

While the United States has a number of diaspora communities and terrorist organizational representatives, the majority of violent threats originate from outside the country. One of the main differences between the Muslim diasporas in the United States and those in the UK is that the US diasporas represent much more diversity, reflecting the Middle East, Asia, and Eastern Europe. It appears that fewer that are drawn to terrorism in the United States. This may be a result of better living conditions, acceptance of immigrants, and more economic opportunities (Hoffman et al. 2007).

The Spread of Organizations

As stated previously, globalization is facilitating the quick exchange and accessibility of information, money, and people through extensive networks. This, of course, includes the movement of radical people, radical ideologies, weapons, and know-how. These flows will widen the reach of globally minded terrorist organizations.

Nationalist and ideological terrorism tend to have a much stricter geographic focus within the region of residence. The fourth wave of religious terrorism seems to be most global in scope. In the world of global Islamist terrorism, killing bin Laden in 2012 may have led to a wider and more geographically dispersed distribution of Islamist terrorist leadership. Rather than end the radical violent ideology that has flourished with al-Qaeda, the killing of bin Laden in 2012 redistributed and further decentralized control throughout the world. The future of al-Qaeda terrorism is unknown, but it is potentially more dangerous and more difficult to suppress a network with globally distributed command and control.

Terrorist organizations throughout the world will have a greater potential for mass destruction. The globalization of scientific technologies, knowledge, and achievement will place more dangerous weapons in the hands of terrorists in the future. The access and construction of CBRN (chemical, biological, radiological, or nuclear) weapons of mass destruction is becoming easier because of access to knowledge, materials, and networks of information and weapons suppliers.

The various aspects of globalization and climate change are certainly revising the potential, locations, and operational pictures of non-state terrorist groups in the twenty-first century. The creators and primary beneficiaries of globalization and climate change (the United States, Western Europe, East Asia) are not the most likely places for the instability resultant from the impacts of these drivers. The future holds an accumulation of subtle changes with interspersed major catastrophic events. Globalization and climate change will compound the existing state weakness, inequity/marginalization, and instability in the regions discussed previously. Instability and conflict have a geographic neighborhood impact, which means the problems diffuse in greater measure to areas in closer proximity. This effect results from the geographic redistribution of people as refugees or economic migrants to adjacent countries, spread of weapons and ideologies, and use of adjacent lands as cross-border havens for terrorists. Those states and political structures most able to limit their social vulnerability to these changes and maintain a capacity to compensate for them will limit their instability and conflict in the future.

REFERENCES

Abuza, Z. (2011) Borderlands, terrorism, and insurgency in Southeast Asia. In *The borderlands of Southeast Asia: Geopolitics, terrorism, and globalization,* ed. Clad, J., McDonald, S. M., and Vaughn, B., chap. 4, 89–106. Institute for National Strategic Studies, National Defense University, Washington, DC.

Barnett, T. (2004) *The Pentagon's new map.* New York: Putnam Inc.

Barnett, J. (2007) Environmental security and peace. *Journal of Human Security* 3: 4–16.

Brown, O. (2007) Climate change and forced migration: Observations, projections and implications. UNDP occasional paper 2007/17.

Buntgen, U., Tegel, W., McCormick, M., Frank, D., Trouet, V., Kaplan, J. O., Herzig, F., Heussner, K.-U., Wanner, H., Luterbacher, J., and Esper, J. (2011) 2500 Years of European climate variability and human susceptibility. *Science* 4:578–582.

Busby, J. W., Smith, T. G., and White, K. L. (2011) Locating climate insecurity: Where are the most vulnerable places in Africa? *CCAPS Policy Brief No. 3.* Austin: Robert S. Strauss Center for International Security and Law.

CARE (2008) In search of shelter: Mapping the effects of climate change on human migration and displacement, 2008. Cooperative for Assistance and Relief Everywhere, Inc. (CARE).

CNA Corporation (2007) National security and the threat of climate change. CNA, Alexandria, VA.

Cochrane, P. (2009) The funding methods of Bangladeshi terrorist groups. *CTC Sentinel,* USMA, 2:5.

Committee on Strategic Directions for the Geographical Sciences in the Next Decade (2010) Understanding the changing planet: Strategic directions for the geographical sciences. National Research Council of the National Academies. Washington, DC.

Cronin, A. K. (2002/2003) Behind the curve: Globalization and international terrorism. *International Security* 27 (3): 30–58.

Devitt, C. and Tol, R. (2011) Civil war, climate change, and development: A scenario study for sub-Saharan Africa. *Journal of Peace Research* 49:129–145.

Hoffman, B., Rosenau, W., Curiel, A. J., and Zimmermann, D. (2007) The radicalization of diasporas and terrorism: A joint conference by the RAND Corporation and the Center for Security Studies, ETH Zurich. Santa Monica, CA: RAND Corporation.

IPCC (1990) *Climate change: The IPCC impacts assessment.* Canberra: Australian Government Publishing Service.

Jarvis, A. et al. (2008) *Climate change 2007: The physical science basis.* Climate change and its effect on conservation and use of plant genetic resources for food and agriculture and associated biodiversity for food security. FAO thematic background study.

Kashyapi, A., Kulkarni, D. A., Bahot, A., and Hage, A. (2012) Asian monsoon in a changing climate—Does it have impact on *kharif* season agriculture? International Conference on Opportunities and Challenges in Monsoon Prediction in a Changing Climate (OCHAMP-2012), Pune, India, February 21–25, 2012.

Kent, R. B. (1993) Geographical dimensions of the Shining Path insurgency in Peru. *Geographical Review* 83 (4): 441–454.

Laczko, F., and Aghazarm, C. (2009) Migration, environment and climate change: Assessing the evidence. Geneva: International Organization for Migration (IOM). Available from http://www.iom.int

Mazo, J. (2009) Darfur: The first modern climate-change conflict, chap. 3. *Adelphi Series* 49 (409): 73–74.

Moran, D. (2011) *Climate change and national security: A country level analysis.* Washington, DC: Georgetown University Press.

Myers, N. (2005) Environmental refugees: An emergent security issue. 13th Economic Forum, Organization for Security and Cooperation in Europe: Prague.

NASA (2012a) Earth observatory. Available from http://earthobservatory.nasa.gov/Features/WorldOfChange/decadaltemp.php

——— (2012b) Global climate change: Vital signs of the planet. Available from http://climate.nasa.gov/effects (last accessed August 2, 2012).

National Intelligence Council (2008) Global trends 2025: A transformed world. Office of the Director of National Intelligence. Washington, DC.

National War College (2002) Combating terrorism in a globalized world. A report by the National War College Student Task Force on Combating Terrorism, May, Washington, DC.

Pew Research Center (2012) On anniversary of bin Laden's death, little backing of al Qaeda. Pew Global Attitudes Project Report. Released April 30, 2012. Available from http://www.pewglobal.org/2012/04/30/on-anniversary-of-bin-ladens-death-little-backing-of-al-qaeda/?src=prc-headline (last accessed July 18, 2012).

Raleigh, C. and Kniveton, D. (2012) Come rain or shine: An analysis of conflict and climate variability in East Africa. *Journal of Peace Research* 49:51–64.

Rice, S. E. and Patrick, S. (2008) Index of state weakness in the developing world. The Brookings Institution. Washington, DC.

Rom, S. (2010) Instability and desperation: The Balkan link to terrorism. *Global Security Studies* 1 (3): 1–110.

Salehi-Isfahani, D. (2010) Human development in the Middle East and North Africa. Human development research paper 2010/26. United Nations Development Program. October.

Scheffran, J., Brzoska, M., Brauch, H. G., Link, P. M., and Schilling, J., eds. (2012) Climate change, human security and violent conflict. In *Challenges for societal stability,* Hexagon Series on human and environmental security and peace, vol. 8. New York: Springer.

Scheffran J., Brzoska, M., Link, P. M., and Schilling, J. (2012) Climate change and violent conflict. *Science* 336 (6083): 869–871.

Simons, A. and Tucker, D. (2007) The misleading problem of failed states: A "socio-geography" of terrorism in the post 9/11 era. *Third World Quarterly* 28 (2): 387–401.

Stewart, N. W. (2008) Sub-Saharan Africa and the global war on terrorism. US Army War College Strategy Research Project. Carlisle, PA.

Sullivan, M. P. (2012) Latin America: Terrorism issues. Congressional Research Service. Washington, DC.

UN (2007) Climate change: Impacts, vulnerabilities and adaptation in developing countries. UN Framework Convention on Climate Change.

USAID (2012) Bangladesh: Population and health. Available from http://transition.usaid.gov/bd/programs/pop.html

Usery, E. L. (2007) Modeling sea-level rise effects on population using global elevation and land-cover data. Association of American Geographers Annual Meeting, San Francisco, CA, April 17–21.

World Resources Institute (2000) Global trends and their implications for business, UNEP.

Zhang, P. et al. (2008) A test of climate, sun, and culture relationships from an 1810-year Chinese cave record, *Science* November 7: 940–942.

Index

B

C

D

E

H

J

T

U

Z

CPSIA information can be obtained
at www.ICGtesting.com
Printed in the USA
BVHW072202090719
552998BV00010B/193/P